SHORELINES

Voices of Southwold Fishermen

Robert Jellicoe

*What a treasury you have gathered here! ... I have enjoyed spending time
in that rich and salty air, made particularly spicy and vivid by the voices of
the people themselves. That world is something that will never return and
you have secured it a place in the memory. Southwold will be grateful to
you, above all for the care and grace with which you have looked after these
inestimably valuable threads and patches of the past.*

Adam Nicolson

BLACK DOG
BOOKS

First published in England 2021
Black Dog Books,
104 Trinity Street, Norwich, Norfolk, NR2 2BJ,
www.blackdogbooks.co.uk

A CIP record of this book is available from the British Library.

ISBN 978-0-9954792-7-2

Managed by Biddles, King's Lynn

Picture Credits

David Barber drawings p.iii, iv, 40, 57, 146, 159, 191, 206, 273;
Southwold Museum p.vi, p.43, 44, 46, 48, 50, 61, 74, 89, 90, 108, 182, 195, 258, plates I & VIII;
Author's collection p.75, 76, 233, 248, 252, plates V, XV & XVI;
Southwold Sailors' Reading Room p.119, 231 & plate IV;
Ian Denny p.217; RIBA Library p.266; Private collections plates II, III & IX;
St Felix School plate VI; Museum of New Zealand plate XI;
Fine Art Society/the Barrow family p.263, plates XII, XIII & XIV;
National Gallery of Victoria, plate VII
Every effort has been made to trace copyright holders

To
The Fishermen of Southwold
For George Ewart Evans who opened my ears
And for
A, D, H & P

Acknowledgements

First, I would like to thank all those who were kind enough to allow me to talk to them, whether or not they are heard in this book: David Aldred; Guy Barber; Jack Bedingfield; Reg Belcher; William Burrell; Robert Cooper; John (Jack) Davies: Jack Denny; Noel Denny; Doris Duncan; William English; Ernest Goldsmith; Joyce James; Philip Jarvis; Edward May; Frederick Rogers; Jack Remblance; Arthur Stannard; Florence Stannard; Millie Stannard; William Spence; Bert Stocks; Rory Tooke; Wally Upcraft,; Tony Warner and Percy Westrup.

Next, my sincere thanks to: David Barber for his enthusiasm, interest and patience in producing the wonderful line drawings; David Butcher, the foremost authority on the history of fishing in Suffolk, in tandem with whom I started this project a long time ago, for all his support and advice; Syd Brown, a great man; Graham Crossley for the initial kick-start and for his help; Ian Denny for the photograph of his grandfather; Gary Doy for his help with fishing nets; Janet Evans for her help with the Crittens; Paul Field who read early drafts and for his advice, support and encouragement; *Wiggy* Goldsmith for many long conversations and Joan Goldsmith for all her help; Simon Loftus for his helpful comments; Robert Macfarlane for his friendship, inspiration and support; Paul McGrane for information about Neil Bell; Adam Nicolson for his support; all at Southwold Museum, especially Jenny Hursell and Paul Scriven; D J Taylor for his support, Stephen Wells, a stalwart at both the Museum and the Southwold Sailors' Reading Room for all his help; John Winter; Stuart Bacon; Tom Cunliffe; Paul Denny; Stephen Hyde; Robert Malster, Frank Upcraft and Hugh Williamson for all their help with enquiries and last but by no means least Peter Tolhurst for his patience, forbearance and faith in publishing this book without whom it would not have been possible.

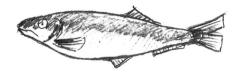

Contents

On Southwold Beach, Arthur Evershed, 1883

The Apparition

First, hand-widths of floating weed, or so their hair appeared, opening and closing on the swell. Then wrinkled white bands of foreheads, below which were sunken eyes, clear sky-blue, and pinched noses that stood out from beards matted and sand-filled. Their faces were no longer with us but they were of us. They moved towards the shore and their ganseys unravelled about their torsos at wrist and waist. They hung unsteadily in the waves sometimes knocked down or shifting on their feet. They never came ashore but were wave-suspended looking at us. To some they held out their hands in a beckoning, to others they smiled and to others still they wailed in shingled voices.

Undone, all undone. That grey vault had given them up. We heard their voices hissing and rattling over the tugging wind so that only snatches reached us. They wanted us join them in the waves, to feel their salty breath in our ears. They wanted us to be their tongues unloosed from their throats.

One raised his hand and gestured with his finger for me to follow. He moved closer to the shore. When I entered the waves he took hold of me and pulled me to him. He smelt of the sea. Weed hung from the strands of his gansey, green and black. His hair and beard framed his bleached face. His teeth had gone so that his lips were pulled back into his mouth. When he spoke it was a hoarse whisper grated out from his throat. "Boy, come along o' me, boy." I could not reply. "Do you know me boy? Do you…?" I looked into his eyes. They were water. "Let me tell you…"

I do not know how I fell into his eyes. Nor can I recall how long I was immersed. His voice was joined by others. They wove about me tight, unseamed like a gansey making patterns as if of the blue wool.

1

Openings

A breeze ruffles the leaves of a book lying on my desk. They lift and roll forward over each other like breaking waves. *Gale's Almanac for 1901* provides, among other things, a Directory which lists the names and addresses of the inhabitants of Southwold,[1] a small coastal town in Suffolk. I am interested in where the longshore fishermen lived at that time and am pleased to discover that they were mostly clustered at the east end of the town in cottages as close as possible to the cliffs that overlook the grey North Sea. Long since the second homes of those who have spent their inheritances on a seaside property, the cottages now bear no resemblance to the basic accommodation they provided over a century ago. Stylishly decorated in fashionable colours, generically furnished in coastal motifs, they parody the concept of the 'fisherman's cottage'. As such they reflect the change that has occurred in the town itself. Said to have the highest incidence of second homes in the country at around sixty percent, Southwold now lives virtually by tourism alone. This was a process already well in motion at the start of the 20th century. Where the sea had always provided an uncertain living, the seaside promised seasonal then year-round opportunities and in this respect, Southwold is no different to many towns and villages around the coast of the British Isles.

In the mid-1970s, I made some tape recordings of fishermen who had been born in these cottages. I had been inspired by George Ewart Evans, a pioneer of oral history, who had come to Southwold in 1976 to deliver a series of W.E.A. lectures. In the 1950s, Evans began recording farmers and farm workers in Suffolk who had worked the land using horse-power. He spoke about the lore surrounding the horse including the ritual of the frog's bone; folklore as an examination of the irrational; about sympathetic magic; dialect and the seasons; old customs like sin-eating or the use of the Rough Band; the cures used by the country people. He peppered the lectures with excerpts from his recordings. It was a joy to hear strong voices speaking authoritatively about their work and beliefs in rich Suffolk accents and dialect.[2] Evans had begun recording at precisely the time when what is now called *agri-business* was sweeping away the old farming practices and cultures. In a generation mass mechanisation had transformed the landscape.[3] Evans made me think that I would like to try to record the remaining Southwold longshoremen who had fished by hand off the beach in open rowing and sailing boats until the end of the First World War. I wondered whether, perhaps like the farmers and farm workers, they too had inherited a way of fishing that might not have changed much over the centuries and that they might be able to talk about their working lives in the same knowledgeable way.

Accordingly I set to work in a stumbling, amateurish fashion. It wasn't difficult to find people who were willing to talk. What was difficult was knowing the best way to conduct an interview. This was at times awkward, the speaker unforthcoming for example, because I had unwittingly asked a closed question. Then the tapes were soon full of noises-off – hooting cuckoo clocks, spontaneous interventions from the speaker's wife, or in one case a daughter taking over from her mother, offers of cups of tea, the flaring of matches to light pipes and roll-ups, low-flying planes and many long silences. Hardly B.B.C. I realised long ago that I should have spoken to more people. I should most certainly have spoken to more women. I should have gone back to follow up in more detail information I was given. I should have covered more topics. In short, I should have conducted real research. But notwithstanding my shortcomings, I was often well rewarded. Like the farm workers, many of the men I recorded were natural storytellers who imparted information about their working lives through narrative in the oral tradition.

It was one thing to have the tapes but to make better sense of them they needed to be contextualised. Fishing is recorded as being practised here before Domesday so I was talking to men who had inherited a tradition that spanned a millennium. The Book tells us that in the time of Edward the Confessor, Southwold yielded 20,000 herrings annually to the Abbot of Bury St Edmunds and that after it the number increased to 25,000. Herring fishing was thus already well organised in Saxon times. The Book also records the presence here of a *heia maris*, literally a sea-hedge, the only one in the county.

This has been defined as a 'woven wicker fish trap set along the shoreline and made up of a number of individual panels.'[4] When the tide flooded over the hedge, flatfish and possibly other species would have been trapped behind it. The Abbott was entitled to a five-eighths share of its catch. The coastline here was very different a millennium ago so it is not really possible to know how or where these fisheries were conducted but fishing is noteworthy in the settlement's earliest written records.

The evidence is not only documentary. Occasionally things way beyond memory surface and connect. On December 21st, 1990, Trevor Knights, a digger contractor, was dredging a section of Buss Creek, the narrow channel that divides Southwold from its neighbour, Reydon. He had been employed by the Southwold and District Freshwater Angling Society. Deep, untangled water would enable better fishing for the Society's members when the season began. At one time this Creek was navigable from the River Blyth. It girdled the town almost islanding the settlement. Knights was clearing the south bank, the Southwold side, about seventy metres west of Might's Bridge, the Creek's only crossing. In the early afternoon he extracted yet another bucket-load and deposited the slub on to the bank. Parts of it began to slither back into the water in a glistening black ribbon. As it did, he noticed something unusual. When Knights got out of the cab to inspect, he spoke to Neville *Dobbin* Harvey, a keen angler, who had been watching him. What appeared to be timbers, black as the slub, were lying exposed on the bank.

Harvey immediately went to see his friend, John *Wiggy* Goldsmith who lived a few hundred yards away. Goldsmith, a District Councillor, was about to attend a meeting in Lowestoft but before he left he located the timbers. He was immediately certain what they were but wanted a second opinion. Back home, he contacted Stuart Bacon, a marine archaeologist based at Orford, director of S.U.S., Suffolk Underwater Studies. Bacon came the following morning, a Thursday, Goldsmith recalled, and with a friend donned diving gear and retrieved other pieces. He too was sure what he was looking at but wanted further investigation. An eighteen foot length of wood broken in two by the digger was returned to the Creek while the other timbers were gathered together, placed in an old trawl-net (donated by the aptly named Colin Upcraft) and left suspended in the water.

Back in Orford, Bacon contacted Valerie Fenwick, founder of the Nautical Archaeology Society. When she came to Southwold with him on Christmas Eve and saw the timbers, she was convinced they were very old. In all, thirty three were recovered. On her advice and with help from Sizewell Nuclear Power Station, samples were later sent for carbon-dating. The results stated that there was a 95% probability that the timbers dated from between 890 to 1155 A.D. and a 65% probability that they were from 970 to 1025. They confirmed what those who had seen them had known at once. Knights had brought to light what is to date, Southwold's earliest-known artefact. The wreck of a boat.[5]

Goldsmith had also recognised that the broken 18ft length was a rudder. 'The top of the steer-board was rounded but the blade was in the process of being cut to shape,' he said. 'That wasn't finished.' And, on some of the other timbers, 'You could clearly see the imprint of the square nails on the planking and the diamond-shaped roves.'[6]

Bacon is convinced that the boat is a Saxon fishing boat grounded in a mud-berth at the Creek's crossing point for the removal and transportation of its catch. Saxon settlers at Reydon or Southwold may have fished this broad or used the Creek to gain access to the sea. The unfinished rudder and possible length of the boat might well suggest a sea-going vessel or one being prepared for it. Other finds in the area, a Saxon log-boat uncovered at Covehithe in 1998 by Rodney Collett was carbon-dated to between 775 and 892 A.D. and two Viking rudders, one trawled up by Robert *Dinks* Cooper 1981, the other, retrieved by Ivan *Nobby* Hutton, washed up on the beach at Easton Bavents in 1986, the finest examples in the world, dated between 850 and 950 A.D., are also witness to the part played by lagoon and sea in our early history. It is tempting to think that the Buss Creek boat may have contributed to the statistics recorded in Domesday but whether it did or not a Saxon craft is a find indeed.

Other places in Southwold attest to its past as a fishery. The Southwold Sailors' Reading Room on top of what used to be called Long Island Cliff, now prosaically East Cliff, is perhaps the best known.

Built in 1864, the philanthropic gift of Frances, the widowed second wife of Charles Rayley R.N., the original purpose of the Room was to provide Southwold's mariners and fishermen with an improving alternative to their other haunts, the public houses. The tone was set at the official opening by the Rev. Mr. Imrie:

'You are fortunate in the possession of a room, where you may meet and read the occurrences of the day, and, better still, you may read and hear words that will make you wise unto salvation. This room is to my mind, very much a harbour of refuge… outside there is rock and storm, whirlpool and destruction; inside quiet, peace and safety. Let this be your public-house. The best side of a public-house is the outside, for the inside has ruined many both body and soul; but the best side of this room is inside, for here is good food for both body and mind.'[7]

Nowadays the Room accommodates Members and public who gather to read the papers, yarn or play snooker in the back but it retains a reverential hush punctuated only by the ticking of the wind-up clock over the now shuttered-off fireplace or the click of snooker balls. One of its many attractions is the accretion of Southwold's maritime past that hangs on every inch of wall space and clutters the cabinet and tables. A *Wunderkammer*. Here are paintings, photographs, newspaper cuttings, posters, model ships and boats, tools, ship's figureheads, and nameboards. This is a testimony to the last one hundred and fifty years. It is impossible not to be intrigued by their silent stories.

Impressively, there are two prints by Peter Henry Emerson, well-known as the late-Victorian pioneering photographer who upset his contemporaries by championing an aesthetic he called Naturalistic Photography. He first came to Southwold in August 1883 on holiday with his family and was soon enchanted. He began taking photographs of the surrounding landscape, the beach and the fishermen. A headstrong man of great energy and enthusiasm, of independent means, from a privileged background, Emerson was one of those Victorian men of leisure whose intellect and curiosity so often pushed the bounds of knowledge. In his case, he abandoned his training as a surgeon to devote himself to exploring the limits of the relatively new medium of photography. He challenged contemporary ideas of the very nature of photography in terms of form and content, characteristically relishing his role as a contrarian and polemicist. He fought against the photographic establishment to argue passionately that the medium was an art form – until in a spectacular *volte-face*, he abandoned the idea in 1891. Teaming up with his friend, the painter T. F. Goodall, Emerson spent much time living on a houseboat on the Norfolk Broads and on Breydon Water near Great Yarmouth. Between 1886 and 1895 he and Goodall published eight volumes of plates of East Anglian life taken on the Broads and in the surrounding landscapes. In some of these books Emerson wrote accompanying texts detailing the working lives and culture of those he photographed. The fourth volume, *Pictures of East Anglian Life* (1888) took as its subject the lives of those he termed 'fisherfolk' and 'peasantry'. It contains a few early photogravure plates of Southwold fishermen as well as providing an extensive written record of their working practices. This is a founding text that gives us for the first time in the millennium a comprehensive account of shore-based fishing in Southwold. Two other institutions, the Alfred Corry Museum at the harbour and the Southwold Museum opposite Bartholomew Green are also rich repositories of beach life.

The Southwold Diary of James Maggs 1818-1876 is another invaluable resource. Maggs was born in 1797 on the other side of the River Blyth in Walberswick. He moved to Southwold in 1818. First as a schoolteacher, then as an auctioneer and through a variety of civic appointments, he became intimately connected with the life of the town. He frequently recorded its maritime activity and the losses associated with it. As an auctioneer he had an interest in wreck. The diaries are only really detailed between 1822 and 1856, but they provide a valuable glimpse of beach life and the perils encountered by the grandfathers and great grandfathers of those I recorded. Maggs's entries are mostly terse facts but another writer who could be said to have fleshed him out was the pseudonymous novelist, Neil Bell. Stephen Critten, was born in 1887 into a family of boatbuilders who, over a century, had built up an unparalleled reputation along the coast. For various reasons Bell rejected his family and became a prolific writer. Two novels in particular, *Bredon And Sons* and *Forgive Us Our*

Trespasses draw extensively on his family history and the life of the fishermen. No account could ignore the work of E.R. Cooper, solicitor, Town Clerk and much more besides. Though he rarely wrote about the men as fishermen, he had unbounded admiration for their skills as seamen, especially in the service of the Lifeboat. The fishermen had no better champion than Cooper who wrote books, pamphlets and articles about the history of the Suffolk coast. The last of these were published in the 1930s by which time Cooper was already aware that this was a life that could not survive. The fishermen were also recorded by artists. If Walberswick is better known as an artists' colony, Southwold too has attracted its share. Recent books have made much of this but some of the lesser known local shore-based painters have escaped attention and are worthy of some notice.

The oral testimonies I have collected are at the heart of this book. One reason why the fishing life was not much recorded was simply that it was taken for granted. It is not surprising that the first to write it down was Emerson, a complete outsider. Notwithstanding the irony that the voices I recorded are here book-bound, they revive the silent Reading Room pictures, complement Emerson's observations, authenticate cultural representations and detail working practices, some that go back little changed to the Saxon boat. It has been rightly objected that to turn the spoken word into a written text is to defeat the object of oral history since the transcription omits essential features of the spoken encounter, the voice, its timbre, its pitch and pace, its accent, the use of pause or emphasis, the expression of emotion and so on. An unsatisfactory way round just one of the above is to suggest the accent selectively by means of phonetics, another to leave dialect constructions as given, the intention being to celebrate the richness of their variety. I hope readers will understand therefore that I have tried to give an echo of the spoken words in the transcriptions, not to homogenise them into Standard English.

My aim is to give some sense of the practice and culture of shore-based fishing in a Suffolk coastal town from the end of the 19th century to the end of the the First World War when motors began to be fitted into the boats. The fishermen were often called *longshoremen* but the word is not very old, the *Shorter Oxford English Dictionary* giving the meaning of 'employed along the shore' as early 19th century but *longshoring* as the occupation of a longshoreman as early 20th. A more particular definition is that longshoremen were 'old sailors settled ashore.'[8] This was certainly true of some of the Southwold men. None of these definitions necessarily imply that the occupation had to be fishing, though what we are talking about at Southwold is the group of fishermen who worked seasonally off the beach more or less within sight of the town whether to north or south in open sailing and rowing boats known as *punts*. Older texts also describe them simply as *fishermen* and in the 19th century as *cliffmen* or *beachmen*, terms, as we shall see, which include fishing as one of several kinds of work that was undertaken.

Sometimes I imagine them drowned. They were not, of course, most of them; they are in their graves mouldering, their white bones earth-browned. But I imagine them beneath the waves. The grey waves. Their grey vault. Sometimes voices and images come to me from that vault. I imagine them regarding their drowned selves, their unlived lives, their swirling depths. Or I see them and imagine talking with them.

Notes

1 This can be found in Southwold Museum

2 These can be heard on the British Library website

3 See Williamson, T. *An Environmental History of Wildlife in England 1650-1950* (Bloomsbury 2013) p. 184. According to Williamson, 'Between 1946 and 1970 4,500 miles of hedgerow were grubbed up annually in England and Wales, with the greatest losses sustained in the eastern counties.' As well as loss of habitat, the use of pesticides and herbicides contributed to wildlife decline. J.A. Baker's *The Peregrine* (1967) written in fierce and startling prose has become recognised as the classic literary response to the use of DDT

4 Butcher, David *Rigged for River and Sea* (North Atlantic Fisheries History Assoc. 2008) p. 88

5 A Bronze Age axe head was found in a Southwold garden but as there was no settlement then it must have been dropped by a traveller. It is on display in Southwold Museum as are the Viking rudders which have been donated permanently by the National Maritime Museum

6 For the full story see Bacon, Stuart *Southwold Suffolk* (Segment Publications 1996) p.18-31

7 Pope, Douglas (compiler) *The Sailors' Reading Room The First 150 Years from 2nd June 1864* (Southwold Press 2013) p.6

8 Rogers, Stanley *Sea-Lore* (Harrap 1929) p.108

2

Benjamin Herrington

One such was Benjamin Herrington (1815-1890) who was born in one of the cottages that used to stand on Southwold beach. 19th century longshoremen, the forebears of those I recorded, made their living from the beach in diverse ways, only one of which was by fishing.

Herrington took to the sea 'like a willock', the dialect word for a guillemot.[1] In his late teens he joined the Navy serving on *H.M.S. Pique* but disliking the life of a bluejacket, he deserted, making his way to London disguised as a tinker. From here he shipped several times to New York and Quebec. When his father died in 1829, he returned to Southwold to take up the beach life, not exactly fitting that definition of a longshoreman as an old sailor settled ashore. He was twenty four.

Leonine, strong and tall, Herrington had all the confidence of one sure of himself and his skills. He knew the sea and the weather in all its changes, he was an expert sailor and above all, fearless. He soon became the principal *cliffman* for the Long Island Cliff Company; he was a lifeboat man for 38 years; he served as a Harbour pilot and occasionally unofficially for Trinity House shipping *brummager* pilots. Threading these jobs he worked the different fishing seasons as the year turned.

During the mid-18th and 19th centuries organisations known as *Beach Companies* were formed all around the East Anglian Coast from Mundesley to Aldeburgh. In Southwold they were called *Cliff Companies*. They were instituted to ship Trinity House pilots to vessels bound for London, to salvage ships in distress and, at Yarmouth and Lowestoft, to service the needs of shipping in the roads. Few records of the Southwold companies have survived. The original *New York Cliff Company* was formed at some point in the mid-eighteenth century. It was superseded in 1810 by the *Long Island Cliff Company* and in 1829 the *Kilcock* or *North Cliff Company* was set up in competition. An Act of Parliament of 1808 made pilotage compulsory for certain foreign and domestic vessels. Eligible ships on the North Sea bound for London now had to be piloted from Orfordness to Gravesend through the shoals and banks off the Essex coast and into the Thames estuary by the *North Channel* pilots. From here the *River* pilots took them in to the Port of London. Although it had been their responsibility since 1514, the 1808 Act effectively gave Trinity House state control of pilotage with some ports excepted; its regulations professionalised the service from which a decent living could now be made. An Account Book in Southwold Museum for a pilot cutter, probably the *William and Mary*, records the fees of four principal pilots over several years in the 1840s and 50s. They were earning up to £250 per annum before expenses from the cutter alone, many times more than a fisherman.

Until the mid-19th century, the Southwold Cliff Companies were jointly owned by small groups of Trinity House pilots and businessmen. Between them they put up the capital to build the *yawls* and *gigs* used for their purposes. Similar groups also owned pilot cutters which worked offshore, sometimes at great distance. After the mid-century for reasons that are not clear, membership of the companies was widened to include that public in the town with a maritime interest, though the pilots and businessmen remained very influential.

The rule was that the first pilot to board a ship flying the *pilot jack* won the job. The Company owners employed the fishermen as *cliffmen* or *beachmen*, to crew, launch and beach their boats and to man the lookouts. These were on or embedded into the cliffs known as *New York, Long Island* and *Kilcock* from where they scanned the horizon intently looking for ships displaying the signal. Competition was the essence of the work. The cliffmen received a *dole* or share of the successful pilot's fee either for acting as a crewman on a yawl or gig or as a *floater* – one who assisted at the launch and beaching of the boat. In addition the pilot gave a sum as beer money to be shared by all. When the pilot's fee was over £9, he doled 5/- for the maintenance of the boat and 5/- for beer money and when less, 2/6d respectively.

Sharp eyes clamped to telescopes were essential in the lookouts. From here signals could be sent to the cutters to proceed to a vessel in the roads or if the pilot was to ship from the shore, a crew and floaters could be quickly mustered from the cliffmen on the beach below. The race was on as soon as the pilot jack was sighted. Rivalry between the companies was intense. At times it turned the cliffmen against each other. Perhaps the worst case, not just at Southwold, occurred on the last day of July in 1855. I have a painting of the incident (Plate I) which often makes me imagine that I hear Herrington telling me what happened.

'There wuz a lot o' rivalry between the two companies,' he begins. 'That made for bad feelin' between neighbours an' that wuz the wust about it. I'll tell yuh this… That wuz the last day o' July 1855. I 'ont never forget it. I wuz sweepin' the horizon from the Long Island lookout about 11 in the mornin' an' I see a brig about 5 mile off, east, pretty much straight off, an' she wuz flyin' the pilot jack. I sent a boy t' the pilot house t' tell him t' come an' I selected a crew o' nine for the yawl. There wuz Andrew Browne, William Bokenham, Frank Palmer, David Winter, James Howlett, Thomas Bugge, William Crickmore, Robert Stannard an' Thomas Rogers. All Long Islanders an' all good sailors. The floaters got our yawl, *Reliance* off quick enough usin' the *sett*, the long pole. Thass a job t' launch a yawl off the beach. That have t' be done right. O' course the Kilcock men had sin the brig an' all, an' they wuz busy launching their yawl, *Swiftsure*. Ben Spence wuz their helmsman. Our pilot, William Simpson, come down the score sharp in his uniform with his ol' black canvas bag an' jumped aboard.

We got off fust. We dursn't make no mistakes 'cos it weren't that long before Spence wuz down t' leeward o' us. Mine wuz a good crew an' we tacked smart every time. I judged the tide right, an' we reached the brig about 12.30. She wuz a Norwegian brig, lyin' in the wind, waitin'. I ordered the sail t' be lowered an' the crew t' row down her starboard side. I hove a rope aboard what Frank Palmer wuz securin' when Spence come up in *Swiftsure* on starboard. There weren't a lot in it, yuh see. Well, he'd lost but instead o' turnin' up t' windward or comin' under the brig t' leeward, like he oughta ha' done, he sailed straight on. He sliced us in two. He did. Sliced us right down t' the keel. You shoulda heard the sound o' the strakes splinterin' an' splittin'. Thass a miracle he din't kill any on us. The crew got out the way quick when they saw he weren't goin' t' head up. Well, we clambered aboard the brig as best we could. The air was blue I can tell yuh. *Reliance* was a wreck. As I wuz climbin' up the side o' the brig, I looked down at

Swiftsure, an' this is the truth. Spence 'ud sailed into us so hard his *bumpkin* wuz embedded in the brig's coverin' board like a harpoon. He'd have skewered any on us if we'd bin in the way. Somehow he got her off an' sailed back t' the beach. An' as it happened the brig wuz bound f' Low'stoft, not London. Simpson took us there an' we all come back t' Sole. So there weren't much t' be doled arter all that effort, on top o' which we'd lost our yawl.

I don't know t' this day what made Spence do it. He coulda avoided us easy. I wonder if he wuz so angry with himself for losin' that he lost his head. He sailed in the Lifeboat along o' me but I wuz wary of him arter that. Well, the Company took the *Kilcock* t' the Admiralty Court in London t' get compensation for the loss o' the *Reliance*. Some judge ordered that *Swiftsure* should be sold an' the money be given t' us. But that seemed t' drag on, an' though *Swiftsure* wuz put up for auction she wuz never sold or else she wuz sold but the money weren't paid. In the end we got about £20 but the expenses wuz near on that for the court case so that wuz a sorry business.

Ol' Ted Syer, you din't know him, he wuz always doin' paintin's o' wrecks an' all that offa here. He done a picture o' the collision what he showed me. Spence is a-comin' up on starboard an' he can see me clear. He know we're there. Ol' Andrew Browne is a-wavin' at him t' turn t' windward, but Spence in't payin' no attention. Rum do boy. That rile me t' this day. He coulda killed us. In the picture I always remember there's dark clouds comin' over the blue sky an' that wuz a dark day, I tell yuh. I'd like t' see that ol' picture agin.

I never heard o' nuthin' like that happenin' nowhere else. There wuz rivalry but nuthin' like that. An' that din't stop the competition between us. About three years later a Roosian ship, *Bajan, Bazan,* suthin' like that, signalled for a pilot an' we went off in our gig, *Teazer* with young William Aldrich, the pilot, an' Kilcock went off in their gig, *Cricketer*. That wuz another close race. We both got there about the same time but *Cricketer* collided with us an' we cast. Ol' William Bokenham, he wuz a tough ol' feller, he wuz seventy if he wuz a day, well he went right under the steamer an' surfaced at her stern. Lucky she wuz anchored an' her screw weren't turnin'. Them ol' Roosians done all they could t' get him aboard an' revive him. *Cricketer* picked the rest o' us up that time. But there weren't no love lost between us. You had t' get there fust. Thass how it wuz yuh see'

While both of these incidents occurred shipping a pilot, when it came to salvage the beachmen had early acquired an unsavoury reputation. George Crabbe, writing of the Aldeburgh men in 1783, described them as 'an artful, surly savage race' itching to see whether a ship in distress would be 'theirs, or the ocean's, miserable prey.' In mitigation, the beachmen's notoriety as 'longshore sharks' has to be seen in a wider context. Before the establishment of lifeboats all along the coast, the only way a ship in difficulties could be saved was by their efforts. It is true that the first exchange between the helmsman of the winning yawl and a ship's Master was a negotiation about salvage fees but once the deal was struck, the beachmen often saved the crew while saving the ship, putting themselves at considerable risk not just to reach the vessel but during the salvage operation itself.

An occupational hazard of launching any boat from the beach was to get her off safely. At Southwold where the beach shelves fast, the tide runs hard and the chop and swell can be steep, this was never easy, particularly in bad weather, which would usually be the case in a salvage incident. To avoid a *broach-to*, the floaters used the *sett*, a long pole with a metal swan-neck attached at one end which hooked over the stern of the boat. The floaters pushed hard on the sett to guide the boat over the first breakers beyond the shoreline. At the same time the crew used their oars to row off while the foresail was being raised. Once it filled the helmsman could steer off in the required direction. This was a tricky operation which mostly, but not always succeeded. On October 24th, 1844 Long Island's yawl, *Jubilee* with Herrington at the helm broached. Herrington, who had hold of an oar, was catapulted to safety on to the beach but one of his crew, Edward Palmer, was drowned, trapped beneath. When the upturned hull was stove-in by James Critten the boatbuilder, Palmer was found to have an agate in his mouth, his gift to the ferryman.

Once safely off and in pursuit, the yawl was sailed hard sometimes with disastrous consequences. On December 22nd, 1845, *Jubilee's* successor, *Endeavour* and Kilcock's *British Tar* were competing to board a pilot when off Lowestoft, Maggs tells us – 'the *Endeavour*, blowing very hard carried away her masts....'[2] One can only imagine that to get to the vessel first, Herrington and crew, having risked full sail in the strong wind, were overpowered and dismasted in a sickening, ear-splitting lurch.

Notwithstanding the risks, the rewards could be considerable. In bad weather several ships could be in difficulty at once. On November 14th 1840 Long Island's yawl, *Jubilee* took the Brig *Latina* to Yarmouth and received £120. On the same day Kilcock's *British Tar* also took the brig *Eliza* of Newcastle there and received £80.[3] £200 taken on the same day doled between the shareholders and cliffmen of each company was good return particularly for the Long Islanders on this occasion. Though not named, it is entirely possible that Herrington was at *Jubilee's* helm.

In Southwold the Cliff companies were economically viable up to around 1863. Various factors ensured their gradual decline. The introduction of steam made it less likely that in bad weather steam-powered ships would be driven on to the lee shore of the shoals and sandbanks that ringed the coast. Trinity House made steady improve-ments to navigation in the form of lighthouses and buoys marking the channels and sandbanks but perhaps the most serious cause followed an incident in 1862 when no *North Channel* pilot cutter was found to be available for service. After investigation and consultation, Trinity House changed the pilotage rules. From 1863 all pilots had to be shipped from cutters at sea in rotation and could only be taken from the shore when no cutter was in sight. This effectively put and end to shore-based pilotage at the same time as opportunities for salvage were diminishing. Though the Companies kept their yawls, gigs and lookouts, their use declined over the remaining years of the century. Finally, in 1899 Trinity House removed all pilots to Harwich. The men I recorded remembered what was left – the lookouts and the remaining yawls on the beach now mostly sailed in the local regattas but recalled no instances of salvage.

By the end of the century the Lifeboat rather than the yawl had become the principal means of rescue for vessels and crews in distress. In Herrington's early days this was not the case. There was no Lifeboat at Southwold until 1840 when a Committee under the chairmanship of Lord Stradbroke set up the Southwold Lifeboat Society and commissioned its first boat, a *Norfolk and Suffolk* type, *Solebay*, which served from 1841 to 1852. Herrington was appointed second cox'n and then cox'n in 1852, a position he held until 1857 when he resigned in a dispute with the Committee. He was appointed cox'n again in 1860 and served until he retired in 1879, an impressive 38 years all told. E.R. Cooper details some of the rescues he made and the awards he received.[4]

One of these, the rescue of the crew of a brig, *Sheraton Grange* was uncanny. Bound for London from Sunderland with a cargo of coal, she was sighted at about 4 p.m. on November 29th, 1853 flying a flag of distress in a S.S.W gale. A vessel in such conditions would be ripe for salvage by the cliffmen and indeed the Long Islanders were prepared to go off in their yawl, *John Bull*. However 'they were deterred from doing so by the united entreaties of a large body of females who were assembled on the cliff, apprehensive of danger to their husbands and children from the approaching darkness and heavy sea; thus creating a panic which rendered the numbers willing to venture their lives to only four.'[5] Not just in Southwold but around the coast of Britain, fear of meeting a woman, even a wife, on the way to the shore was a common superstition indicating that bad luck would follow. The image of long-skirted, head-scarved women congregated on the cliff in the gathering darkness remonstrating in the shriek of the gale with their husbands, sweethearts, brothers and sons is an immensely powerful one. They must have knowingly invoked the taboo.

By now it was dark. In defiance, Herrington and William Waters, the second cox'n, assembled a crew and went off in *Solebay's* successor, *Harriett*. Herrington spent an hour searching for the vessel working against wind and tide. When they found her she was deserted. Not giving up they dropped astern; the crew of nine were eventually found in the long boat and taken on board. All of them were saved. At considerable risk the crew then boarded the brig to try to pump her free of water but with the seas breaking over her they abandoned the attempt. Soon the brig grounded and the Lifeboat returned to the shore.

This incident exemplifies an important rule observed by the Southwold men. Salvage was primarily the task of the Cliff companies who manned their yawls for the purpose. Lifeboat work, motivated by the humanitarian principle, was only undertaken as the last resort. Herrington's son put it like this, 'You see they used their large beach yawls mostly [for salvage]. It would be bad weather indeed for them to use a Lifeboat.'[6]

Herrington's dispute with the Committee in 1857, concerning the salvage of a brig, *Pensher,* demonstrates his plain speaking. 'His contribution to the meeting was to thump [the key of the Lifeboat shed] on the table and inform the startled gentry, in the bluntest of sailor "lingo" what they could do with it.'[7] Reinstated in 1860 and cox'n for another nineteen years, Herrington undertook many more rescues some but not all successful. Of the latter, his attempt to save the the crew of the brig *Billy* of Whitby is regarded as the greatest service ever undertaken at Southwold.

'...the wind, bor, the wind. You in't never heard nuthin' like it...nuthin' like it...Howlin'...shriekin'...you couln't hear nuthin' else....'

On January 13th, 1866 at about 11 a.m. the brig was seen approaching from the south flying a flag of distress in a heavy southwest gale. Before the Lifeboat could launch, the brig foundered on the *Kaneway*, the shoal directly opposite the town. The shock caused her masts to fall overboard. After a successful launch, Herrington crossed the shoal, anchored to windward and attempted to veer down to the wreck, but the severity of the storm meant the anchor did not hold. He recrossed the shoal and beached. Fifty floaters then pulled the boat into a position windward of the brig from where Herrington made a second attempt and with reefed sails again approached. As before, the anchor failed and he came back over the shoal for a second time. Another anchor was found and put on board. He sailed off and veered down again, this time successfully. By now all the crew bar one was lost. Herrington urged the terrified survivor to go the stern of the brig to be rescued but in moving aft he was washed overboard. Herrington cut the anchor cables and went in search to no avail. Appearing on wave tops and disappearing into troughs

Herrington finally crossed the shoal for the third time and beached the lifeboat in front of the town. He later declared this was the worst sea he had ever experienced.[8] His son wrote that the lifeboat's iron tiller was so bent by his exertions that it had to be repaired by Blowers, the town's blacksmith. [9]

Herrington was never a Trinity Pilot but from time to time he shipped *brummagers*. Trinity House allowed the use of unlicensed pilots to escort vessels to London when no licensed pilots were available. These were often longshoremen who knew the waters as well as the pilots. Pejoratively known as *brummagers* or *brummagens* they were named for the perceived second-rate products of Birmingham. Maggs records two occasions when they were used.[10]

Unscrupulous brummagers often posed as Trinity House pilots, poaching their work. A serial offender was the Southwold longshore-man, John Fish. He led an eventful life. He escaped drowning in a capsize when off trawling with John Braham on September 6th, 1847.[11] The following year on July 11th, the Trinity House Pilotage Committee in London received a letter from Newson Garret of Aldeburgh who had written on behalf of pilot Robert McCowan. McCowan had super-seded Fish who had fraudulently taken charge of a foreign vessel. In what appears to have been a fit of fury, Fish threw McCowan's coat and trousers overboard. The Committee solemnly advised that this was an assault which should be pursued in a Magistrate's court.[12]

Temper he may have had but he was also brave. On December 4th of the same year (1848), as a crew member of the Lifeboat, *Solebay* with Herrington as second cox'n, Fish rescued two men from the dismasted *Ury* of Sunderland which had struck on the Barnard Sands. A yawl from Kessingland was unable to reach her so a messenger was sent to Southwold by horse to alert the Lifeboat. According to E.R. Cooper:

'The Lifeboat was launched and reached the wreck in about half-an-hour. She was on her broadside with the decks blown out and a tremendous sea breaking over her. The Lifeboat anchored to windward and veering down rescued a man fast to a rope amongst the wreck, another man was seen and ropes thrown to him, but ineffectually, as he was in a state of insensibility, thereupon John Fish, one of the lifeboatmen, got on to one of the masts which was floating attached to the wreck and running along it succeeded in rescuing the man in circumstances of the utmost peril, having the utmost difficulty in breaking his grip upon the rigging...'

Lloyds of London awarded the whole crew £19.10s, £5 of which was for Fish. He was also awarded a Silver Medal by the Royal National Shipwreck Association, presented to him in the Town Hall on March 29th, 1849 which he received to a 'burst of applause loud and long.'[13] With this medal Fish headed a Roll of Honour to which many brave Lifeboatmen in the town including Herrington have been added for their outstanding service. And yet such was the life of a long-shoreman that, on December 14th, just ten days after the rescue, Fish and three other longshoremen again capsized as they came in to beach and, 'had not immediate assistance been at hand they must have perish'd- the boat being whelm'd over them. Providentially they were rescued, but greatly exhausted.'[14]

Herrington is on record as shipping brummagers to vessels in his boat *Dart*. As lifeboat cox'n and a well respected cliffman, it is unlikely that he was ever underhand.

Before he left Southwold to join the navy, Herrington had been a Southwold Harbour Pilot, a job he recommenced on his return. Harbour pilots were quite distinct from Trinity pilots, the latter having far higher status. A Harbour pilot was engaged to take merchant and other vessels over the bar and in and out of the port. The Harbour entrance, often silted and impassable in the 18th and 19th centuries, was always potentially perilous. Whereas Trinity House Pilots had to pass exams, a probationary period and an annual review, Harbour Pilots, usually longshoremen, were appointed by the Harbour Commissioners, an organisation of local gentry. If successful, the Commissioners issued the applicant with an annual Warrant.

A vessel wishing to enter the port of Southwold could only ship a pilot between Dunwich Church to the south and Covehithe Church to the north, though these boundaries appear to have been changed from time to time. The pilot who first got alongside the vessel within these limits was entitled to the pilotage in and out of the port. It appears that there were two *stations* from which the pilots shipped, one at Covehithe and the other Dunwich. Exactly what these were is unclear, perhaps some kind of shelter erected on the beach in which the pilots and their crews waited for vessels in the offing. Pilots were only allowed to ship from a boat that had a crew of four so we must imagine the stations were crowded and that there must have been competition to get the pilot aboard. A ghost story recorded by A.B. Jenkins involves Herrington going to the station at Covehithe which was known as the *Horse Pond*.[15] Other evidence suggests that the pilots disliked these stations as waiting there took them away from the town and in winter were felt to be injurious to their health. They petitioned the Commissioners to allow them to ship from the beach at Southwold as the Trinity House pilots did, but to no avail. Only when Trinity House prevented pilots being shipped from the shore following the 1863 rule change did the Commissioners relent.

Interlacing these jobs, Herrington went fishing. One of his boats was *Dart*, a twenty-one foot punt passed down to him by his father, Jonas. A phenomenon longshoremen dreaded was sudden summer storms or those occurring at the equinoxes which rapidly turned blue skies grey and whipped up the waves. (Some years ago I saw one of these. Several funnel winds descended from the skies and moved across the surface like clawing fingers.) In such circumstances it was best to beach as soon as possible. Herrington was once out fishing '…I'd run off in *Dart*,' I hear him saying,

'when that come on t' blow from the south-east an' before we'd even had time t' haul the nets, the sea had roughed up bad. That wuz a dark night an' a heavy thunderstorm had come on an' all. I din't have no choice then, I had t' run for the shore, thass all I could do.

Somehow I reefed the sails an' ran ahid o' the storm, but what I din't know wuz where I should make the beach. I reckoned that what with the time we'd bin off we musta bin near the *Barnard* [sandbank] an' I knew if we run abreast o' it, that'd be the end on us. We'd ha' bin on the lee shore an' would ha' drowned. That wuz rainin' torrents, an' I had sheet lightnin' coming down one side o' me an' fork lightin' th'other. I had two ol' men along o' me what shoulda really hev bin at hoom sittin' over the fire. I tried talkin' t' 'em t' tell 'em what I wuz doin', but they din't make no answer. They wuz scairt as hell, boy.

As I wuz lookin' ahid, in a flash o' lightnin', I see a church tower light up as plain as day. I say t' them ol' boys, "We can't do better'n aim for that, 'cos if thass Kessin'land we'll go in through Pakefield gat, an' if thass Cothy [Covehithe], we shall miss the Barnard," but they never said nuthin'. I wuz on my own.

One sea come roarin' up behind us an' if that had broke over us we'd 'a bin done for but somehow we only got the run o' it arter it wuz spent so that only come over the stern with a barrer load o' water. That wave lifted us over the southern end o' the Barnard an' we struck the beach at Cothy. If we'd a' gone a bit further north we'd a' bin lost. The sea wuz so bad that seemed impossible the boat could a' brought us through. One on 'em say, " Thank God!" when we beached an' that wuz the fust words I heard spoke. O'course there weren't nuthin' on the beach t' haul her up with, no crabs nor nuthin', an we hardly had the strength t' do it, so we had t' leave her where she wuz.

I'd lost my sou' wester offa my hid in the storm. I knew I ha' t' get t' Sole t' get help. So I took my sea boots off an' run all the way there on top o' th' cliff in my stockinged feet. I knew they'd all be a-thinkin' we wuz lost 'cos the gale wuz so bad an' a terrible sea wuz runnin'. I wuz right about that. I han't bin married long an' my wife an' my mother'd bin on the beach all night. They thought we wuz done for 'cos all the other boats what'd bin out had got back safe. My poor wife weren't in no condition t' take it, bein' with child, she wuz so distracted. Day wuz breakin' an' they wuz sweepin' the sea from the lookouts with their telescopes when one on 'em at Kilcock what had his trained on Easton cry out, "There's someone on the cliff comin' this way. He hin't got nuthin' on his hid but by the size o' him, thass Ben!" Others then looked an' say, "Yeh, thass him all right!" They told my wife an' mother that I wuz safe but kept from them what they feared, which wuz that we had capsized an' I'd lost my hat swimmin' ashore an' that the ol' men wuz drowned. I wuz met by Joe Beaumont an' he an' others helped to get up the boat. Hell o' a do, boy.'

Fearlessness, courage, physical strength, determination, character. Herrington was an exceptional longshoreman but it was a life shared by many on that strip of beach making a precarious living from the sea. Herrington died aged 75 in 1890. 'At his funeral such a number of people followed that I much question,' wrote his son, 'whether such a long procession has been seen either before or since… flags were all half-mast and every shop in the place closed during the funeral procession.'

Notes

1   Cooper, E.R. *Storm Warriors of the Suffolk Coast* p.23

2   *The Southwold Diary of James Maggs 1818-1876* Vol. 1 p.130

3   Ibid p.109

4   *Storm Warriors* p. 24-27

5   *Ipswich Journal* November 29th, 1853

6   Herrington, J.C. *The Story of a Cliffman* Chapt. X p.6-7, Southwold Museum

7   *Storm Warriors* p. 25

8   Cooper, E.R. *Seventy Years' Work of the Southwold Lifeboats* p. 22-23

9   Letter to Cooper, E.R. by Herrington J.C., Southwold Museum

10 *Maggs* Vol. 2 p. 68

11 *Maggs* Vol. 1 p.138

12 *Pilotage Committee Minutes Vol 17 July 11th, 1848*. Ms. 30158, Records of The Corporation of Trinity House

13 *Seventy Years* p. 12-13

14 *Maggs* Vol. 2 p.16

15 Jenkins, A.B. *A Selection of Ghost Stories Smuggling Stories and Poems Connected With Southwold* p. 4

Voice

I heard, or thought I heard him speak — it was not always easy over the wind and the waves. Words came in spasms with long gaps between.

Boy, the words began, there's

> *Nuthin' here but ebb an' flood*
> *Nuthin' here but sand an' mud*
> *Nuthin' here but fish an' eels*
> *Nuthin' here but flukes an' keels*
> *Nuthin' here but banks an' shoals*
> *Nuthin' here but flints an' coals*
> *Nuthin' here but weed an' shells*
> *Nuthin' here but bricks an' bells*
> *Nuthin' here but trunks an' trees*
> *Nuthin' here but wind an' seas*
> *Nuthin' here but tusks an' hoof*
> *Nuthin' here but bone an' tooth*
> *No-one here but drowned folk be*
> *No-one here but them an' me*

Then the wind and the waves seemed to calm and the water in which I had been standing, held tight by his grip, rose and washed over me. I had no sense of drowning. Rather I felt only gentle motion, a floating, a letting go. I felt neither cold nor fatigued. A calmness, a floating as I say, borne up by the water beneath. I heard the waves rolling over the top of me, a hissing in my ears and as my eyes adjusted, I saw green and grey.

He was ahead of me, beckoning again. I followed, though I cannot say how it was that I moved. Shapes loomed up and then receded. Seals perhaps, others of the drowned, and I know at times there were anchors and wrecks, twisted silently in skeletal shapes, ribs protruding.

We looped arms around the branches of a tree, sat somehow on its smoothed bleached trunk. I made out the watery blue of his eyes, watched his moving lips.

I went off with my boy, the two on us, he began, *like we allus done, very early that day, t' get the top o' the flood. I pushed the boat down the ways into the breakers, an' he rowed off. When we'd cleared, he hauled up the mains'l an' away we go down into the bight. We had a good tow. Heaved th' trawl up an' then over again t' tow back down t' the town on the ebb.*

We wuz towin' fine, but the sky blackened on a sudden, an' this squall come outa nowhere, an' before I knew it we wuz cast, the boat fillin' so quick she went down by the stern. We musta been two mile off. I tried holdin' on to him but he wuz pulled away so quick an' then my boots wuz all full o' water an' there wuz nuthin' I could do.

Thass so lonely here. I keep lookin' an' lookin'. If I could only find him. Thass why I come back. Ha' you sin him? Can you tell me suthin'? An' my wife, an' the other children…

He trailed off and there was no blue in his eyes, just grey water and his beard floating round his face.

3

Childhoods

Edward (Ted) *Closh* Rogers and his son, Esau were drowned while trawling off Dunwich on Friday 14th June, 1901 when their punt, *Clara* was swamped in a sudden storm. *Clara* was washed up on the Sunday, and that evening a special memorial service was held in St Edmund's Parish Church. A large congregation attended including many longshoremen. At the end of the service £15 17s 1d was collected for the widow and her remaining children. *Closh's* body was later recovered by *Spot* May; Esau was never found. *Closh* Rogers was forty eight, Esau twelve.

At the turn of the 19th century the Rogers were one of several fishing families in Southwold working from off the beach in open boats known as *punts* powered by sail and oar. Using wind, tide and muscle, they worked an annual round of short fishing seasons throughout the year, trawling, drift-net fishing, longlining and sometimes drag-netting.

Life for such families was tough. There was no certainty as to the supply of fish, its marketing or its prices. Winter, when fishing was restricted between December and April, was a time of shortage and dread. If enough money had not been earned or put aside to see it through, the family faced real hardship. An annual soup-kitchen held weekly in the Church Rooms was an institution and in times of severe want appeals for extra funds were launched, as in 1868/9 when a Special Relief Fund Committee was set up. Subscriptions were urgently requested on account of 'the almost total failure in the fishing of last season', which had caused an 'unprecedented amount of distress… among the poor of Southwold.' £112.7.6 was raised. 800 quarten loaves, 350 quarts of soup and ten to twelve pounds of tea were distributed every Tuesday and Friday.'[1]

Frederick Bertie Rogers was born in 1889, almost two years after Esau. The middle of three children, he had an older brother, William, poor-sighted *Blind Billy*, and a younger sister, Ellen. Mr Rogers' father, Benjamin, a longshoreman, and his wife, Eliza scraped a living together as best they could in a town with few opportunities for such as them.

'I can tell you one thing about it in those days, they were darned hard times. I tell you that. Father just relied on the longshore fishin' t' get a shillin' or two, this wuz when I wuz a real youngster you know. Sometimes he used t'bring home a shillin', sometimes nuthin'. We were pretty hard up, I tell you that; they were proper hard ol' times they were. When I wuz bit older, Mother say, "You're goin' t' school boy." I say, "Well, I don't know. I don't think I'm a-goin'." She say, "Yis you are. You'll go t' school," she say. I had t' go.

We never had nuthin', so if father earned a shillin' fishin', he'd say, "Here y' are. You better go an' get three pennyworth o' pieces o' meat." You used t' get that at ol' *Fryett's*.[2] We used t' call 'em *block ornaments*, little bits o' meat what had been cut off an' what somebody had too much of an' din't want. We used t' get them an' p'raps mother'd make up a stew with dumplin's so we used t' have a sumptuous dinner. You never used t' get a lot 'cos there wuz five o' us all together. Still we struggled through.

As regard anythin' t' spend or pocket money, we never had any unless we *run herren* for somebody an' got a ha'penny. Coh! Bless me, yes! I used t' run all over Southwold an' p'raps get a penny. "Boy, what you done with that penny?" "I bought some sweets." "Sweets! You want t' get some bread or suthin', don't you?" he'd say. "No," I say, "I bought some sweets." "Oh. You better go without your bread, then." So we did. Used t' get about an ounce o' tea. That used t' be about a penny. Anything like that.

Firewood we used to make out with goin' over the common an' pull out stumps. Used t' get stumps an' pull 'em up, that wuz when I wuz a little older, o' course. We din't used t' bring the tops, just the stalk, the stem, probably the root an' all. Always used t' have a fire on. That used t' make a blinkin' stink too. So we went on like that.'

Education was rudimentary. Mr Rogers, a reluctant scholar, went to the National School. His mother, hoping that education might keep him away from fishing was disappointed. He lasted until he was twelve and a half.

Philip Jarvis, a decade or so younger than Mr Rogers was born into another fishing family.

'I wuz born in 1903. All I could hear about wuz fishin' from mornin' till night. At that time I had three brothers fishin' out o' Low'stoft. Two were engineers an' one wuz a mate, on drifters. O' course they had t' cycle t' Low'stoft in them days or walk by the beach t' get down there by seven o'clock t' go t' sea…But fishin' wuz talked of from mornin' t' night by my father an' my mother used t' talk o' her father a-goin' t' sea, so I couldn't help but know how that went on.

My mother used t' say, an' this is the truth, "Your father, out o' fishin', never kept one o' you." Out o' fishin'. Things were hard in them days. The women used t' take in washin'; the boys an' girls used t' chop firewood, take it round in linen baskets, sell it. Anythin' t' get a sixpence – well if you got a penny you were lucky. O' course there wuz always ways an' means.

You used to live nearly off fish. Your father, if he'd been out early in the mornin', he'd come ashore on the beach an' the fish would be cleaned in the boat an' they'd be nicely on a string hangin' on the *thole-pins* to dry, an' they'd go straight in the pan soon as you got home. On a Sunday, o' course meat wuz cheap in those days, a bullock's heart used t' be a luxury, a real luxury. If it wuz winter time, my father'd go out at night, like a lot more would, up t' Easton cliffs an' you had a swede or two an' turnip tops, after dark, mind you. I've sat there many a night an' mother would say, "Your father'll be home soon, bring us some swedes." An' we'd have a boil-up o' swedes. In the winter time, they used t' go out with *eel-picks* an' possibly they'd get a few pounds o' eels an' you'd have eel stew.

When things got really bad, an' I can remember that, they had a soup-kitchen down Mill Lane. That used t' be the church hall there. You used t' go down with a basin or a can an' get it but you'd got t' be artful on that. They'd say, "Don't go too early, otherwise you 'on't get the meat an' carrots what are on the bottom." So we used t' wait back an' go an' get the thick stuff off the bottom. The longshore fishermen always relied on gettin' a good sprat fishin' in, 'cos thass when they stood a good chance o' makin' some money, though the price weren't much. Sixpence a bushel that could get down to if there wuz a glut, five shillin's would be the top if there wuzn't many. Well you never got a livin' by gettin' a few fish, you got a livin' by gettin' a lot. That seem a backhanded way o' sayin' it, but you made more money by gettin' a bulk than you did just a few now an' agin. Mr Alderton's shop near the lighthouse, he used t' sell oilskins, waterboots, groceries an' everythin'. He used t' let you run an account on the understandin' that you would pay him off in the sprattin' time. A lot used t' do that. You had the money t' pay then but he'd let you go till the sprattin' time an' then you'd pay him off.'

A longshoreman could not support his family without the help of his wife turning her hand to washing and other work. Taking in washing was one activity. It was dried on lines strung out the beach or spread over the gorse on Whin Hill opposite Skilman's Hill absorbing its coconut-like aroma.[3] Another practice was to accommodate visitors during the holiday season. Sometimes the family was moved out of the house to a garden shed to free up a room or two, or else children were sent out to stay with relatives in the country. Joyce James was the daughter of a fish merchant whose premises were at 6, Trinity Street in an old pub facing east formerly known as *The Rising Sun*.

'When I was young, Southwold was a very poor place. Church Street was the poorest street in Southwold. You wouldn't think that now to see it but there were tremendously big families there.[4] That, of course, was where a lot of the fishing fraternity came from. The wives used to have to take in washing. That kind of thing. And in the very early days, the women used to take washing down and have lines on the beach and dry the washing down there. And they'd hang it on the gorse too. Oh yes that was a regular thing, to use the gorse for laundry.

Mother used to help dad in the shop in the season. She would have to work very hard in the summer to help eke out the winter and we were sent away as children so they could use our bedrooms for visitors. In those days they called them *apartments*. The people would write to mother and say had she got two bedrooms and a sitting room? And then they would do the shopping and mother would do the cooking. When I was allowed to be at home, I used to have to lay the table and serve the meals. Take the plates and the dishes, then clear away. So I was really a maid-of-all-work you might say.'

To eke out the winter makes clear it was not only the fishing families but those dependent on their catches who also had to make sure they could survive the winter months. Emerson criticised the longshoremen for their improvidence in having large families. He was equally disparaging of their attitude to domestic economy. The fishermen handed over their earnings directly to their wives, he noted, 'for it saves them much bother', adding that the women 'were unequal to the honour.'[5] The resulting poverty, as far as he was concerned, was of their own making.

Not all were so judgemental. Sympathetic shopkeepers like Mr Alderton and Mr Eastaugh, extended credit to fishing families, a practice called *living on tick*. Emerson wrote that in his time the shopkeepers had had enough of it and were trying to extract ready cash. He recorded cunning ways the longshoremen might try to avoid paying up, such as entering the shop jangling a few coppers, buying what was required then telling the bested shopkeeper to book it. Nevertheless the *pay-book system* as he called it continued into the twentieth century. William *Rory* Tooke:

'Livin' on tick. Oh yes. Half the town done that. More'n half the town. My mother an' father used to. Eastaugh the baker, he wuz a very understandin' man.[6] Sometimes my mother used t' owe him six or seven pounds, a lot o' money in them days. I'd see my father go in there every Saturday night with a little red book. But no sooner were you cleared up, signed an' sealed but winter time wuz on us again. Really thass all we used t' get t' eat for tea, a piece o' bread an' drippin' with some salt sprinkled on. They just hadn't got it, poor ol' dears.'

And when they hadn't got it, they resorted to theft:

'The winters were very severe when you were at sea. I've told you the story o' a family that lived at the back here? All they had wuz a piece o' toast in the mornin' when they went t' school, nuthin' when they went home. The man wuz desperate t' get his children some food. He got his grapplin' irons an' the lines he used for catchin' cod, walked up t' Easton cliffs where there wuz a field o' swedes. He knew quite well they were guarded like gold. The only way he could get 'em, he had a sack, he crawled up the ground an' then he took 'em home, skinned 'em, sliced 'em up an' boiled 'em, brought the children outa bed to have a feed.'

Mr Rogers was right about firewood. The poorest families scavenged gorse stalks off the common and brought them home for burning. Emerson, much taken with the gorse, usually referenced it aesthetically, 'covered in snowy linen' for example,[7] but he did record that he had seen 'an old woman, too poor to buy even the penny faggots, digging and scratching among the burnt stalks and filling her apron with the dry roots' and that sometimes 'children in ragged clothing collect in groups to dig up these roots in order to carry them away in their bag for fuel'.[8] He even made a photograph of them doing it.

If life was hard, it was not all bad. Trinity Fair, an annual Charter fair granted by Henry VII, was held on the three days after Trinity Sunday. It stretched from the top of South Green to the bottom bringing much excitement. In 1900 'the white booths, the swings, the steam horses, the shows, the shooting galleries, the cocoa-nut shies and all the fun of the fair [were] looked forward to for weeks beforehand, and [were] enjoyed more than any other event of the year.'[9] Accompanied by much civic pomp, including a hearty and usually self-congratulatory Mayor's luncheon, it wasn't only children who forgot themselves for its duration.

As a boy, Mr Rogers took part in the annual Model Yacht Regattas held first at the pond on Ferry Road and then after 1900, at the pond at the north end of town by the newly built pier. These regattas were serious, organised events attended by summer visitors and run according to strict rules. The yachts were made by the fishermen and the race Committee ensured that there were specific races for 'Fisher Boys and Girls'. The yachts had to race to the other side of the pond and back by wind power alone. Having the sails correctly adjusted to the wind was crucial. Once the competitors released their yachts from a fixed station at the start, they hared round to the far bank where, in one swift movement, they turned the yachts to windward and adjusted the mainsail for the return. They then ran back to the start to loud cheers from the banks. Some of the boats were modelled on the beach yawls and pilot cutters and the regattas were miniature versions of the real ones that took place annually at sea. Mr Rogers entered *Lily* and *Happy New Year* in the races for Fisher Boys and Girls in August 1902.[10] The regattas are still held today, still using only wind-power. They are unique in the country and while boat design has been modernised, it is possible to see some of the older yawls and cutters gracing the pond, even winning. The Whit-Monday sports held on the common each year included 'rural sports' for the town's children including an egg and spoon race, a three-legged race, and flat races for boys and girls enthusiastically attended and vigorously pursued.

Guy *Toby* Barber, born in 1896 lived in Primrose Alley though when he lived there it was called Shitting Alley as that was its function for passers-by. Recalling his early years, Mr Barber wrote in an auto-biography he lent me:

'We had to wear patched knickers. These were cut down from someone else's trousers and more often than not the patches were of an entirely different cloth and colours.'

He wrote about some of the games he played on South Green. Football with a rag ball was a favourite as was *sheep*, a variant of hide-and-seek, 'a game much loved by all and boy, did we have some fun with the girls!' He also told of the South Green longshoremen's children being taken to The Dutch Barn on Ferry Road each Christmas for a tea-party organised by Mr Monier-Williams. 'Southwold,' he wrote, 'then had the rich and the poor, but the rich never let the starvation of the South Green poor go unnoticed.'[11]

Born in 1907, William *Blucher* English talked to me about growing up in Walberswick during the First World War. One thing I discovered was that he was a beachcomber of some skill, for at the back of his cottage he had displayed his finds. Some of these spoke of deep history from times before the severance of Doggerland – fossilised remains of land mammals, gouts of amber and so on while others, more recent, were the debris of the drowned or the careless, coins, buckles, bottles, rings. Mr English spoke and I wrote down *verbatim* what he told me:

'T' grow up in Walberswick wuz really good. We wuz all working class. We wuz all fishin' folk, this end [the east end]. We had some funny ol' chaps an' dears. If anyone wuz sick or ill, they all rallied round, help each other out. All the houses were lived in. Thass surprisin' how many there wuz – fishin' folk, there.

When I went t' school there wuz twenty-eight t' thirty-two kids. We had an Infants teacher. We used t' have t' call her *Governess*. The ones what lived further away, the farm people an' the marsh people, well their kids used t' bring their dinners t' school – sandwiches, cold tea, an' the close ones 'ud go home.

That went right through t' the roof; lovely airy ol' place. The Infants were the sea end an' the others, the other. I can remember first goin' makin' pot-hooks an' hangers. There were open, old-fashioned fire-places at each end. There wuz a caretaker t' light every mornin' an' t' sweep up when we were done. When we first started, we had the slate an' the slate pencil. When you were in the Standard 4, you had books an' that sorta thing. We had bricks an' a frame with so many beads on each line an' thass the way we used t' learn t' count. The bricks were at different angles an' you had t' fit them together, triangular, rectangular an' [crescent] moon ones, t' help you get used t' shapes. The books, they were *Ten Little Nigger Boys* an' then there were nine, an' thass how we learned t' count. They wouldn't allow that now. They rhymed as they went from the ten down. We had nursery rhyme books an' all that, *Three Little Pigs and the Wolf, Jack and the Beanstalk*, all them things we had t' read. Easy, easy t' start t' learn with, an' thass what they taught us t' read with. The tables were all put in rhymes so a kid could pick 'em up easier. We had the Three Rs. In the bigger class, you stood up an' read, *Little Women*, them kind o' books. We had silent readin' an' then class readin'. You stood up an' read what she said, the chapter or whatever.

It went *Infants, Standard 4, 5, 6*. You went with the Infant teacher until you went in *Standard 4* with the *Governess*. There wuz only seven of us in *Standard 4*. They'd give *Standard 4* suthin' t' do, then *Standard 5*, then *Standard 6* but mostly 5 an' 6 went t' gether.

The fust morning you fust went, they come an' ring a bell out on the green 'cos that wuz the playground. The porch wuz this end an' thass where you hung your hats an' coats, pegs all round. Then you went in. They'd call the register fust. You'd have t' answer, "Yes Ma'm" or "Yes Governess". Then we had a hymn an' the Governess would read a verse outa the Bible. An' then the upper class started off with their Diary. The way o' the wind wuz put down, then what the weather wuz like that mornin', fine or sunny or anythin', then there wuz a rain-gauge in the garden an' a boy wuz sent out an' brought it in an' that wuz measured. What the boys used t' do with it wuz no-one's business! I always remember one day the Governess asked a boy, "Where is the wind today, George?" "Outside, Ma'm!" Coh! He got six o' the best! Three cuts on each hand an' boy she could bring 'em down too. Hand used t' smart the rest o' the day. If you saw a flower out early or a bird, you put that down, anythin' you'd seen over an' above your daily weather-report. Eclipses, all that wuz put down. You had it for the whole year, except that wuzn't filled in holiday times. We never got the holidays you have now, never got half-terms. For full attendance for a Quarter, you got Friday afternoons off.

The ol' Governess, she lived in the village durin' the week. Every Friday she'd catch the train from Walberswick Station t' Beccles. A cab from *The Anchor* 'ud turn up an' take her from the school t' the station. Nice ol' gal she wuz, Scotch too, Mrs Bellingham. We used t' have some decent teachers, all girls, young women to us. But when the Governess retired, we had a Miss Tooke from Halesworth. I din't get on well with her at all.

I wuz seven when the War broke out. A few days after that I came seven. If the Lifeboat gun went, the school became empty. You'd just take up your hat an' go down t' the river t' watch. When mines were washed ashore, different things, I remember a steamboat comin' ashore, well we just went, never asked. When there wuz anythin' washed ashore, I remember walnuts, oranges, margarine, candles, butter, soap, we'd just take the day an' go an' collect it. We never got into trouble. The next mornin' she'd say, "You all went yesterday so now you'll write an essay on it." She'd give us a tickin' off but she'd make us do suthin' useful with the experience o' it.

In the winter time when that wuz sharp weather, we'd go down on the Town marshes by the side o' the fence an' go skatin' Someone 'ud say, "Thass fit t' bear," an' we'd all go. When the time came for us t' go back t' school, someone 'ud come up an' take the clapper out so they couldn't get us. "We never heard no bell, Ma'm!" we used t' say. Then someone 'ud take it outa his pocket later on an' hook it back on.

We used t' go *birds'-egging* on a Saturday mornin' in the spring time. You took a spoon on a stick an' you went on the marshes after plover, teal, snipe, water hens, duck, redshank. We'd sometimes come home with thirty t' forty eggs apiece. Take a basket or a bag an' then we'd dole 'em out. Take 'em home t' your mothers. You were allowed then. No-one said nuthin' about it.

In the summer-time we'd go *butt-stampin'*. There'd be pools o' water in the dikes up here. You'd walk barefoot an' you'd feel 'em underneath your feet an' you'd just bend down an' take it out, throw it on the bank. The biggest you'd keep an' the smallest you'd put back, let go again. *Black-butts* – flounders. We'd make reed boats. You know, the leaf into a sail by

34

bendin' it over an' we'd have races with them. In them days we had t' make our own fun.

After the wind had blown the dust away on the roads in March, they'd be hard an' flat an we'd have races with our tops. We had all different kinds o' tops, *Flying Dutchman* an' the ordinary sort with a hobnail in the toe. Used t' go t' the blacksmith's an' get him t' put it in. We'd have races up an' down the street. On the Green we'd play marbles where the grass wuz off. We'd play *Big Ring*. Four o' you'd put in say, ten each. A big glass one wuz called an *alley* an' you'd flick all the smaller ones out an' they were yours. You'd even make your own when they were doin' the roads, out o' clay. Come home an' ask mother t' bake 'em in the oven.

On May 1st, we had the Maypole on the Green. Kids used t' take turns t' dance round it an' bind it down. Then you'd go the opposite hand an' unloosen it. The mothers 'ud turn out t' watch us. We had the little'uns an' the big'uns an' we'd each take our turns t' do the dancin'. Hoops wuz another thing we'd play, either an iron hoop which the blacksmith 'ud make or an ol' bike wheel. I'd like an ol' bike wheel. We'd take 'em with us doin' errands. Say somebody wanted suthin' in Southwold, they'd give us a penny f' the ferry an' a penny f' usselves an' you'd take the hoop an' you'd be there in no time – rollin' it along the wall. You'd leave it outside the shop when you went in. I done that many a time.

It wuz surprisin' what you could buy with a penny. Champs in Southwold [57, High St] you could get a halfpenny comic an' a halfpenny Lucky Dip with a toy an' sweets. Charlie Boy's toffees were four a halfpenny, eight a penny. Or you'd get a pennyworth o' broken biscuits. They'd mix 'em all up an' the broken ones they'd sell us kids. We'd drop the tins an' make a few more!'

Even though the First World War spanned his schooldays, a childhood like this is inconceivable today. One cannot ignore the institutionalised racism but the freedom, the attention to the world outside and the lack of care are a long way from the anxieties perplexing modern children. This is not to idealise. Though the fisher boys and girls had their high summer days to look forward to, winter was never far away and its uncertainties had to be borne as best they could by the 'poor ol dears' and their dependents.

Notes

1   *Southwold Parish Magazine* May 1869, Southwold Museum

2   James Fryett ran a butcher's at 71, High Street, elsewhere remembered as, 'very good to poor people and fond of a joke.' John Fryett, his son, ran a pork butchers, poulterers and greengrocers shop at 32, East Street

3   Shakespeare records this ancient practice in *Henry 1V Part 1* when Falstaff says, '…they'll find linen enough on every hedge.' Act 4 Sc 2. l. 45

4   Cottages in Church Street currently sell for around £600,000

5   Emerson, P. H. *Pictures of East Anglian Life* p.33

6   Frederick Eastaugh 64, High Street, Southwold

7   *Pictures of East Anglian Life* p.45

8   Ibid p.92 Regarding the penny faggots, the cutter got a halfpenny, the Corporation of Southwold a farthing, and the carter a farthing.

9   Newspaper cutting, June 11th, 1900, Southwold Museum 2006:62.1

10 *Scrapbook* Eaton W. Moore p.4, Southwold Museum

11 Barber, Guy *My Life Story*

Trace

He left me there. I saw his shape merge into the sand-filled water, a dim outline, then nothing.

Shoals of fish, dark or silver depending on how light caught them. Waves moving on the top, swelling and falling. As the tide strengthened, I was forced to hold fast to the tree for fear of being swept away. Come night, the wind dropped and the sea shushed and sighed. As in sleep there were moments of silence as if it had stopped breathing. Then it started again stilly restless.

A grey seal loomed up, eyed me curiously and flipped away, air bubbles escaping its mouth.

I became aware of words as a kind of bubbling, stringing past my ears like ribbons of weed.

> *The three o' you… on the beach, heavin'…faces white…gulls screamin'…*
> *Red-eyed… holdin' tight together…long-leavin'*
> *My tears are bladderwrack blisters… foam-flung by the tide…*
> *Yours fall on salted boots…tide-marked, white and dried…*

4

Lost

Southwold, encircled on three sides by marsh, river and creek, rises to face the North Sea on top of cliffs formed by glacial deposits. Sky falls huge to the horizons. The surrounding marshes run south to the River Blyth and north to Buss Creek, so that the town feels not just sky-landed but almost-islanded (Plate I I). Southwold beach heads north-north-east for a little over a mile from the harbour pier to its boundary with the hamlet of Easton. Composed of sand and shingle in ever-shifting proportions, it lies on a bed of Norwich Crag.

At the end of the 19th century the town in which these children were born was in the grip of progress. The railway, opened in 1879, an eccentric branch-line that connected to Halesworth and the national network beyond, began to bring increasing numbers of visitors. The town used to end at St James's Green but development in 1882 started expansion northwards when the first of a series of sea-facing terraced villas was built. In 1890 a lighthouse was erected in the town itself, visible for seventeen miles at sea. It challenged St Edmund's Church, a Perpendicular masterpiece, whose tower had been a land and sea mark for centuries so that now the one which had ever proclaimed the saving of souls was joined by the other, a beacon for the saving of bodies. Then in 1898 the newly formed Coast Development Company purchased forty acres of the Town Farm Estate from the Corporation and acted in earnest. By the following year it had opened *Pier Avenue*, a thoroughfare from the station to the beach, laid the foundations of what was to be the *Grand Hotel*, offered 123 building plots for sale on the fields of the old Town Farm and announced the erection of a pier. The Company operated a fleet of paddle steamers, the *Belles* that made excursions from London to Great Yarmouth and back. The new pier would allow visitors to embark and disembark, to stay at the Grand Hotel and to return to London by sea or rail if preferred. Abel Penfold, the Company Chairman was bullish. 'Southwold', he declared, 'would be one of the most prosperous and frequented places on the East Coast of England.'[1]

Such change alarmed. If the preferred destinations of the London trippers were Clacton, Lowestoft and Yarmouth, Southwold was being modernised against its will. At least that was the view of some. 'LOST' wailed a notice. 'Between the months of September 1888 and August 1900, a quaint little fishing village answering to the name of Southwold, age unknown, colour black and brown with green spots, clothed simply and prettily. When last seen was being chased by the East Coast Development Company. Anyone giving advice and information which will lead to its recovery will receive hearty thanks of its friends and well-wishers.'[2]

Whatever Southwold's other attractions, the beach was one of its best, weather permitting. Here the summer visitors could bathe, promenade, doze, read the papers, daub with paints, in short, enjoy a family holiday. But such ease was at odds with the fishermen for whom the beach was principally a workplace. For them visitors were a seasonal irritant. Photographs of Gun Hill show them bunched amongst the fishermen's boats and gear, their different interests plainly juxtaposed.

Nevertheless Southwold beach at the turn of the century retained many features of its working past. If you walked north from the harbour pier, the first structures you would have seen were the Lifeboat Sheds about halfway along the beach to Gun Hill. Here were the *Alfred Corry*, the principal boat, and *Rescue*, a surf-lifeboat used for quick snatches from shoaled vessels just offshore. When the first Lifeboat had been commissioned in 1840, it had been stationed under the town at *Kilcock* or *North Cliff* but after the shed was severely damaged in a storm in 1862, the R.N.L.I. moved it south. Sam May had superseded John (Jack) Cragie as cox'n in 1898. Whenever the lifeboat was called out, this was a busy place, often cold and windy with a sea running, surf in a white fury pounding the shoals, a boat to launch and a crew to board. Arthur Grubbe, a member of the Lifeboat Committee, recorded in his diary that between sixty and as many as 140 men gathered to help launch the boat.[3]

Behind the Lifeboat sheds, bordering the marshes, was the Model Yacht Pond built in 1892, adjacent to which stood the old *Sail Loft*, once used for manufacturing sails for wherries and next to it, a

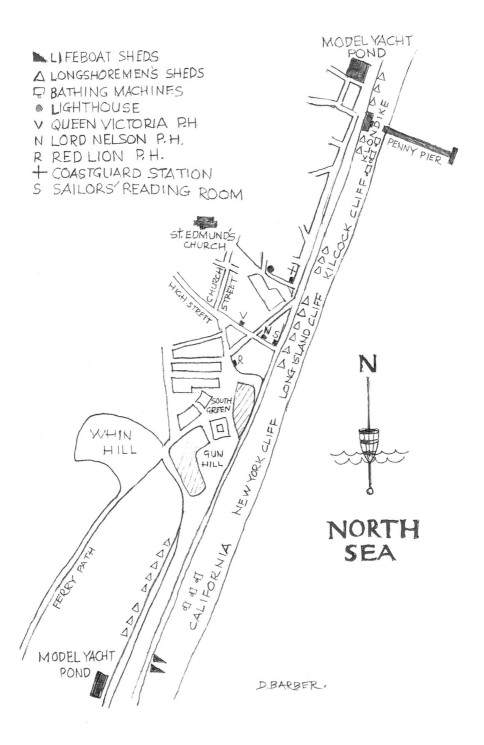

LIFEBOAT SHEDS
△ LONGSHOREMEN'S SHEDS
⊡ BATHING MACHINES
● LIGHTHOUSE
V QUEEN VICTORIA P.H.
N LORD NELSON P.H.
R RED LION P.H.
＋ COASTGUARD STATION
S SAILORS' READING ROOM

MODEL YACHT POND

PENNY PIER

KILCOCK CLIFF

LONDON DIKE

St. EDMUND'S CHURCH

CHURCH STREET

HIGH STREET

LONG ISLAND CLIFF

NEW YORK CLIFF

SOUTH GREEN

WHIN HILL

GUN HILL

FERRY PATH

CALIFORNIA

MODEL YACHT POND

N

NORTH SEA

D. BARBER.

workshop. Running from here to the foot of Gun Hill were the fishermen's sheds or *shods*, tarred wooden constructions with red pantiled roofs, used for storing nets, sails and gear, as well as for repairs. Some, more narrow, were smokehouses. The fishermen would gather here when not at sea to yarn and smoke while mending nets, baiting lines, or patching sails. Opposite the sheds, hauled up above the high tide-line, the fishermen kept their boats, their *punts*. They ran from the foot of Gun Hill back to the Lifeboat sheds, an impressive sight, surrounded by the detritus of their trade, beam-trawls, nets, net-barrows, anchors, ropes, buckets, cables, whatever was in seasonal use. The punts, mostly weighing two or three tons, were hauled up the beach by means of winches known as *crabs*. In summer Gun Hill was a favoured part of the beach, visitors drawn here by the bathing machine enterprise run by cox'n Sam May and his brother, Jack. Huge in frame and character, May was a well-known, much-loved figure in the town.

Ever vulnerable to attack from the sea, the cliffs at Gun Hill and just north at New York Cliff were defended by wooden breastworks known as Vs. Severe damage during the last decades of the 19th century meant that controversy still raged in the town about the best method of defence. In order to build up the beach, the Town Council favoured the construction of groynes to counter scouring and longshore drift. But the fishermen dissented arguing that groynes flattened out the beach, made launching more difficult and beaching more hazardous at high tide because they were then invisible. It was an argument that would not go away. An entry in the diary of Arthur Grubbe, on January 15th, 1891 gives a clear indication of the power of the sea at the undefended extremities of the town and thus some idea of the threat faced:

'Last night about 12 o'clock was the highest tide that has been known for many years…The sea broke over the foot of the Gun Hill badly, and coming down the slope made a pond all around the 'shods'… damaging one man's (May) very much and several others badly…The beachmen didn't expect this tide and were engaged all night with their boats and shods. Some of the former are knocked about considerably… Between the north cliff and the Easton cliff, the sea swept over freely the whole way…This part is a dismal vista now whilst the marshes running back to the Buss Creek wall are one big sea. Not much damage was done under the town. We have had north winds for the last two or three days, but not enough I should have thought for this abnormal swelling of Neptune.'[4]

Mr Rogers recalled the layout of the beach before the pier was built in 1900.

'The boats used t' lay all along the beach. They started at *California* [the area between the Lifeboat shed and Gun Hill], so many boats there at the foot o' the Gun Hill. From the Gun Hill there weren't nuthin' again until you got t' *Kilcock Cliff* [under St James's Green] an' thass where they used t' start again. There used t' be two boats in a berth, a certain amount o' beach for 'em, yuh see, an' the next one the same like that. That'd be so-an'-so's berth, we used t' call 'em *barth*. I can remember at California, there used t' be us, before us used t' be ol' *Champagne* Rogers to the south. Then us. Then come ol' Deal, *Prim* Deal's father. Then we come up to the Herringtons – they'd be at the foot o' the Gun Hill. The ol' *Rapid* used t' lay there – there's a model o' her in the Sailors' Reading Room. There used t' be ol' Ben Herrington an' Will Herrington, an' they were proper ol' fishermen, they were. An' thass how the boats used t' be paced out till you come t' ol' Ben Lowsey. He used t' have pleasure boats an' that. My brother worked there one summer season along with him. He used t' have the *camera obscura* on the Gun Hill an' you used t' stand in there an' turn it round an' see people on the beach. That wuz-sort of coloured-like an' that showed down on the table…'

Mr Barber knew this end well, having been born in Primrose or Shitting Alley, only a short distance above on New York Cliff:

'At the bottom o' the Gun Hill, that wuz a well-known plairce for all the gentry that used t' come t' the town. There were a lot o' big houses on the Gun Hill, Stone House, Aaron Villa, that wuz Sir Charles Blois's, an' a tremendous lot o' well-to-do families used t' come t' Southwold an' they nearly all used t' go t' the Gun Hill for some reason or another. They had all these ol'-fashioned machines on the high wheels that they used t' push down. The lairdies used t' walk up the long plank t' git inside. Some would want the machine pushed into the waters. When they went out the front nobody could see till they got in the waters, all covered up. The chief man down that end wuz, o' course, ol' Sam May. He wuz cox'n o' the Lifeboat, well-known figure in Southwold, an' I think that wuz partly the attraction at that end.'

A lone longshoreman stands amid summer visitors at Gun Hill

Some idea of relations between the fishermen and the visitors can be understood from the following anecdotes. A well-known incident, told by Mr Barber, took place during November spratting season at *Klondike* near the pier, a short time after it was built.

'On Sundays they all had a lot o' sprats [in the November season] an' they'd probably all be on the beach, *Claifornians* an' *Klondikers*. The Klondikers' wuz where I wuz this particular mornin'. The people comin' out o' church, quite a lot o'people, used t' come on North Parade, walk down that way, watch the fishermen shairkin' the sprats out. Well, there wuz an ol' man an' his son, ol' Mr Hurr [Benjamin or *Tope*], his son wuz Herbie, Herbie Hurr, father an' son in that boat, an' they were shairkin' the sprats out. The ol' man wuz deaf. He had a gret ol' brown beard an' an ol' slouch sorta hat, pulled down. Herbie wuz at the *lint* an' the ol' man wuz on the other part with the corks an' some people, some lairdies, said t' Mr Hurr, "That's cold this morning isn't it, Mr Hurr?" An' the ol' man looked. "What do the lairdies say, Herbert?" "They say thass cold, father." "COLD! Thass bloody perishin' bloody cold!" Very abrupt they were, very abrupt.'

Mr Tooke recalled this:

'Some o' the ol' fishermen were hardy ol' boys. Some were very rude, very insultin'. Ol' Jack Davy, he wuz an uncouth ol' man, very fond o' pinchin' you where you daren't show your teacher! One day he wuz leanin' over the rail on the cliff lookin' out at sea. A lady come along, a visitor, this wuz summer time, with two young daughters, about sixteen or seventeen. Full o' the joys o' spring they were, beautiful summer mornin', skippin' along. "Ah! Good morning, fisherman." He never turned his head or nuthin' like that. He just went, "Uh!" "Is it going to rain today?" "Uh!" Just then the mother arrived. She said, "Good morning, fisherman." "Uh!" Can you tell me the way to Dunwich?" He lifted his leg up sideways. "Along there." They got so used t' the beach, they took possession o' it. They even turned visitors off! They firmly believed the beach wuz theirs. They claimed it wuz their heritage. They thought so.

Winner (standing) *and Bull Smith.* Winner wears his characteristic bowler

Ol' *Winner* Smith wuz very famous for his bowler hat. Somebody said, "Your hat is getting a bit past it." It was a black one in the first place an' that had turned a lovely russet colour. Some saucy bugger spoke t' him one day on the cliff. "I see your hat is due for another change." What he really meant wuz that he ought t' git a new one an' ol' *Winner* thought he wuz

44

referrin' t' the colour! He turned round an' give this feller a crack across the head with this ol' stick. He said, "If you don't like it," he said, "you can send me another." This feller wuz so amused, despite the bruise on his head, he told his friends in his club in London. They sent him a bloody sackful o' bowler hats! Must have had about a dozen, with the compliments o' so-an'-so's club in London. He wuz like that. You din't speak t' him first, you let him open the conversation.'

Decorum, then, did not come naturally to some of the fishermen. John *Dusso* Winter related a story about how a lady visitor bought some herrings off the beach from Captain Jarvis who offered to take them up to her bus. As they moved from Trinity Street into East Street the lady saw her transport approaching. "Here's my bus," she informed Captain Jarvis worriedly. He immediately dropped the cases and yelled at the top of his voice, "Hold that fuckin' bus!"

It wasn't just visitors; the longshoremen shunned their own children. Mr Cooper told me:

'As boys you weren't allowed down there [on the beach], not 'til you started fishin'. You weren't even allowed in the *Red Lion* with 'em, not in the pub without you din't speak. You could go in an' have a half-pint but you mustn't say anythin'. If you did they'd hit you round the ears with a hat, bowler or whatever it wuz, they blinkin' well would, yes! They used t' get up to some tricks! No, you weren't allowed on the beach…You'd got t' be very careful when you were boys with them ol' lot. There wuz ol' *Winkle* Hurr, *Champagne* Rogers, *Crikey* Rogers, they all had nicknames, *Jimbo* Hurr, an' they were blinkin' gret blokes. Some on 'em were six-foot four, six-foot five an' big-built. That wouldn't do for one o' 'em t' hit you anyhow.'

Mr Barber remained baffled all his life:

'When I first come up against this, I wuz goin' t' school at the time an' all the boys used t' go on the beach t' see their fathers shairkin' out the sprats. Thass how that started with us. An' we used t' go down an' see these men with their beards an' oilskins on, an' if you went anywhere near them, "Clear outa this!" They used t' call us *kittyhawks*. "Clear out, you bloody *kitty-hawks*!" An' that wuz your own father tellin' on you t' clear out. Weren't allowed near 'em! They used t' grease the iron on the *ways*, what they used t' run the boats down on, an' if there wuz one o' 'em ways an' you stepped your foot on it, boy you were right for a proper dinger! They idolised them. They used t' have a jar an' the wife used t' have grease in it an' thass what they used t' dab on the runners an' help the boat slip in easy, an' that wuz kept in the bow o' the boat. No! They would swear at you, probably throw suthin' at you if you went near 'em. I could never make out why it wuz, 'cos you weren't doin' no harm, 'cos you merely went down onto the beach t' watch your father. Instead o' bein' sociable, like a parent ought t' be, it wuz, "Get out the bloody way! What you doin' down here? Clear out!" They wanted the whole beach t' theirself. Thass the truth.'

From Gun Hill, the beach ran beneath New York Cliff without further interruption to the central Long Island Cliff, on top of which the Sailors' Reading Room kept the more abstemious fishermen from the pubs. They gathered on the bench outside like seagulls to yarn and squint seaward. Immediately below, dug into the cliff face, was what was left of the *Long Island Cliff Company's* lookout or *clift-house*. The other lookout, better built, belonging to the *Kilcock* or *North Cliff Company* stood a little further along beneath the corner of St James's Green.

The Kilcock Cliff Company's Lookout with Critten's workshop at the foot of the score

Mr Barber and Mr Rogers remembered these, the last remnants of the old Cliff Companies. Mr Barber:

'There were two *clift-houses*, one in front o' the Sailors' Reading Room an' one wuz where the toilets now are…They were only for fishermen. As you heard me say before, the only thing fishermen smoked wuz counter-shag an' in a confined space there wuz nuthin' more horrible than the stink o' shag, overnight shag! You can imagine what this ol' plairce wuz like. That wuz long. In the front o' it wuz two wide half-doors; each side o' that wuz two openin's without winders an' in each winder wuz two brackets. On the walls at the back wuz two or three ol' spyglasses, gret ol' things. If some-body say, "Look at her runnin' down there!" Well, on go the glass. "Oh, ar, there's a brigantine runnin' down there." An' me, bein' a boy, or somebody else, would come down the steps an' come an' have a look in the winder. "Clear outa this!" An' away you had t' go in a bloody hurry. You weren't allowed near 'em. The one at the Readin' Room wuz just the same. Thass where they kept in there, for hours an' hours.'

Mr Rogers related what happened to him in the same lookout when he got too curious:

'Between California an' Klondike at Kilcock cliff, where the lavatories now are, that wuz a lookout. I remember when I wuz a boy, I got in there one day an' ol' *Bull* Smith wuz in there. We used t' call it the *clift-house*. Well, there used t' be two, that one an' one down the score where the Read-ing Room is. That one used t' be a rough ol' place but the Kilcock one wuz select, posh place, wooden floor that had. Ol' *Bull* Smith used t' be in there a good bit; it used t' be a longshoremen's retreat really. They used t' get in there, yarn an' spit an' gob. I went in there one day when there wuz nobody about. I thought t' myself, "Well, they're off trawlin' better have a look in the clift-house." 'Cos I wuz s'posed t' be at school then. I got the spyin' glass out, used t' be in a little ol' case, wuz gazin' out lookin' over t' Cov-ehithe. Suddenly a voice came out. "You can put that up as quick as you got it out!" That wuz ol' *Bull* Smith. "All right, Mr Smith," I say, "I wuz just havin' a look." "Well you look up there," he say. "Put it back where you got it." 'Cos you weren't allowed in there, us boys weren't. "Go on," he say. "Now hop off home." Another time I went in there. Thought t' myself, "I won-der what's in that cupboard." I pulled out any amount o' these little ol' flags. "Cor!" I thought. "What a lovely lot o' flags." Sortin' on 'em out, I wuz , when a voice said, "What do you think you're doin' with them flags? Go on. Put you 'em up, do I'll put my foot up your stern!" I say, "All right mis-ter. I'll put 'em back." "I know you will. I'll see you do it, too! Now," he say, "you don't want t' come in here." "All right, mister." "Garn!" he say. "Outa this!" I had t'go.

That wuz a proper lookout. No playin' about in that one. But the one near the Readin' Room used t' be a proper ol' pig-sty. There used t' be an ol' urinal-place there against it. When you got as far as the *Nelson*, you could smell it. Pooh! Heck! Especially if the wind wuz out at sea a little! Us boys got in there one night – you din't know ol' Sammy Green – anyway he say, "Are you goin' down the clift-house?" I say, "Yis, let's have a look in." Coh! That used t' stink when you went in. Howsomever we got in. "Coh! Hell! I don't half want t' pump ship," he say. "Wait a minute." So we all got in that ol' shit-place. Somebody stood behind him. He say, "What dirty bugger have bin an' pissed over my trousers? Look at this! Regular steamin'!" he say. We laughed. After a time we never went no more, packed that up 'cos a tide come an' took that away.'

Loss of The Long Island Cliff House, March 13th, 1906

On the beach itself from Long Island to Kilcock Cliff, remains of an earlier beach village could still be seen. including a row of two-storey brick sheds which were photographed by Emerson in 1886. One building of singular importance was Critten's boatbuilding shed.

Below Kilcock Cliff beneath St James's Green another group of fishermen had long since erected their sheds, planted their crabs and beached their punts. By the end of the century some remained but a movement northwards was under way. It is not possible now to know exactly why this happened but a combination of circumstances might explain it. Development on top of the cliff had added two sets of terraced villas from 1882 though these had no immediate impact on the fishermen. More decisively, two storms in 1897 wreaked havoc on the boats and sheds of the Kilcock men, so much so that after the second one in November, a Fisherman's Fund was got up to provide relief. £192.0.10 was raised and divided amongst the fishermen according to need. Most of the donors were London visitors.[5] The construction of the Grand Hotel in 1901 further urbanised the remaining North cliff. Perhaps feeling too overlooked, too much encroached on by pesky visitors, and ready to start again after the losses of the storm, the Kilcock fishermen moved mostly north, either side of the newly built pier. They called this place *Klondike*, a topical reference to the recent Yukon goldrush and a witty riposte to the Coast Development Company who were Klondiking in earnest and had frozen them out. The longshoremen knew that they would never get rich quick, though they might hit the odd lucky strike. *California* and *Klondike* continued the tradition of naming parts of the beach for the New World as in *Long Island Cliff* and *New York Cliff*. The Klondikers built new sheds or transported the remains of their old ones so that now, after 1901 the two groups mirrored each other working with their backs to the marshes south and north at the extremities of the expanding town.

Mr Barber recalled the sheds here:

'Now if a man had a boat, he'd have his shed what he used f' storin' his gear. At Klondike – I'll talk about the ones at Klondike – there wuz about six sheds this side o' the pier an' on the other side [north] there wuz a long row on' em, about twenty or thirty. These sheds were all black an' they were all wood. They had a pitched roof an' nearly all on 'em were pantiled. In front wuz two half-doors so they could have the top half open an' hauled back an' the bottom half shut when they were in there mendin' their nets an' lookin' out to sea. Below the eaves, that would be cut off, an' the top part up t' the roof wuz called the *loft* an' that wuz where they used t' keep all their nets. They were nearly all alike, these sheds. O' course some were bigger 'n others but in design they were nearly all alike. Some people, take Mr. Jack Cragie, f'r instance, he wuz a teetotaller, he never drunk no beer,

An unknown longshoreman outside his shed.
Note the relief models of ships' hulls on the door.

he never smoked an' he saved his money an' therefore he had a better class o' shed than what some o' the others did. But they were all the same. As you went along this row, you'd see p'raps one or two little narrer ones goin' way up. They were smokehouses what they used t' smoke the herren in an' sprats an' that. They stood all along there, a long row on 'em an' o' course, there wuz all sorts o' rubbish around 'em you know, nets an' beams an' ways an' all that. Then all the ol' crabs what they used t' haul the boats up with, they all stood in front o' the sheds in a row. They were a pretty sight. I'd like to see 'em again.

They kept everythin' in these sheds, all the gear, sails an' everythin' an' no-one ever locked 'em up in 'em days, never locked 'em up. The shed doors were shut, the loop put on an' ol' wooden peg put in. They never thought about robbin' one another in 'em days. No they din't! Thass true! Some on 'em had a board over the top o' the door off some ship that had come ashore. They'd found it on the beach, brought it up an' fixed it on the shed door. At the California end, 'cos their sheds stood on what is now the Ferry Road, down there wuz the only brick an' stone shed. It's now one o' those little ol' bungalows, belonged t' Mr Herrington.'

Emerson noted the fishermen's honesty, 'Theft is unknown amongst them.'

The name boards were: *Royalist, Spectator, Belle Isle, Rosebud, Nyl-Ghau, Billy* (of Whitby), *Brittania, Alma, Era, Nordhavet* and *Betsey* each with its story to tell. Photographs reveal another feature of the sheds not mentioned by either Mr. Rogers or Mr. Barber. On the open tops of the half-doors the longshoremen had made relief models of their boats, some just the hulls, others with masts and sails.

If use of the beach was contested, at least in summer, the sea bed off the beach was the fishermen's alone. They had to know what lay beneath the waves to avoid fouling their gear on obstructions, the whereabouts of the shoals and banks and the depths of the waters they were in. To the north was a shoal off Benacre Broad (also known as *Little Broad*). This was the southern limit of the extensive Barnard shoal, a dangerous place on a low tide and an opposing wind. Off Easton Broad, just to the north of the town in nine to eleven fathoms, lay *The Stones*, 'gret ol' stones from when Easton was a headland' as one fisherman put it. And also in eleven fathoms,

The Oysters, a large deposit of shells. Off the town an inner shoal ran parallel to the beach and an outer shoal lay further off a few hundred yards. The water between the two shoals was called the *Kaneway*, but the name was also used of the inner shoal itself. Just north of the Harbour pier another shoal, called the *Hayle* built up from river deposits and shifting sands made entry to the harbour tricky especially on low tides. South, off *Dingle Marsh* were the *Dingle Rocks* close in to the beach; off Dunwich Cliff was *Dunwich Bank*, and close in, hard-pan, known as the *Oven Lids*. *Sizewell Bank*, a long shoal, ran from Dunwich to Thorpe, very shallow off the sluice on Minsmere beach, and just off Thorpe above Aldeburgh, *Thorpe Rocks* were to be avoided. The fishermen gauged depth by means of lead-lines ribboned off in fathoms and half-fathoms and the ground they were on attached itself to tallow smeared on the bottom of the lead weight.

As Southwold itself, the beach was a place in flux at the turn of the century, undermined by a building wave action, the incursion of visitors on an ever larger scale. Lost. *Klondike* ironically expressed it. There was money to be made but it wasn't likely to come the longshoremen's way unless they moved with the times.

The fishermen's conviction that the beach belonged to them was not without foundation. The depth of the fishing culture at Southwold was unexpectedly revealed to me in this story Mr Rogers told about his uncle's shed:

'The fishermen used the sheds t' stow nets in, where they'd got the room, an' all th' rest o' their gear. My ol' uncle though, he'd got a sorta posh shed down along the Ferry Road. Next door t' th' *Inch* that used t' be. A man called Aldrich bought it when he died an' turned it into a posh bungalow. O' course that got washed away in the '53 flood. That wuz a good shed. There wuz a couple o' little winders on either side o' th' door. Th' ol'man used t' sit in there an' do his sailmakin'. He never used t' want t' know the time, he'd just look up at the sky, where the sun wuz. "Ah! twelve o'clock," he'd say, "better get outa this." Home he used t' go. One day he say t' me, "You can mend that net while I'm gone." "All right, uncle." I started mendin' on it an' o' course I went wrong in one or two meshes. That din't suit the ol' man. "Done it wrong, there, look," he say. "You oughta done so-an'-so." I say, "Did I?"

He say, "Yis. Instead o' that your picked up a mesh where you din't ought t' an' your made another one." That had t' be right along o' the ol' man.

One time I thought I'd make myself what they called a *barmskin*, thass an ol' oily apron. I made it outa an oily, sewed it, done it well. The feller next door, he say, "Partner, your done that all right." See me ol' uncle. He say, "What you got there, bor?" Say, "I've made myself a barmskin, look." "Ah!" he say, "if your'd a' put the stitches so-an'-so, that woulda come better." "Well. Thass all right for a barmskin in it?" "You might as well a-done it properly as done it like that. Your stitches are wrong. They in't right there. Look." "Ah," I say, "That'll do." "Yeh, that'll do." "Well, I'd blinkin' like t' do suthin' right along o' you once in a while," I say.

Then the ol man got so queer, he couldn't get down the Ferry Road. He say, "You look arter all that. I'll make it right for you." I say, "Thass all right, uncle, you don't want t' worry about that." I sorta half-nursed him while I could, when he wuz queer, before he died.

He'd got about half-a-dozen ol' cats he used t' have down there. Sometimes one on' em 'ud get the bait off a hook an' git the hook in its gills. "Bloody ol' cat," he'd say, "got a hook in its mouth. Come here. Let me get it out." The ol' chap' 'ud pull it out.

Connected up t' the shed wuz an ol' smokehouse where they smoked herren, sprats, that sorta thing. The ol' boys used t' sit outside there, *speet* the sprats or herren up. They used t' look lovely too. Then they'd hang 'em up an' let 'em smoke. Whenever that wuz a-blowin' or they coul'n't get off, they'd overhaul the nets in the shed, have a look at 'em an' they'd mend any holes that wanted mendin' or put any rope or lines that wanted t' be put on. A couple o' the ol' sheds were decorated. Ol' *Bayther* Rogers – used t' live in Church Street – he had an ol' sign on his called *Nyl-Ghau* an' Jack May, next to us, he had one called *Nordhavet*. They were nameboards that had come off ships an' got washed ashore.'

It is worth dwelling on the etymology of *barmskin*. *Barm* is Old English and means *bosom* or *lap*. A *barmcloth* is thus an apron, a *barmskin*, an apron made of leather. Chaucer uses *barmcloth* in his description of Alisoun in *The Miller's Tale*:

> 'A ceynt she werde barred al of silk
> A barmclooth eek as whyte as the morne milk
> Upon her lendes, ful of many a gore...'

To emphasise her slender waist (she is described as being shaped like a weasel), Alisoun wears a belt (*ceynt*) of striped silk. Her apron (*barmclooth*) is as white as the morning milk before the cream has risen. Its many pleats (*gore*) swing about her thighs (*lendes*). I doubt if Mr Rogers in his oily apron was as sexy as Alisoun but what is of real interest is that he was using the Old English word in its original sense. It is exciting because its use by a 20th century longshoreman takes us back to pre-Conquest Sudwald, the settlement that yielded 20,000 herrings to Bury, perhaps even to those who worked the boat found in Buss Creek. Maybe this is why the longshoremen thought the beach belonged to them; it had been theirs from the start.

And further back in time way beyond the Saxons, headlands at Easton to the north and Dunwich to the south, made the unnamed almost-island, the centre of a stagged bay. Wave action, longshore drift and destructive storms slowly dehorned the headlands, depositing the debris in the banks and shoals. What the sea took, it also revealed. With every cliff-fall, older worlds were gradually brought to light, remainders of ancient seas and reminders of our continental connection: fossilised tusks, ribs and vertebrae of whales and walrus, bones of sabre-tooth, leopard, horse, gazelle and deer, while further north at Pakefield, 700,000 year old flint shards have been discovered,[6] until very recently evidence of the earliest northern European hominids. Dunwich, a mere medieval town beneath the sea, is Britain's Atlantis. All has tumbled into that grey vault, rolled and rounded, now thrown up on the beach, now sucked south. Little wonder this shore gives rise to melancholy and the eerie.

Notes

1 Box, Peter *The Belles of the East Coast* p.53

2 The Gooding Collection Vol. A. p.225, Southwold Museum

3 The Diary of Arthur Grubbe Ms. Archive Drawer B5, Southwold Museum

4 Ibid

5 Cooper, E.R. *Old Southwold* Scrapbook, Vol. 2 p.2, Southwold Museum

6 Butcher, David *Medieval Lowestoft: The Origins and Growth of a Suffolk Coastal Community* p.1 Subsequent finds at Happisburgh in Norfolk have been dated to almost a million years, including the earliest known footprints outside Africa

5

The White Threshold

On holiday on the Isle of Lewis a few years ago, I went to the Museum at Uig where the crofting life is magnificently displayed. An unattributed quotation about the crofter's relationship with his boat arrested me:

'...The character and nature of the boats were very varied. Some were stout-hearted, some timid, dependable-unreliable, honest-treacherous, fast and slow, good-natured, bad-tempered, sluggish-lively, tough and delicate etc.

All must be understood to be handled properly before the best is realised. They must be humoured, driven, coaxed, nursed or bullied according to their character, before they respond...There must be trustworthiness, courage and mutual affection between a boat and the helmsman...'

This reminded me of words spoken by Mr Barber, words which unite fishermen from about as far apart in the United Kingdom as it is possible to be:

'They [the longshoremen] were rough an' tough [but] the boat they went fishin' in wuz their god. They looked after it an' treated it so well. That wuz painted each year, that wuz scrubbed out every day, washed out. Always in the bow wuz a jar o' ol' grease an' the wood they used t' hoist her up on [the *ways*] had an iron plate on 'em which they greased, an' when they were done with 'em, they were stood up with the grease towards the boat, off the sand, so the starlin's shouldn't pick the grease off 'em. Everythin' wuz so neatly done with 'em, they could go down there in the pitch dark an' put their hand on exactly what they wanted, they could.'

Whether at Uig or Southwold, the boat was to be understood, served and husbanded. Florence Stannard told me that when a longshoreman got married, his boat was beautifully adorned; it was a vital part of the union.

The longshoremen's lives and livelihoods depended on their boats as much as on their skill in handling them. Just as the blacksmith was a kind of Vulcan in the rural community, the boatbuilder commanded high status amongst fishermen. In the days of sail and oar, fishing towns and villages had their boatbuilders fashioning craft by hand, eye and tradition, expertly adapted to local conditions.

The Southwold beach boat was one such craft. 107 boats mostly weighing two or three tons were registered at Southwold in 1903. They belonged to sixty four owners.[1] A meticulously detailed model of *Rapid* (LT 835) is on display in the Sailors' Reading Room. Emerson recorded basic details about the boats which, in his day, were built for a sovereign a foot and cost about £60 complete with gear. His is invaluable first-hand evidence but we can get closer to the real thing from those who worked them.

'The longshore boats,' Mr English told me, 'or *punts* as we used t' call 'em, were built at Southwold by Critten, Billy Ladd or Aldrich.[2] They were between seventeen an' nineteen foot long an' had a beam o' about seven foot – plenty o' beam they used t' give 'em so they looked a bit like a soap-dish. We never used t' like a narrow-gutted thing like the ships' lifeboats that sometimes got washed up ashore. Most of 'em who had 'em built, named 'em after their sons or daughters. Ol' Joe Palmer f'r instance, his wuz called the *Arthur and Phyllis* (LT 431) an' the one I had wuz called the *Maud Ellen* (LT 810). I bought that off Goldsmith an' that wuz the name o' his daughter. You never changed the name, you see, 'cos that wuz bad luck.

They had a mainmast, a *standing-mizzen* mast an' an outrigger an' they were clinker-built. The mainmast wuz supported by a stay called a *burton* which you moved t' the weather-side every time you went about an' the only other rope wuz the *halyard* which pulled the sail up. The mains'l wuz a *dipping-lug* which meant that every time you came about on a tack, you had t' lower it, bring it round the mast aft an' haul it up the other side. T' do that you had t' undo the *tack* o' the sail from the *bumkin* – that wuz an *s*-shaped bit o' iron that stuck out o' the *stem* – undo that, change the *burton* t' weather, lower the sail an' haul it up again. An' that could be quite a business sometimes, I can tell you!

The sail itself wuz attached t' a *yard* an' on the *yard* wuz a *thimble* an' this here *thimble* hooked on t' the *traveller* which wuz an iron ring which went round the mast. This wuz attached t' the *halyard* so when you pulled down on that, the whole thing went up. The sails were o' *sailcloth*, white, an' some would keep 'em white until they got dirty an' then they'd be tanned in *cutch* which helped t' preserve 'em.[3] They were made by Jeckells an' they

were all in strips t' get the shape an' the pull right. They had up t' five sets o'
reefs so you could *reef* down for bad weather an' that.

The mizzen wuz a *standing-mizzen* that pulled up the same [as the main-
sail] an' that wuz hooked t' a point on the side o' the mast. It wuz attached t'
an *outrigger* which wuz about six foot long an' which ran through the stern
an' fixed into a square metal clasp which wuz bolted t' the back thwart. There
wuz a pulley in the back end o' the pole through which the rope from the
clew o' the mizzen ran an' which wuz cleated t' a point inside the stern. The
mizzen kept the boat up into the wind; that wuz the point o' it, you see.

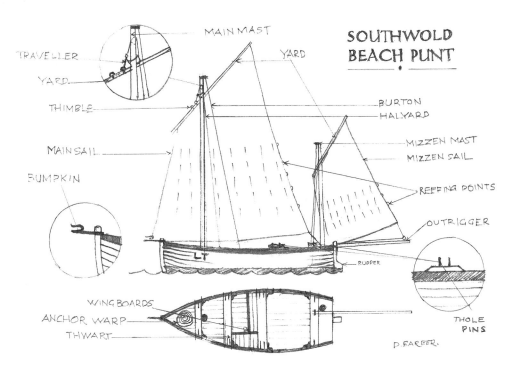

Inside you carried a *lee-board* which wuz about six to seven foot long an'
about nine t' eighteen inches wide. It wuz made out o' elm, tapered at the edges
an' had a rounded bottom. On the top wuz a rope which you hooked over the
thole-pin so that it would keep it in place when you used it. An' o' course you
always dropped it over the lee side. The function o' the lee-board wuz like a
centre-board in a modern dinghy, it helped t' stop the boat from slidin' across
the water when goin' t' windward an' t' make it sail closer t' the wind.

They carried two pair o' oars, or *sweeps* as we used t' call 'em but they were so heavy you only used a pair at a time. Along the gunwales were pairs o' holes what the *thole-pins* went in; you used 'em for rowin' or attachin' things to, also for when you were trawlin' an' that. Another thing you always carried wuz bags o' shingle for ballast an' you shifted 'em about accordin' t' the weather.

There wuz a bulkhead under the main thwart which wuz divided by wooden boards t' form *wings* an' you used 'em t' put your fish in. Runnin' the length o' the boat were the *bottom boards* an' triangular-shaped *stern sheets* at the aft end which were raised. The rudder wuz hooked on t' *pintles* but as a precaution a bit o' rope wuz cleated inside so if you unshipped you wouldn't lose it. All the boats, o' course, were lettered an' numbered LT so-an'-so, whatever it might be. They were mostly white with tarred or red bottoms an' black or blue gunwales.'

Other gear carried for use when trawling were a *drogue-sail* and a *lead-line*, each of which we will hear about in context.

Longshore boats were run on a share system. The boat took a share of any catch for its maintenance as did the owner. Mr Barber:

'If a man had a boat, he had his shed, he had his gear, nets, lines an' everythin'. Now he couldn't go sprattin', he couldn't go longlinin' without he took two men with him. Well, the owner got a share for his boat, an' the owner got a share for his gear an' the other men got one share each. That man who owned the boat an' gear had got t' put so much away, if he wuz a careful man, so he could buy new gear or pay for anythin' that needed replenishn' in the boat....Take Mr Cragie. I allus think o' his name 'cos he's allus in my mind when I start talkin' about longshorin', I knew him so well. Right, he's got a longshore boat, kept in good condition. He would say: "How would you like t' come sprattin' along o' me, when the time come?" "All right. Yis. I don't mind." "Well you know how the rules run don't you? I shall have my two shares an' you'll have yours." So there'd be three shares an' if you agreed you'd say, "Yis, all right." Well, thass how you went along with it. There wuz no argument about, no quar-rellin' about it.

Well now, if that wuz a seventeen foot longshore boat, a bigger one, carry a few more nets, well then they'd have three on there, an' that meant

you'd got three shares. More in't there? But that din't make no difference t'
th' owner, he still had his two shares, you had yours, the partner had his.
That wuz the same with all on 'em. It wuz an ol' traditional sort o' thing, I
s'pose. An' after all's said an' done, the owner did really want two shares,
as I say, 'cos he's got the upkeep o' the nets an' the upkeep o' th' boats an'
the shed an' all th' gear. He'd got t' look after it all.'

One of the most hazardous of the longshoremen's activities was
the launching and beaching of their punts, the crossing of the shore-
breaking waves and then of the *Kaneway* just off.

'There wuz quite an art t' *larchin'* the boats. Summer time goin' a-
shrimpin', they used t' go alone; when they got t' trawlin' they'd have two
in a boat; herrenin', p'raps three an' when they got t' sprattin' they used t'
have three or four. Shrimpin' an' trawlin' wuz in the fine summer months
so that weren't so difficult but when they were goin' after the herren in
October time that wuz gettin' a bit bad; but now, gettin' on a month, November, beginnin' o' December, sprats, that wuz gettin' rough. But they'd
go off if that wuz a rough mornin', they din't care about the seas a-breakin'.

They'd get their boats down on the ways; every one wuz greased an'
kept in order. P'raps there'd be three or four goin' in the boat. They'd larch
her down t' the water, let her lay down. They used t' call it *keelin' over*, keel
her down on the bilge an' they used t' get everythin' they wanted t' put in it.
I'll talk now just as they used t' talk. "*Keel her up!*" Used t' keel her up on
t' her keel. If there wuz a nasty sea a-runnin', as there might be November,
December, they had what they called a *sett*. Now, there wuz always someone
there t' help you shove her off, never wanted t' worry there weren't anybody
there t' help you off. The sett wuz like a scaffold pole. It wuz long an' as it
went along, it tapered at the end. On the end o' it wuz an iron band t' stop it
from splittin' an' there wuz a *swan-neck*, an iron that came out with a curve
on it which they used t' hook over the stern o' the boat. That laid on the
stern o' the boat so when it wuz afloat, all they'd got t' do was pull it off an'
let it drop in th' water.

These ol' boys used t' man the pole, maybe four, maybe six. The crew,
all but one, would get in the boat. Two would sit on the forethwart with a
pair o' oars, all ready; the other one would get on the afterthwart with his
two oars. Now the skipper, who wuz in charge, he'd have hold o' the stern

o' the boat an' he'd watch till the waves come t' what they called a *smooth*. I could show you now if I wuz on the beach. In a gale o' wind, there's always a time, for a second or two, when the water's smooth, always. They'd wait for this. He'd holler out, "*Let her go!*" They'd shove with the sett an' he'd run down with the boat into the water an' hop up on the nets onto the stern. These ol' boys would shove her off an' away they'd go.

They'd always watch for a *smooth* comin' back. The danger o' comin' back t' the beach in a punt in them days wuz what they called *casting* o' her. If you come back t' the beach winter time in a heavy sea, you got t' come *straight on*. If you din't wait for a smooth t' come on an' you came in there when the seas were a-rollin', very likely a breaker 'ud lift you up an' you'd go broadside on, throw everythin' out, you an' all.

When they're comin' back, let's take *Mop* Smith come back t' the beach. There's him an' his two brothers. They've got several *bushels* o' sprats, which mean the boat is heavy. They're down at the boat but up at the *crab*, there's someone waitin' for 'em. The crab is made o' wood an' what the rope go round is called the *bull*. Thass got a square head what the bar go in. They'll stand there, p'raps one or two, p'raps more, they've got the bar. They've already pulled the bolt an' chain down t' the boat. One man 'll hop out the boat. His job is t' gather up the chain, put it through the hole in the stem, through the crab-rope an' sing out, "*Heave up!*" As soon as they sing out, "*Heave up!*" whoever's at the crab, they put the bar in the hole an' away they go round with it, all the way round, till they've heaved her right up.

They'd pull her out o' the water an' there's one man holdin' on her up, on the keel, an' there's other ones a-puttin' the ways, the wood, underneath, an' thass how they heave her up. When they get her far enough out o' the water, they put her in on what they call the *swivel*. Thass one made t' swivel round. It has two high cheeks. They put her in an' there's an iron pin go through this. When the swivel is half-way along the keel, they'll stop an' turn the boat round so she's pointin' out ready t' go t' sea again. Then they shove the two *stools* under [to keep the boat upright]. Oh! Thass quite a method. An' you know quite a lot o' the' longshoremen in them days were ruptured, had a hernia, some had a double hernia through liftin' an' pullin' an' pushin' an' they never done nuthin' about it. I know one ol' man in Victoria Street, ol' *Jimbo* Hurr, that could hardly walk, he wuz in such misery, tied an' lashed up. They woul'nt do anythin' like go t' the doctor's. They thought they were too tough.

The longshoremen each had a *berth* for their boats, thass what the crab signified. Along the beach, say this is my shed here, now straight ahead o' that, thass my crab standin' there facin' the sea. Well I've got t' come t' there an' the [next crab] is over there but far enough so that when you're heavin' your boats up [they] don't clash. Thass how they were all spaced out, like that. Now if you were a-comin' t' the beach, say that wuz a-blowin' very hard, you might be one o' the last, or you might be the last, somebody'd know that wuz where your berth is an' they'd wave you further along t' come ashore at somebody else's. Help you that way. Yes, each fisherman had his berth an' there wuz room there for about two or three boats in the width o' the beach they had.

A laden punt beaching in rough breakers. It was essential to avoid *casting*

They were a marvellous race o' people, that they were. When I look back on the things I've sin my father do an' I've sin some o' the other ol' men do, that really frighten you! T' see 'em *go off* in a gale o' bloody wind, an' I've sin 'em down the California end one winter time when the sprattin' season wuz on, an' us boys always used t' be on the beach, an' they were *goin' off*. There'd be two boats an' they'd amalgamate. They'd say, "Look, Jack, you lend us a hand, an' we'll lend you a hand." They wanted t' get the low water. They din't care what the sea looked like. They got the two gangs, six people, plenty more there on the *setts*, ready. They'd put one crew into one boat, two people, an' they'd shove her off. Them two people 'ud row off, clear the breakers an' lay there. Then all the others would man the other one. They'd shove her off. They'd go alongside the other one, put the other man aboard o' her an' then they'd both go out.'

Mr Barber's account emphasises the potential dangers and some of the methods of crossing the border between beach and sea and sea and beach, *the white threshold* of the poet, W.S.Graham. They are the physical rituals of transition, as old as going to sea itself, 'the sphere of chance-in-play' as Adam Nicolson has put it. The beach at this moment, according to Nicolson, is the place of 'promise', 'threat', 'ambiguity' or *in extremis*, of 'grief'.[4] Maggs recorded several instances of death by drowning on the threshold. This one involved two boys:

'1830 Nov 30th Saml Jarvis and Job Spoore two lads were accidentally drowned by the upsetting of their boat upon the beach. Same day held an Inquest upon the body of Job Spoore and upon the body Saml Jarvis the following day, who was carried into the Harbour by the tide. Verdict in both cases, accidental death.'[5]

Mostly though, *going-off* was about taking to the other element, pulling the punt clear of the breakers with the oars, sensing the wind, hauling up the sail, feeling the boat transform from a dead weight to a living thing responsive to handling, about hearing the slap of the waves against the bow and watching the foam seething aft, about the way the boat is lifted by the waves and the way the body responds. By contrast beaching was a lurching moment of uncertainty, hope and skill until the boat became a dead weight again and the long-shoremen eased her up the shingle and turned her seaward ready once more.

Learning to sail a punt was rite-of-passage often picked up in a rough and ready way as boys. Mr Rogers:

'... the ol' man asked if I'd go a-shrimpin' with him. I say, "Yis. I'll come along." So we went up t' Dunwich an' when we done shrimpin' up there, he say t' me, "Well, we got a few shrimps." Shrimps never used t' make much in them days. Used t' get about half-a-crown a *peck*. Well we got about a couple o' pecks, I 'spect. "You can sail her home while I clean the net." "All right, father." I wuz as bold as brass sittin' aft there, steerin' along. There wuz a stiff breeze o' wind from the nor' west. That wuz all right comin' under Dunwich Bight, till we come t' the harbour. I thought t' myself, Coh! She's goin' t' turn over! I shoved the tiller as hard as I could away from me. The ol' chap roared at me! "What are you doin' on? You'll make the harbour." "Coh! Father," I say, "She's a-goin' t' turn over." "She 'on't turn over," he say. "Don't you do that sorta thing!" Anyhow we made the beach. Got ashore.'

Mr Jarvis also had a nervy experience:

'Jack Cragie wuz a man short once. I went with him. I got swore at too! My father an' him an' myself – 'cos Bob Palmer used t' go an' he wuz ill. An' Jack Cragie say, "We'll take your boy." There wuz a lot o' wind. We were goin' away off an' we reefed the sail. We put two reefs in – 'cos they had four or five reef-points in 'em. They done that end an' I done this, an' somehow, I got hold o' the third reef-point an' tied it an' they'd gone two. So when they set the sail all the weight came on the third reef-point. Coh! There wuz some swearin' about! "Lower that sail! You'll rend her all t' pieces!" 'Cos they valued their sails. Coh! He let fly at me.

I'll tell you another thing. I wuz with ol' Herrington. He used t' go her-renin', him an' a man by the name o' Stuart Welton. I wuz a boy then an' all the ol' boats, when you used t' haul the nets an' shoot 'em away again, o' course you got a lot o' water in 'em, so you had t' pull the stern-sheets up an' bail it out. I wuz a-bailin' out an' the bailer wuz a hand-cup an' the edges had frayed. They used t' put the plug in from the inside, but the plug-hole, over the years, had worn, so they'd got a great plug with a cloth round it. Well, as I bailed out, I suddenly caught the cloth an' out come the plug an' the water poured up. "Coh! I don't know what! Look Mr Herrington, I pulled the plug out." An' calm, he say, "Put your hat over it, boy!" An' I had t' put my hat down an' stand on it till I found the plug t' put in again. As cool as a cucumber. I wuz frightened, boy. I thought it wuz goin't' sink. It wuz pourin' in. He said, " Put your hat over it, boy!" '

Not only did the longshoremen have to know the ground on which they were fishing but, when trawling, they had to know the obstructions on the sea-bed in order to avoid fouling their nets. Mr English told me how they did this using what were called *long marks* and *breast-marks*. This was a system of triangulation between the boat at sea, a land mark at a further distance from it and another land mark nearer to it:

'The longshoremen had t' know the exact depth of water. You'd use your *lead-line* all the time for that. An' they also had t' know marks, *straight-in* or *on the beam*. They marked wrecks, anchors, cannons, that sorta thing. You had t' know 'em otherwise you'd get *fast* an' lose your gear.

How did we use the marks? Well, s'pose you'd leave the beach or harbour about four in the mornin' – this is in the sailin' days – reach off t' *The Brig* [the wreck of a brigantine off Walberswick] an' set your net t' tow south. You'd tow right through *Dunwich Bight*, keepin clear o' anchors an' wrecks, t' haul up at *Chimneys-in-One*. [The aligned chimneys at the Coastguards' houses on the cliff at Dunwich]. After cleanin' the net, you'd set again at *Road Open* [a road visible from the sea] t' tow across *Sizewell Bank*, then haul up again an' come outside the Sizewell Bank Buoy, t' set again an' tow on the slack tide. You'd be nearly six hours doin' that, then you'd either tow some o' the way home so you could reach the harbour with a fair wind, or just sail straight home, that all depends what you got, the amount o' fish. If you hadn't got much fish, you had another tow down, what they called a *saver*. You'd be back in the harbour or on the beach again about two o'clock.

All the time when you were off, you'd be aware o' these wrecks. As you got near one o' 'em, you'd have your lead-line goin' so you could steer inside or outside o' whichever wreck it wuz. That'd be the same goin' north, you'd tow off there in the same way.

For takin' the mark, say you were goin' t' The Brig in *quarter-less seven fathom*. When you were gettin' near to it, you would watch for your mark straight-in, that'd be your *breast-mark* an' for your mark *on the beam* that'd be your *long-mark*. You'd keep your eyes goin' all the time till they lined up, then you'd keep clear.

On the Aldeburgh grounds, some o' the Low'stoft steam trawlers would come an' tow if they heard any o' us were gettin' fish. I've heard sparks flyin' when they got caught 'cos they didn't know where the wrecks were.

They'd shift 'em about too, pull 'em out o' line, specially the anchors, so sometimes we'd get caught on 'em as well, you see. You'd go for weeks without gettin' caught, then you'd catch one o' 'em. Some o' the wrecks have laid there hundreds o' years, like *The Brig*. Now there's new ones like aeroplanes, that sorta thing. If you *got fast* on a wreck, you had t' wait for a tide t' finish before pullin' back the opposite way again. I hung a good six hours on a wreck once below the *Belle* pier. That wuz *Joe's Wreck* an' I just lost a *lute-head* but I got the net all right when the tide went away.'

This triangulation enabled the longshoremen to navigate paths of avoidance, a simple, effective and self-sufficient solution to the problem. Not long after I learnt this, Mr Cooper agreed, over a pint or two, to tell me the marks he used. Thus, for example:

The Brig: in seven fathom
Breast-mark: Walberswick Church over the west chimney of Westwood Lodge.
Long mark: Lighthouse over Centre Cliff.

Wally (*Snipe*) Upcraft, one time Trinity Pilot and Harbourmaster, put it like this:

'You've heard talk o' *The Brig* in the bight? Well, the breast mark for that, there's a great house at Walberswick [Westwood Lodge] with three chimneys. Now, Walberswick church is right behind the westernmost chimney. Thass a breast-mark. For a long mark, before the Centre Cliff wuz pulled down there wuz a big dome on each end, the lighthouse used t' be right in line with the outer dome. That'd be your long mark. So you knew what t' look for when you were comin' close up to it. You'd got t' keep clear. But you couldn't tell everybody, anybody really, all the marks that you know, 'cos you'd forget 'em yourself until you spotted one mark, then the other'd come t' you.'

Knowledge of the marks then, was part of the *mystery* of long-shoring which you kept to yourself. I have never seen the marks written down in any document so those Mr Cooper passed on would have been lost forever. These days GPS and computer-generated images of the sea-floor solve all such problems.

A known hazard was one thing but the unknown was potentially fatal. The longshoremen in their small punts were always vulnerable to sudden squalls and storms and fog was particularly perilous, the possibility of being run down, unseen by a larger boat, all too real. Maggs records fatalities in such circumstances while others were reported in the local papers.

Until the end of the First World War the longshore fishery was conducted from off the beach in punts powered by sail and oar. Thereafter, with the introduction of first, petrol and then diesel engines, the traditional method came to an end. Since the engine made the punts heavier, it made sense at Southwold to berth them in the harbour as launching or beaching with the engine aboard would have made an already hazardous operation even more so. Mr English described the change:

'I think Joe Palmer wuz one o' the first t' have a motor in his boat, but by the late 1920's an' early 30's, they all started t' get 'em.[6] They were petrol or paraffin powered. I had an Amco an' any Ford part 'ud fit it. That wuz a four an' a half horse-power single-cylinder job. The advantage o' a motor wuz firstly 'cos it made less work for you. It wuzn't so hard. I mean, with a sail, when you were trawlin' for example, you were completely dependent on the wind for your tow, but with a motor, you could set your course an' that wuz that. You kept your mizzen o' course, but the motors made things much easier generally. They stared comin' in the harbour after a while an' workin' from there 'cos it wuz a hard job haulin' the boat up an' down the beach an' in the end most o' 'em were workin' from there. When the boats had motors put in, they had t' be fitted with an extra nine or ten inches on the gunwales 'cos the weight o' the engine drew it down when you were under way an' o' course the engine wuz right in the middle o' the boat so you had plenty o' width about you.'

Percy Westrup, a longshoreman from Thorpeness, told me about this:

'Two o' my boats were built at Southwold. My biggest one wuz built at Southwold. Eighteen foot. That cost eighteen pounds when that wuz built, man by th' name o' Ladd…Pound a foot! 'Cos, they could build 'em at Southwold, better'n what they can at Woodbridge. I can remember takin' my big boat t' Woodbridge. I wanted so much put on t' make it higher [to accommodate the engine]. When I went there, there wuz this apprentice-boy. "Oh," he say, "I can see where this boat wuz built, it was built at South-wold." I say, "Yis, boy. They can't build one at Woodbridge like it." That shut him up! They can build a boat at Woodbridge for the river but as for the beach they can't, not like they can at Southwold.'

Notes

1 *Flood's Register of Vessels of the Port of Lowestoft* February 1903, Author's collection
2 Critten was on the beach at Kilcock; Ladd was at the bottom of South Green; Aldrich was at California opposite the Lifeboat sheds
3 '… a resin of the Far Eastern tree *Acacia catechu* which was used as a preservative…' Butcher, David *Fishing Talk: The Language of a Lost Industry Drawn Mainly from East Anglian Sources* p.38
4 Nicolson, Adam *The Mighty Dead: Why Homer Matters* p.29-30
5 Maggs Vol 1. p.74
6 Palmer's engine was a Thorneycroft. He was engineer on the Lifeboat and never missed a call-out. His nickname was *Satan*

6

Critten And Sons

'The clock in the square grey tower of Senwich church had just struck four, but already, under the lowering November sky, darkness was come and in the boat-building shop of Bredon and Sons the five hanging oil lamps were lit and the shutters closed and checked, with the exception of one wedged half open on the lee side. Without, a southerly gale bombarded the timbered sides with an incessant fusillade, and at regular intervals the sea spray drove hissingly against the barred swing door which occupied the whole eastern end of the sturdy squat building that for eighty years had crouched defiantly under the cliff…'[1]

So begins *Bredon And Sons*, Neil Bell's 1934 novel about the business into which he had been born. Bell, born Stephen Critten, wrote that the novel was 'the story of my father's people over a hundred years of boat-building and I knew I could tell it well for part of it was also my own story in its earliest years. I was born there; I knew the people; knew the way of life: it was in my blood.'[2]

Crittens and boat-building had been synonymous since at least the eighteenth century. William Critten (1744-1807) had businesses both in Southwold and at Aldeburgh. His will bequeathed his house, work-shop and its gear to his wife, Mary, as well as shares in a yawl and a pilot cutter. In addition he owned two other properties occupied by the Trinity House pilots, Edward Syer and Ashmenall Baldry. William may well have apprenticed his eighth child, James (c.1783-1852) to the Aldeburgh shop because a hastily arranged marriage with Mary Richardson took place there in April 1805, two days after the third banns were read. After the marriage the couple moved back to South-wold where their first child, James (1805-1879) was born in June.

Having succeeded his father, James senior later leased a plot on the beach from the Town Council 'North of Long Island Cliff' and continued the business.[3] It is possible that the shop he built there was destroyed because in 1837 James junior, having already built another, took out a further lease for 75 years. He signed the indenture on February

19th, 1841, in a beautiful hand, elegant, controlled and confident, exactly the hand to build a boat.[4] This shop was wrecked by the high tide of November 20th, 1863 which also destroyed the original Lifeboat shed, whose door was later found washed up on Dunwich beach. Rebuilt, father and son consolidated the Critten reputation as the pre-eminent boat builders on this part of the coast.

The heyday of the business spanned the lives of the Jameses about whom a few scraps of information have survived, most notably this entry in Maggs dated Thursday April 12th, 1849:

'… Mr Jas Critten-boat builder – and his son Jas – brother George and a boy of Wm Pott Spence, on their way from Covehithe in an open boat were accidentally upset- Jas. Critten Snr and his brother George swam to the Shore- Jas. Critten Jnr. being entangled in the sail & rigging, after extricating himself therefrom – he then proceeded to the safety of the boy whom he extricated from a watery grave, but very much exhausted, so much so that medical aid was applied and the next day the boy came home.'[5]

This suggests a terrifying episode in lethal conditions beyond the control even of master boat-builders during which the younger James was nothing short of a hero.

Another scrap concerns a formal complaint lodged at the Town Hall on May 24th, 1850 and witnessed by the Mayor, Peter Palmer, in which the younger James stated that his uncle, George, 'did unlawfully assault and beat him.'[6] We do not know the circumstances or the outcome but clearly something serious had taken place. George, described elsewhere as a shipwright, may well have been in partnership with his brother, and the assault may have had something to do with work. Was there bad feeling in the shop? How well did brothers and sons get on?

This is of interest because in *Bredon And Sons*, Bell characterises the siblings of each generation as either worthy or prodigal. The novel opens tempestuously in a north-west gale which despatches George Bredon to his death as he tries to save the shop that has stood on the beach for eighty years. George represents one side of the Bredon character: hard-working, skilled, successful, stubborn, proud. The other surfaces in his dead brother, Bob who possesses 'that queer, dark outcropping taint'[7] manifest in 'the laughing and not caring, and the recklessness, the shiftlessness, and all the mad spending and drinking. And hating the work in the shop.'[8] This binary pattern of inherited characteristics repeats itself with variations in each generation. If Bell's view of the Bredons is determinist, the lives themselves are played out against the shifting backdrop of history and the local affairs of Southwold and beyond.

For half the novel Bell fictionalises faithfully, if not always chronologically, 19th century Southwold, particularly in its relationship with the sea. In some respects these chapters could be read as fleshed-out versions of Maggs. Senwich, as the town is called, is topographically accurate. A scene set in the *Red Lion* seems taken from life, as does the shop with its large east-facing door, its five oil lamps, grindstone and steam room. The Bredon protagonists engage in controversies that gripped the Town such as whether a self-righting lifeboat, as James Bredon (unconvincingly) and mistakenly believes, is the right sort for the conditions at Southwold rather than the 'wet boat' favoured by the cox'n. Bell describes real shipwrecks and brave rescues made first by the cliffmen in their yawls and then, as time moves on, by the lifeboatmen.

Bell is excellent on detail. The process of constructing a beach punt is clearly explained; he uses the real lease the younger James signed in 1841 as the one his fictional James has drawn up for him; adopts his father's indentures for those he gives the fictional Arthur. He describes accurately the rhythms of life in the town revolving round the fishing seasons, the summer visitors, the Regatta and the sports, the winter storms and wrecks, the lifeboat rescues and the deaths of the longshoremen at sea. In dialogue he captures his characters' accent and dialect faithfully.

Although the town changes slowly through the century, there are two constants. 'New names and new faces in the streets' appear in James's lifetime:

'But if on the beach there were new faces, the old names had not changed. Busy with their nets and tackle, hauling up their boats as they circled round the "crab", counting catches, cursing the ravenous gulls, smoking their Dunwich clays, growling with mock ferocity at the children tripping over ropes and clambering into the boats were the Mays, the Hurrs, the Watsons, Palmers, Crickmores, Bences, Stannards, Greens, Herringtons, Bensteads, Waters, Craigies, Pecks, Coopers, Fishes, Crisps and Muirs. And on their lips were the nicknames that were as old as the town: Rory, Plucky, Toshes, Mop, Pincher, Forty, Ducker, Crooker, Brushey and a dozen more.'[9]

And then there is the sea. In an impressive passage near the start in which the dying George Bredon relives his life, he muses on the sea's influence on the town:

'A sort of doom it was. The doom of the sea…The doom that destroyed Dunwich and Easton Bavents. There was no beating the sea. It could wait. But it had what it waited for at last, towns, ships and men.'[10]

The business reaches its zenith in the life of James Bredon in the mid-century. Though he keeps building punts for the longshoremen, the demand for yawls starts to decline. James's hope to revive his fortunes by investing in the new railway, which promises the possibility of sending fish direct to the London market, comes to nothing. As prosperity slowly ebbs out of the once flourishing business, the Bredon wives lose their servants and take to accommodating summer visitors for the season. After James's heroic death, the business falters on till it can no longer support two families and the break between James's sons, Arthur and Richard, occurs. Richard leaves for Stourhampton to work for a large boat-building firm. Arthur carries on as best he can, apprenticing his boys, believing that the business will at least give them a living, but when the shop is destroyed in another storm and Arthur, like his grandfather, dies trying to save it, the end has come. The doom of the sea has triumphed. The second half of the novel deals with the ways the succeeding generations fare as they enter the new century.

Two types of craft which made the real Jameses famous, were the yawls and gigs used by the Cliff companies. Yawls have been described as 'undoubtedly the most exciting working sailing craft ever developed in Britain'.[11] Their design was much influenced by that of the Viking longships which once raided this coast. Earlier yawls had three masts, later reduced to two with a consequent increase in the size of the foresail. Their long sweeping lines, narrow beam and shallow depth made them craft of astonishing beauty and speed.

Many were over 50ft long. Lug-rigged, they carried a crew of up to twenty-five, or more if salvage required it. Apart from the helmsman, the most important person aboard was the foresheet-man whose skill in handling the huge fore-lug sail was critical for stability and speed. Never cleated, the sheet was wound two or three times round the appropriately named *sampson-post* in the main tabernacle. The other crew were employed in windward work – changing the foresail from side to side when tacking, bailing out and shifting the bags of ballast to prevent capsizing. Lacking a centreboard, yawls were poor sailing into the wind but could reach astounding speeds off it. When a ship flying the pilot-jack was spotted from the lookouts, the cliffmen scrambled to launch their *yolls*. Veteran yawlmen interviewed by E. J. March 'confirmed that at times, when hard pressed, the lee gunwale would sink from six inches to a foot *under water*, but so fast was the boat going that only a trickle came aboard.'[12] There can have been few finer sights than to stand on Long Island or Kilcock Cliff and watch the competing Critten-built yawls reach off to a vessel. Gigs were also used to board pilots especially in smooth weather. These too were long, up to 35 to 40ft and narrow with the same fine lines as yawls. They carried six or eight oars, each painted with a white circle to ensure that wherever they sat the crew would provide an even pull. 'The boat, steered by a yoke and long lines, fairly flew through the water under the powerful strokes of the crew and in light weather could easily beat a yawl making for the same ship...'[13]

A flurry of yawl and gig building in the mid-century reflected both the quality of Critten workmanship and the Cliff companies' optimism that there was money to be made. Between 1846 and 1870 five yawls were built. It is hard to imagine how crowded the seas must have been at the time with passing shipping and the opportunities they offered. An eyewitness, E.E. Middleton, the first person to sail a yacht single-handed around the English coast, writing of Southwold, in 1869, recorded that, '...the beach or the promenade by the pilots' houses affords a view of shipping rarely to be seen – one day presenting a fleet of four or five hundred vessels streaming out of Yarmouth and Lowestoft Roads...'.[14] During his stay in the town he somehow joined the crew of the lifeboat, launched to go to the aid of a vessel, seven miles off, that had blown its canvas. A yawl, which Middleton calls a launch, was already a mile ahead. Comparing the two types of craft, he observed that the lifeboat was superior going to windward and could carry full sail, while the yawl, sailing off the wind, had to tack more than once dipping its close-reefed lug foresail. The weather on this occasion was only suitable for the lifeboat so the fact that the yawl was prepared to take the risk shows how far the companies would go to secure a job. The prize gained was thirty shillings a head for the cliffmen who reached the ship first but 'at great risk to life.'[15]

The last but one yawl laid down by the Crittens was the 50ft *Nil Desperandum*, otherwise the *Nellie*, commissioned by the Kilcock Company in 1856 and built for £1.6s.6d per foot. A drawing of her lines hangs in the Reading Room. But the last of all the Southwold yawls was the Beechings Brothers-built *Bittern* commissioned in 1892 which lay under Kilcock Cliff until finally broken up in 1926. John Critten's son, Andrew saved her rudder. It seems astonishing today that such craft could have been allowed to pass unpreserved. Bell includes a ghostly tale of her imperatives, even while lying moribund on the beach:

'On dark nights of winter, the wrack hiding the moon and stars and a northeast gale blowing, when the crash of the signal gun echoed over the town for the lifeboat crew, the old *Bittern* would slip down towards the sea, her shattered timbers, her broken mast, her vanished sails miraculously renewed. Manned and launched by the ghosts of dead men she plunged through the breakers and set off for the ship whose call for help had raised the town. "And many a time," the tale would end, "as the lifeboat drove through the seas towards the wreck, she'd see old *Bittern* ahead of her." And if the listener, on a half-inquisitive, half-dubious note, asked, "And what happened then?" The invariable answer came impatiently, almost irritably, "Why nawthin'! She come back o' course. Layin' over there under [the]… Cliff aren't she. Gew an' look at her." '[16]

The prosperity in the Critten business at this time allowed James junior to educate his children as best he could. After the death of his first wife, Hannah, he remarried. The two oldest boys were John (1848-96) and George (1852-1923). John was my great, great uncle by marriage and George the father of Stephen (1887-1964) who became Neil Bell.

The yawl *Bittern* standing alone and forlorn. Note her length and fine lines

I have inherited John's grammar and arithmetic textbooks, printed in Dublin which his mother, Sarah (1811-1886), a Roman Catholic, had procured. Both are bound in brown linen, the grammar having an additional home-made linen cover, the flap-ends of which are sewn together with thread. The covers are named, JOHN CRITTEN, place-named, Southwold and dated in black ink in his own hand, May 29th, 1860 for the grammar and Feb 22nd, 1861 for the arithmetic. He hadn't quite worked out spacing because he failed to fit his capitalised name across the cover of the grammar and had to hypertext the final EN above the TT. He didn't make the same mistake with the arithmetic.

Words came before numbers and the words of the grammar were Catholic strictures. 'The object of English Grammar,' it intoned, 'is to teach those who use the English Language to express their thoughts correctly, either in speaking or writing.' Then it asked him to parse sentences such as this:

'If we knew how much the pleasures of this life deceive and betray their unhappy votaries and reflected on the disappointments in pursuit, the dissatisfaction in enjoyment, or the uncertainty of possession, which every-where attend them, we should cease to be enamoured of these brittle and transient joys, and should wisely fix our hearts on those virtuous attainments which the world can neither give nor take away.'

This was Catholic finger-wagging as much as an exercise in the naming and relationship of parts. The grammar led him through orthography, etymology, syntax and prosody in much the same vein. The arithmetic just got on with it: Numeration, Notation, Addition, Subtraction, Multiplication, Division, Reduction, Weights and Measures, Simple and Compound Proportion, Bills of Parcels, Bills of Book Debts, Tare and Tret, Simple and Compound Interest, Commission, Brokerage, Insurance, Buying and Selling Stocks, Barter, Profit and Loss, Partnership, Vulgar Fractions, Decimals, Involution, Evolution, Extraction of the Cube Root, Duodecimal Multiplication and Mental Arithmetic. John clearly learnt to master the many mathematical skills he needed as a boat builder and businessman but at school even he may have struggled with: 'If 3/16ths of a ship cost 273 and 1/8th l., what is 5/32nds of her worth?'[17]

John Critten's grammar and arithmetic text books

However they managed to survive this, both boys were apprenticed for seven years to their father when they were fourteen. George's indentures required him, in the standardised language of such contracts, to abstain from fornication and marriage, never to play at cards or dice tables, never to haunt taverns or playhouses, never to absent himself without permission but to serve as a faithful apprentice and behave himself towards his Master. Were these the transient and brittle pleasures the Grammar had in mind? Both apprentice and Master signed it – James junior, now the patriarch, as James Critten Snr, in that same bold hand, George, nervously, in the hand of a child.[18] Duly apprenticed they learned their craft from their father, as he had from his, and the Critten cycle revolved again.

Of three known photographs of the interior of the workshop, one shows it in some detail. Light streams in from the south-facing windows and open side doors on to a *punt* under construction. The back wall at the cliff-end, is made of pebble flints, their rounded ends embedded into mortar in the vernacular style, so that they resemble lines of eggs. Beams span the width of the shop which are jointed to the wall-studs in true boat-building style by brackets called *knees*.

The interior of Critten's workshop at the bottom of Haines's Score, 1896

Three figures form a triangle, two at work on the punt, the third at the bench. At the apex of the triangle on the punt's stern is the apprentice, John's son, Andrew. He is wearing a cap and a light drill or canvas working-jacket buttoned at the top. His left hand rests on the port *quarter-knee*, a curved piece of wood that joins the gunwale to the transom. Behind him, suspended from a stud, hangs a pair of leather crotch boots. Jumbled timbers, planks and ropes litter the wall.

To his left near the port bow stands an older man, square-faced with a grizzled grey-beard. He wears a nautical cap, a gansey, flap-fronted trousers and leather boots. He is holding something small, a copper nail perhaps, between both sets of fingers while guardedly eyeing the lens. He looks experienced, sure of his skills and that he doesn't suffer fools. Cantilevered over the gunwale is a sway-brace, its bit point-up, gleaming in the sunlight as if he has just put it there for the duration of the photograph before taking it up again. The clink-ered, roved oak planks sweep out from the stem in a beautiful curved line by his legs. The copper nails which fasten them, space out evenly along their length. The keel is balanced precisely on its strong-back and is held upright by three struts on each side. On the floor are curled planings, wood-fleece. It is posssible, but not certain, that he might be John's great uncle, the George who assaulted his father.

Completing the triangle at the work-bench lining the south wall is the heavily bearded John, dressed similarly to Andrew in cap and working jacket; he wouldn't look out of place today in Shoreditch. His white trousers are dirty and stained. He is box-planing a piece of wood which is gripped in the bench's vice. Shavings are curled beneath it exuding a resinous smell. Further along the bench is a long white timber, American oak perhaps, running its length and out of the picture. At the back of the bench, behind a metal bar, tools are massed to hand, chisels, augers, set-squares, pincers vying for attention. A bow-saw hangs at head height from one of the knees by the window. It just obscures the one object in the shop that would provide us definitively with the date the picture was taken – a calendar.

The top half shows a photograph of St. Edmund's Church centrally placed, around which are other Southwold views framed in elaborate curled tendrils. The calendar has been torn off to reveal that the month is April and that the 1st began on a Wednesday. Assuming it has been kept up to date, the strong sunshine streaming through the windows and doors confirms this indeed may be spring. Crucially though, the year is obscured by the top bar of the bow-saw. The evidence that most strongly suggests 1896 is the presence of Andrew born in 1880, who looks about fifteen or sixteen. There is no sign of John's brother, George. As for the punt, it might be *Ellen Louisa*

(LT 864) which was built in that year for James Denny, a fisherman at Kilcock. John Critten was forty-eight, in April 1896, at the height of his powers – and just months from his premature death.

According to Bell, John and George 'built good sturdy craft for one of them, built in the year I was born, was still in service up till a few years ago.'[19] Nevertheless by 1897 'the boat-building business had gone on the rocks, owing to the competition of the big boatbuilding yards at Lowestoft and Yarmouth and to my father's inability to pass a public house without putting his head in to see if a crony was there. One usually was.'[20] But this wasn't the whole truth. John died suddenly in December 1896 within two days of the onset of 'unfavourable symptoms' which 'until the last few hours' did not anticipate the outcome.[21] George's weaknesses contrasted with John's uprightness, 'a quiet and sterling character ... widely known and esteemed.' He was a former member of the Corporation and a member of the Sole Bay Lodge of Oddfellows. A Memorandum in his hand, sent to E.R. Cooper, the Town Clerk, on July 16th, 1896 is like his father's, strong and clear. On the day of the funeral, January 4th, 1897, 'Flags were at half-mast and most of the blinds of the houses were drawn.'[22] Were the Crittens really a riven family or did Bell exaggerate for the purposes of the novel? Stephen was contemptuous of his father who had clearly disregarded the terms of his apprenticeship and their relationship deteriorated so badly that he later changed his name by deed-poll to Stephen Southwold.

And then within a year the shop was completely destroyed in the storm of November 1897 for which the Fisherman's Fund, already mentioned, was set up. The business which had lasted for at least a century was no more. Not wishing to begin again in Southwold, George made the break. He moved to New Brompton, Kent close to where he had gained employment at Chatham Docks. Stephen was sent to St Mark's school whose sole function was to train boys to gain apprenticeships in the yards, one of which he won, though he lasted only seven weeks. His highest marks in the tests were in English composition. After spells as teacher and war service in the R.A.M.C., he went on to become a prolific author adopting various pseudonyms, one of which was Neil Bell.

The years that followed must have been difficult for John's wife, Adelaide, and her two boys, Andrew and John, adrift from the work that had defined the family name. Nevertheless they were resilient. In 1909 Andrew, with his wife, Ida, went into business manufacturing clothing, joined in 1910 by John. They called their enterprise *The Southwold Home Knit and Hosiery Company*. Enabling enmeshing ran deep. As it prospered, Andrew continued his father's commitment to civic duty, becoming first a councillor, then an Alderman and on nine occasions, Mayor. He became a man of substance in the Town,

Critten's Boatbuilding Shop, etching by Arthur Evershed

eventually occupying Manor House in the centre of the High Street, the building according to Pevsner which is the town's finest. In his capacity as Mayor he hosted dinners to entertain the longshoremen 'who were working on the beach when in his earlier days he was associated with his father's business.' Andrew's wife and her 'lady friends' acted as the 'waitresses'. Such was the Mayor's hospitality that in terms of food and particularly drink, 'the tide remained at the flood.' With dinner completed, Andrew rose to toast the Fishermen of Southwold, saying 'it gave him greatest pleasure to meet all his old friends of the beach, and one would have to go far to find a more genuine set of men. The early days he spent with them were full of pleasure and he wished all a happy and prosperous year.' Charles (*Beefy*) Jarvis, the cox'n and Harry Smith replied in kind and a 'merry time was spent with toasts and songs and stories, some of the latter reminiscent of adventures and perils encountered amid the the tumbling waters of Sole Bay when whipped by the wind and flecked by the foam fresh from the North Sea.'[23]

Notes

1 Bell, Neil *Bredon And Sons* p.3

2 Bell, Neil *My Writing Life* p.163

3 Town Leases. Archive Drawer B4, Southwold Museum

4 Lowestoft Records Office 491/13/6/2

5 Maggs Vol 2 p.20

6 Copy in author's Collection

7 *Bredon And Sons* p.50

8 Ibid p.51

9 Ibid p.174

10 Ibid p.54

11 Cunliffe, Tom *Pilot Cutters Under Sail Pilots and Pilotage in Britain and Northern Europe* p.128

12 March, Edgar J. *Inshore Craft of Great Britain in the Days of Sail and Oar* p.168

13 Ibid p.175

14 Middleton E. E. *The Cruise of the Kate* (Edition unknown) Photocopy p.242

15 Ibid p.243

16 *Bredon And Sons* p.159

17 Answer: £ 227 12s. 1d

18 Miscellaneous Ephemera Archive Box 1 995-64, Southwold Museum

19 *My Writing Life* p.13

20 Ibid p.14

21 Newspaper cutting January 1897, Southwold Museum.

22 Ibid

23 *Catholic Parish Magazine* March 1922, Southwold Museum

The Seabirds

Another appeared from the gloom.

Tide allus pullin' south then north, north then south. I like t' watch th' sun risin' east. Sometimes that fire up the surface so that the water glow above the grey an' green, all a-shimmer, like I remember leaves on autumn trees.

An' when I turn sunwise, I see the sand-streaked cliffs up Easton linin' the shore, lit up like amber. An' the pockmarked holes pepperin' the top layer. Like dark cave-mouths they are, inches wide, sand martins shootin' in 'n out an' unceasin' in spring. An' sometimes, a windhover, sun-bronzed on the whitened branches of a dead tree. Watchin'.

Once I was walkin' up there an' stickin' outa the cliff wuz this curved shape an' that come to a point. That wuz a tusk, fossil tusk of a mammoth. Thass the truth. I liked poulterin' for fossils. I kept 'em down there in the shod. I like t' think about 'em.

I want t' hear the sea birds cry agin.

The wheelin' cobs' mews
The sprat-loons' kowkin's
The willocks' muurrrs
The kitties' kitty-weekin's
The rixies' kreaars
The sea-pies' kleep keepin's
The pickmires' kuk-kuk-keears.

But most I want
T' hear the curlews' lonely crewees
Carryin' across the marsh.

I am curlew.

7

A Right Royal Lot

Who were these longshoremen who claimed the beach belonged to them, bought their boats from the Crittens and still sometimes used the old words?

Mr Barber once told me that they were 'a right royal lot' by which he meant not only that they thought they owned the beach. He might have meant they were demanding or petulant but I think he was touching on something deeper, a kind of majesty of self-reliance. He clearly admired their skills, for all their brusqueness and apparent hostility to their own kind, even their own children. It was a quality bred of the sea. Every time a longshoreman went off alone or with others, he entrusted his life to those things he had learnt to master: his skill in launching and beaching, his ability to know and handle the boat, his knowledge of wind and tide, his reading of landmarks and the grounds on which he fished, his understanding of the habits of the species he pursued. In addition he had to have personal and physical qualities commensurate with the work – courage, strength, endurance, nerve to name a few. Trusting in himself was all he could do, knowing that it was always possible that what was beyond his control could drown him. This engendered self-reliance, stubbornness and superstitiousness. The longshoreman didn't need anyone to tell him anything. And this was the characteristic that irritated P.H.Emerson above all.

Emerson first arrived in Southwold with his family for a short holiday in August 1883.[1] An Anglo-American, he had come to England in 1869 following the early death of his father, Henry Emerson, a distant cousin of Ralph Waldo Emerson, who had made his fortune first in coffee and then in sugar on slave-run plantations in Cuba. His mother, a Cornish woman, wound up the business and returned to England where Emerson was educated at Cranleigh School. He excelled as an all-rounder exhibiting a competitive spirit. Having decided to follow medicine, Emerson had already taken one degree at King's College, London, and was now at Clare College, Cambridge completing a second. He was regarded as very able. His mother having died in 1881, the twenty-eight year old who arrived in Southwold was a wealthy man of independent means, intelligent, strong-willed, self-confident, energetic and on the verge of a glittering career.

Emerson had bought a camera in 1881 to use on ornithological trips and had also experimented with photography for scientific purposes at Cambridge. In the summer of 1882, he had used the camera on Skye to photograph the local people, at the same time noting their agricultural customs and practices. Two prints submitted to the annual Pall Mall exhibition run by the Photographic Society of Great Britain were accepted.

Emerson had never been to Suffolk before and at Southwold something happened. Profoundly affected by place, he became enchanted. The land and seascapes entered his soul. He began to photograph intently. The epiphany was so overwhelming that his whole life changed direction. Although he completed his second degree he never practised medicine. Instead for the next few years and with the help of his friend, the painter T.F. Goodall, Emerson dedicated himself to photographing life and landscape in Norfolk and Suffolk.

The next spring, 1884, Emerson left Cambridge with his family and returned to Southwold where he rented Wellesley House which overlooks the common. The landscape continued to enchant. Of the view from his upstairs windows looking down across the marshes that stretch beneath the common to the harbour, he wrote:

'Here....the trees seem to grow in fantastic shapes and cluster in weird and mysterious groups, while nothing more beautiful can be imagined than the ever-changing tints of the reeds, the silvery lines of the marsh-fringed dikes and the sombre greens and glowing yellows of the gorses. Perhaps the great charm to be felt in this country is the ever-changing aspect of the landscape...'[2]

This is the language of a visual artist, alert to colour, tone, line and texture. Returning to Southwold at weekends, Emerson photographed the longshoremen at work on the beach and the farm workers he encountered when out driving his dog-cart in the surrounding country. Just as he had on Skye, he noted their working practices. He got to know Charles Nunn, a Reydon farmer, some of whose employees he photographed and John (Jack) Cragie, longshoreman and cox'n of the Southwold lifeboat, *London Coal Exchange*.

Pictures of East Anglian Life (1888), the result of some of this work, contains thirty-two photogravures and fifteen small prints. Many of the images are seminal examples of what Emerson called 'Naturalistic photography', the idea that an image should represent nature as far as possible. In practice this meant avoiding sharpness in the image to make the photograph represent what is actually seen by the eye. This aesthetic challenged the dominant mode of Victorian photography, exemplified in the work of Henry Peach Robinson whose moralising, narrative images made by combining multiple negatives in the dark room were pre-eminent. Emerson took on the establishment with characteristic bullishness arguing passionately that his kind of photography should be considered art. Much as he enjoyed being a contrarian, it was nevertheless typical of his mercurial nature that in a sudden *volte-face*, he summarily renounced all he had believed in so passionately. In 1891 he published a pamphlet edged in black in which he mourned *The Death of Naturalistic Photography*. The cause was his acknowledgement that, unlike an artist, a photographer could not alter the tones of the image at will and thus that photography could be no more than a mechanical process. It was ruled 'by a physical law and not by inspiration.'[3]

While Emerson's attempts to elevate photography into art have been well documented, far less attention has been paid to the accompanying texts included in some of the books in which, sometimes helped by Goodall, he detailed the lives and working practices of their subjects, Broads marshmen, farm workers and longshoremen.

In the *Preface* Emerson declared that his aim was to produce 'truthful pictures' of those he termed 'peasants' and 'fisherfolk'. This held for both the images and the text. With regard to the text he set out his working methods:

'I made ample notes....so that all the information was gained by actual observation afterwards amplified and corrected by information gathered from the lips of specialists in the various subjects.'

In relation to the fishermen he referenced his sources. Jack Cragie, and 'other sailors, coastguardsmen and longshoremen' supplied tales of shipwreck. Ghost stories were taken from 'the lips of those who saw them, the names of those persons being in my possession'. Everything appertaining to longshoring was 'taken direct from the sea and the fisherfolk'. The result Emerson hoped might 'form a humble contribution to a Natural History of the English Peasantry and Fisherfolk.'[4]

Thus Emerson figured himself as a scientist, a natural historian, whose aim, 'truth to nature', was paramount. To achieve this he went to the field to take direct observation modified if necessary after consultation with specialists. But the figure also cast his subjects as specimens. The terms *English, Peasantry* and *Fisherfolk* further suggest that Emerson's relationship to them was from a foreign perspective, historically muddled and nostalgic. If the only thing that mattered in terms of image and text was objective 'truth to nature', Emerson did not have to engage with his subjects, merely observe them.

Nevertheless, John Taylor has written that Emerson admired his subjects because he felt 'they represented an older, truer England.'[5] This was signalled in the epigraph he chose from Goldsmith's *The Deserted Villlage*:

> But a bold peasantry, their country's pride
> When once destroyed can never be supplied.

Both 'peasants' and 'fisherfolk' were still engaged in mainly pre-industrial activities. They were ruled by the seasons and worked by hand – and indeed hands are almost always at work in Emerson's early photographs. Demographically both groups were now in a minority as England had ceased to be a fully agricultural nation in 1850. Even though they were neither 'peasants', nor 'folk', Emerson thought these groups represented an older order, disrupted specifically by the effects of agricultural depression in Norfolk and Suffolk and more generally by the machine age. Taylor has pointed out that one way this disruption was being experienced in the 1880s was through the incursion of urban holidaymakers and day-trippers by railway or coastal steamer in to the Broads and resorts such as Great

Yarmouth and Cromer. He could have added Southwold. Despite the fact that Emerson and Goodall lived on the Broads in their houseboat, *Lucy*, for long periods, they did not regard themselves as trippers. 'Peasants' and 'fisherfolk' – elsewhere even called 'natives' – on the other hand, were part of a 'natural' order in which everyone knew their place and existed in mutual relationship; they appealed to the values of upper-middle class Victorian men who, according to Taylor, had a 'fondness for hierarchy, for a necessary and fixed order of being.'[6] Thus Emerson was outspoken in his criticism of some farmers for neglect of their workers in the depression but this has to be understood as arising from his outraged sense of a betrayal of responsibility on the farmers' part rather from any desire to challenge that relationship. The same is true of his defence of poachers.

There is something nostalgic about this. Raymond Williams identified a persistent trope in English Literature, the idea that life in the country was always better in the past, though it is not confined to Literature alone.[7] Emerson's privileging of 'peasants' and 'fisherfolk' over the modern urban majority could be argued to be in this tradition But while he may have admired them, he did not idealise them. If there is one thing that characterises his account of the fishermen, it is his criticism of their faults which finds expression in a condescending tone. A social Darwinist, Emerson believed in the innate superiority of some (people like himself) over others. 'Equality there can never be, he wrote, 'the stern law of heredity forbids that *in utero*.'[8] Doubt-less he would have argued that he was being dispassionately objective in his observations but we must approach the only account we have of the Southwold longshoremen in eight hundred years, the first to fill that absence, in the knowledge that is is coloured by its author's ambiguous relationship of admiration and condescension.

Emerson set out his study of the 'fisherfolk' methodically. Under the headings: *Character and Intelligence, Religion, Superstitions, Ghost-stories, Fishermen's Materia Medica and Medicine, Politics, Habits and Customs* and *Dealing with Tradesmen*, he aimed for 'truth to nature'. Accompanying some of the plates he described long-shoring practices and the work of the Lifeboat. Emerson once described himself as an 'anthropologist of types' and an unintended consequence of his work was that he recorded ways of life that were soon to be forever lost or changed.

The men I recorded (and I fully acknowledge the failing here) were born at the end of the 19th century and the start of the 20th, the children of those Emerson encountered. Unlike his methodical approach, mine was random and poorly thought out. Nevertheless it is possible to give a picture of some aspects of the longshoremen's lives based on what I was told which, unsurprisingly, often complement Emerson's findings in fact though not in tone.

The fishermen generally had large families and uncertain incomes. Poverty gnawed at their doors. Without the contributions of their wives, already burdened with child-rearing, it could have been much worse, especially in winter. Emerson noted that the fishermen were faithful to their wives, and that the younger men, were not as given to 'immorality' as their rural counterparts. Some were also, as we have heard, fine physical specimens.

The large families were also closely interrelated. Some married their cousins or second cousins while others acknowledged the adopted family in middle names, such as in the Hurr family which in 1905 included *Ballantine Brown* Hurr, George *Watson* Hurr and Benjamin *Lowsey* Hurr. Emerson recorded that in his day, the fishermen had begun to marry country girls who came into the town to go in to service. Thus Florence Barber and Millie Soames, became sisters-in-law by marrying into the Stannard family. Romance began for Florence Barber, she told me, when William Stannard, who lived in Pinkney's Lane, where she worked, passed her on hands and knees scrubbing a doorstep and told her to put the whiting the right way up.

Emerson noted that the fishermen were distinguished by nicknames. Donald J. Gooding who recorded them, wrote:

'Nicknames are almost universal amongst the fishermen – the definition given by most dictionaries 'a term of contempt and reproach' is quite incorrect in this instance as most of the soubriquets are given in the most friendly spirit and generally completely supersede the Christian names – in some cases the nicknames are hereditary sometimes with the addition 'young' conferred on a younger member of the family. Some of them are called after different nationalities such as *Rooshian* (Russian), *Frenchman, Dutchman* from a fancied resemblance to the natives of those countries. But most are given in early boyhood.'[9]

He listed 152 nicknames from 42 families. *Dogs* Howlett for example, was named for his habit of eating dog-fish and once named, boys (being boys) used to bark at him. The Hurrs were among the most numerous being between them: *Bollosus, Bungs, Corky, Dace, Dod, Dry Bread, Dubber, Ekey, Fitz, Gipsy Will, Jumbo, Nibble, 'Oodens, Roker, Sharper, Sprunt, Swivel Eye, Tup* and *Winkle*. The list did not include: *Jonty, Moor, Saddler, Sloper Sweaters and Tope*. William English explained it saying:

'I suppose some of 'em were things they'd done or said. It could be that 'cos there were several from the same family, that it was a way t' distinguish 'em.'

He then told me the Walberswick names he could recall: *Billy D, Blucher, Boko, Boss-eye, Chivers, Dinks, Doddy, Gilbert, Scarboro', Slinger, Spider, Summer Dew, Sykes, Swift, Tow, Treacl, Weary* and *Whiskers*. His own name, *Blucher*, came about, he said, because, 'Guy Fawkes, I used to dress up in a hat and someone said, "He look like ol' Blucher." '

In terms of *character and intelligence*, Emerson's judgement was that the Southwold longshoremen were 'as curious a mixture as the peasantry'.[10] In this mix vices far outweighed virtues. First they were venal, 'The fisherman loves money as dearly does the peasant,' he wrote, 'and will resort to all sorts of cunning devices to obtain it' because, 'like the peasant he is always poor.' When selling fish to the public, he 'prefers not to fix a price but will cunningly "leave it tew yew, sir".' If forced to name a price to a merchant, he 'often manages to "best" him of a shilling.' Dealing with a stranger, he liked 'to feel his way into his character' and to 'slavishly echo' his opinions in the hope of reward – in short to become 'all things to all men.' Annoyingly fond of singing their own praises, the long-shoremen were hypocrites, according to Emerson, who claimed that while others would not hesitate to take advantage they would do no such thing.

Moreover, the younger men were slow and lazy 'and, though avaricious, [would] not exert themselves much for money.' Emerson overheard them refuse offers of five shillings an hour from holiday-makers wanting a pleasure trip in their boats. Though there were more boats on the beach than necessary, the younger men refused to join the navy or merchant service because they had heard tales of bullying. In the past longshoring was undertaken by ex-men-of-war sailors to supplement their naval pensions, but now it had become a necessity for a younger generation who lacked enterprise. After a voyage or two away, they returned and married 'on nothing'. The resulting poverty, by implication, was their own fault. Their children exhibited 'unboundless cruelty to animals.'

Emerson noted the way the fishermen dressed – slop, 'beverteen' trousers and sou' westers or wide-awake hats and in winter, oileys, ganseys and duffle trousers. In this respect they were unmistakable. It was also a subject on which those I recorded were forthcoming. Mr Upcraft recalled:

Patched-arsed Solemen looking out to sea. Sketch by Charles Keene

'There used t' be the ol' *slop* as we called 'em an' *gansey, gansey* an' *slop.*Though they used t' wear all types o' caps. Some o' 'em would have a *cheesecutter*, some would have a trilby, the ordinary peaked cap; one or two I remember used t' wear a bowler hat. O' course the trousers always used t' be t' pieces. They called 'em *patched-arsed Solemen.'*

The style can clearly be seen in Emerson's photographs, *Baiting the Line* or *East Coast Fishermen*, for example, both taken in 1886. Joseph Southall's painting, *Up from the Sea* (1920) is also typical. The patch was adopted when a longshoreman had a new pair of trousers; duffel from the previous pair was sewn into the seat to prevent wear caused by rowing.

Tanned slops, ganseys, head gear, Dunwich clays. Longshoremen at South Green

Jack Denny was a tailor working in the Market Place who started his apprenticeship under his father in 1927. Apart from the general public (one of whom was Eric Blair, later George Orwell), his customers were farmers, gamekeepers, farm workers and occasionally fishermen:

Plate I 'Collition' between the *Swiftsure* & *Reliance* Ted Syer

Plate II Southwold 1588 The creek almost islands the town A proposed fort is at its seaward end

Plate III *Fatal Accident at Southwold February 27th 1858* Ted Syer

Plate IV *Loss of the Elizabeth Kilner Feb15 1892* Ben Lowsey

Plate V Dust Jacket of *A Suffolk Coast Garland*
1928 E.R. Cooper

Plate VI *Below East Cliff* Walter Crane 1886

Plate VII *Southwold Suffolk* c. 1875 Edwin Edwards

Plate VIII *Kill Cock Cliff*
c. 1840 Henry Davy

'Fishermen would have a very heavy serge suit for best and make it last years and years. Very, very heavy cloth up to twenty-seven, twenty-eight ounce serge. It was nearly always blue serge, nearly always blue-black. People in the Potteries, they had theirs in a much brighter blue. Fishermen's slops were the easiest pattern to make. They were based on the old *magyr* which was just a square-cut, T-shape, with a hole in the top with two seams up the sides. They wore them white on Sundays and the tanned ones for work and the rest of the week. Saturday nights and Sundays they always stood here [in the Market Place] by the pillar box and by the pump and they'd walk in twos and walk just the length of a boat, backwards and forwards, just about four steps, as they talked. Then when their white slops got stained and dirty, when they tanned the nets, they used to put the slop in with the nets. So you only got two colours, never a blue slop, the factory slop, just the white and the tanned one. Another thing was their pipes. They always smoked their pipes upside down, so the wind didn't blow their tobacco about.'

The gansey was worn by fishermen around the coasts of Britain. It was a dark blue woollen jumper knitted in such a way that made it virtually wind and sprayproof. Fashioned in the round or in parts later sewn together, they were patterned with motifs that reflected the fishing life and which could be displayed vertically through the whole jumper or horizontally across the chest or yoke. The sleeves were short to prevent them being caught on longlines or in nets and freedom of movement was allowed by gussets inserted under the arms. Motifs included marriage lines, cables, anchors, the tree of life, diamonds, zig-zags, flags and more.

It is a common assumption that the pattern represented a place and that a fisherman could be identified by it, say if he was drowned and washed up away from home. For this to be true it would mean that each fishery had a unique style not replicated elsewhere. The Moray Firth Gansey Project concluded that there was no definitive evidence for this although variations occurred between the North and South Moray Firth patterns.[11] Peter Tolhurst has reached the same conclusion about North Norfolk ganseys.[12] Southwold had no particular style, and if one looks at photographs of other fisheries, Sheringham or Scarborough for example, a variety of patterns is the norm. In certain communities though such as Filey, the owner's initials were sometimes knitted in above the welt. Choice of patterning may have appeared random but Gladys Thompson, who made a definitive study of ganseys, quoted Catherine Gillies of Inverness talking about those worn on Barra in the Outer Hebrides:

'The complicated designs on fishermen's dark-blue jerseys round the British coast are not just haphazard or worked in from whim. The symbols have conveyed messages for several hundred years.'[13]

The messages conveyed the fishing life in single motifs, for example, parallel zig-zags represented waves; double moss stitch, sands; cable stitch, rope and so on. Motifs in combination became narrative. Thus if the yoke of the jersey represented home and in the middle was an open diamond, this represented a window. If the diamond had a heart inside it, it meant "the heart is in the home". In this way the gansey could thus be read as a text, a signifier of meaning rather than randomly patterned. Peter Tolhurst has written interestingly of superstitions held by knitters, such as, 'women were sure not to wind wool after sunset or they would soon be making shrouds for their husbands.'[14]

In the Southall painting, the longshoremen are shown wearing long leather sea-boots. William *Billy* Spence (b.1894) a tall, thin angular man, deep of voice, gentle and kind, was one of the first people I recorded. He was a cobbler or *shumakker* and remembered making these boots. He gave me his foot-measurer, a hook and a leather handpiece heavily padded on the palm which he used for stitching through tough leather which I later donated to the Museum where they are currently on display.

'My father wuz an all-round craftsman. He used t' make a lot o' fishermen's boots in them days. All the fishermen here. That wuz all leather-work o' course. There wuz no such thing as rubber then. We used t' make all what they call *thigh-boots* now; they used t' call 'em *crotch-boots* in those days. They were thirty-six inches long an' went right up t' the crotch. They all came in raw *hides* an' they had t' be *closed together*, all up each side, inside out an' then they had t' be turned t' the original. That wuz a job y' see, 'cos that wuz all done with grease an' you had a heck o' a job t' keep the pincers on t' pull 'em inside out. When that job wuz done we had t' use very heavy thread for sewin' the soles on an' the welts. We used t' use *sixteen-cord* o' green hemp, well waxed, t' sew the welts in with an' also t' sew the sole on. They were what we call *clumped* on with an *oversole* o' brass rivets. That wuz £2 for a pair o' those an' that wuz three days' solid work.

They used t' call us cobblers or *shumakkers*. The farm-workers would come in after harvest as a rule, when they had been paid, t' be measured. It wuz the same with the fishin' industry. The chaps used t' go outa here from Low'stoft. If they had a good *home-voyage* [herring fishing in the autumn] they'd come an' order a pair o' *walkin'-out* shoes. In those days they had a high heel an' they always wanted a pointed toe-cap, well decorated. They looked smart! Then they used t' go from here on what they called the *Westward* voyage [fishing from Newlyn in the winter]. If they had a good Westward voyage, then they'd think about havin' a new pair o' thigh-boots…

When it came t' my time, there wuz no need t' do so much makin' then 'cos the rubber boots came into the industry. That changed everythin' with regard t' the sea-boots 'cos they became more expensive. You could go an' buy a pair of rubber *thigh-boots* or *three-quarter boots* for £1. 10s. – in fact we used t' sell 'em as a sideline. That wuz the trouble, once the rubber business came in, that did really have a big effect on the trade.'

Mr Jarvis recalled the crotch-boots and the dress generally:

'My brothers all had theirs in brass tacks, done by Spence o' Southwold, these leather boots made an' the names worked in the soles. If they got drowned an' they were picked up, they'd easily tell [who they were]. Another thing if somebody pinched their boots too. Thass the same as these different types o' ganseys that they wear. Different ports had different patterns an' they could always tell the body by the gansey he wore.

They all wore slops, these tanned slops, which they now sell in the shops which people go about in in the summer. But if you wore one in my day you were looked down on at school – you were a fisherman's son. But they were good things. They kept you clean, there wuz no buttons t' catch the nets. That wuz the idea – no buttons anywhere, nothin' t' hook on the nets. If you wore an oily coat in a boat, thass a nuisance, you'd get your buttons [caught]. Some of 'em wore earrings. That wuz a fad but there used t' be a sayin' that they made the eyesight better. I don't think that. I think that sorta wuz a status symbol if they had their ears pierced, 'em gold rings in. Tattoos on the arm, that wuz another way o' tellin' 'em. Most fishermen had tattoos. My father had tattoos on his arm.'

Mr. Jarvis's belief that the gansey was a signifier of place is, as we have seen, common but not necessarily accurate. There is no unique Southwold pattern. There is evidence however of the 19th century Southwold Trinity House pilots having their initials tattooed on their wrists, arguably a more reliable means of identification than a sodden, rolled gansey on a decomposing corpse. Other things Mr. Jarvis said clearly reveal the low status of fishermen, the practicality of the clothing, and personal decoration in the form of earrings and tattoos.

Longshoremen were dirty and unkempt according to Emerson 'they neglect cutting their hair and bathing is a thing that does not occur to them.' They ostracised anyone who had 'the itch or *pediculi*.' I was told nothing much about this though Mr Winter told me that Scrivener Waters used to enjoy going beachcombing or *poultering* as it was called. In those days, *buffs* which were used to keep deep-sea drift-nets afloat, were sometimes lost at sea and could be sold at Lowestoft for half-a-crown each. Spying a buff beneath the pier, a rounded canvas-covered shape, and thinking he was in luck, Waters approached, only to discover the buff was a crouching *Winner* Smith who often used the underside of the pier to defecate. It was clearly an alternative to Shitting Alley.

Both Emerson and Mr Denny commented on the longshoremen's fondness for smoking. Jack Bedingfield (b.1894) recalled this incident about *Bull* Smith:

'One [of the Smiths] wuz *Bull* – a gret big ol' boy with a white slop on an' a gret big ol' trilby. He always used t' be a-smokin' his ol' *calabash*, 'em little ol' pipes they used t' smoke, little ol' clay pipes. Sometimes they used t' break 'em when they were doin' somethin' an' they used t' get 'em in the mouth with just a bit o' stem in the bowl an' they used t' smoke 'em until they were right black. Black as ink they were. All dark shag. Coh! Not only that, after they'd finish smokin' they used t' get the *chow* out. They'd *chow* – chew tobacca – they used t' say *chow*. They used t' get a piece, rub it up an' put it in the side o' their mouth an' squirt out the juice.'

The pipes were called *Dunwich clays*. There was no mistaking the *patched-arsed Solemen* then, with their individual headgear, white or tanned slops, ganseys, patched trousers, sea-boots, their curious nick-names, their blackened pipes, their habit of squirting tobacco juice from their mouths, their basic habits, their unkempt appearances.

Emerson recorded that drinking was a curse amongst some of the longshoremen. It was a long-standing problem. The Reading Room, established in 1864, was built specifically in order to keep them out of the pubs and while it was effective in some cases, it didn't stop them all. He mentioned two groups of fishermen working from the beach, and the one clustered to the south beneath Gun Hill, at some time called the *Californians*, was generally regarded as being more fond of alcohol than the other group. Mr Rogers recalled:

'Drinkin'! Yes they done a lot o' that if they got the chance. Coh! Blimey! Yes! Drinkin', not half! Many on 'em used t' be three-parts drunk if they done all right, whensoever they got the money. They used the *Victoria* an' the *Red Lion*.¹⁵ Ol' *Red Lion*, my uncle told me, they used t' take the lines up there an' bait 'em in the kitchen. He say, "Boy, you'd be up t' your knees in beer on the floor." Now that may be an exaggeration, but before the ol' boy died, thass what he told me. "Coh!" I say, "Uncle, thass some lot o' beer." "Ah!" he say, "They used t' capsize it! Swim about in it!" They used t' bait lines in there. "Rum place t' bait lines," I say. "Yes, they used t'." I weren't allowed in there, o' course, I weren't old enough. Those two were the favourite pubs. Down the street wuz out o' bounds, you din't go there. *Victoria*, Saturday nights, there used t' be a crowd on 'em get in that back room, used t' be full. They'd tell yarns, tell the biggest lies a-goin' I s'pose. Somebody say, "Give us a song." Well, I had a brother, he wuz very fond o' that. Used t' very often give 'em a song. "Go on," he say, "have another pint." Beer used t' be floatin' about there like anythin'.'

'When they done all right,' corroborates exactly Emerson's observation that the fishermen's domestic philosophy was to spend when they had money, buying provisions after a good fishing or having prospered in other ways but that 'as a rule they [were] careless of their money and will run into debt with a light heart,' especially if drink was involved. One remarked, 'they lay up their money for a rainy day and when the first rainy day comes they spend it in the pub.'

Once there, singing was never far away. Mr Rogers:

'There wuz an ol' song called *The New Look* or *The New Front* or suthin'. That wuz all about women, you know, who used t' wear these tight dresses, that sorta thing. I remember one line they used t' sing:

> See it from the front, it's very plain, you understand,
> But from the back, it's absolutely grand!

Coh! There used t' be uproar in there! "Go on!" they'd yell. "Give us another bit on it!" My brother generally used t' do that. *Shade of the Old Apple Tree* used t' be another. *The Bay of Biscay.* Used t' have a proper high night in there, Saturday nights. 'Cos us youngsters used t' be in there along o' the ol' men as well. "Go on, boy, you can sing suthin'." They used t' keep you up till you did try an' do suthin'. You could hear it all over East Street. There weren't no music, anythin' like that, just shoutin' an' hollerin' in there singin' ol' songs. That used t' amuse the ol' fishermen y' know. There were some hectic Saturday nights in there, especially if they'd done a bit o' fishin'. O' course when they never got anythin' the place 'ud be dead, nobody there. There weren't many local songs, not that I can remember. Only the Lifeboat, *Bravo Lifeboatmen*, it wuz called. I only know about one line:

> When danger's nigh, who'll stand by?
> Why, the cox'n and his Lifeboat crew.

The ol' boys used t' bawl that one out. There wuz a good ol' song there once, a feller used t' sing. It wuz called, *It's the Poor That Help the Poor*. That wuz a touchin' ol' song too, quite nice really, if anyone took an interest in it. All about a litle ol' boy, a ragged urchin. He han't got much t' eat, only what he could scrounge. Another ol' feller come up an' he [the boy] say, "You can half my bread, mister. You can have half, though I'm hungry too." Coh! That right nearly made you howl, that ol' song did. I know one line. That used t' say:

> Up came a beggar with his clothes threadbare
> "Turn him away," said the master there.

The boss turned him away, you see, an' this here boy gave him half his bread. That wuz called, *It's the Poor That Help the Poor*. "Thass right enough, too!" some on' em used t' yell. "You can't get a rich man t' help you." "No," they say, "that they 'ont." '

The songs sung in the *Victoria* then, were a mixture of the traditional and the popular, the latter being quite new. *It's the Poor that Help the Poor* was written in 1904 by Alan Mills and Harry Castling. The lyrics were printed as a poem beneath a photo-image of the boy halving his bread and giving it to the destitute who stands outside the big house of the master, one of the Living Pictures series of postcards which were printed at around the same time.[16] *In the Shade of the Old Apple Tree* was another highly sentimental song written in 1905 by Harry Williams and Egbert Van Alstyne about a young man coming from the city to place flowers on the grave of his lost love. *The Bay of Biscay*, a traditional song, tells of a crew being rescued from their wrecked ship when all hope seems lost. However *The Bay of Biscay* or *Bay of Biscay* is also a song of the *night-visiting* genre in which the ghost of the drowned sailor, Willie, appears to his wife after an absence of seven years. It is a song that plays on the fears of wives who never knew if they would see their husbands again once they had gone to sea. In the early nineteenth century they would have no photographs of their loved ones and any messages that were sent by their husbands could take years to arrive. Willie's appearance to his wife, Mary in the middle of the night occurs at that time when the body is sleep-bound but the brain is active, a time when people often have vivid experiences of lost or loved ones. *Bravo Lifeboatmen* would also have reflected the longshoremen's experiences. Mr. Rogers's memories provide another layer to what we know about the tradition of singing in the town adding to what was discovered by Katie Howson and others of the East Anglian Traditional Music Trust regarding a visit to the town in 1910 by Ralph Vaughan Williams and George Butterworth who were collecting folk songs. The composers wrote down eleven songs from three of the Hurr brothers, William (*Dubber*), Robert and Ben.[17]

As far as religion was concerned, Emerson thought the longshoremen hypocritical. They believed in a Supreme Being but were actually fatalists, more interested in material rather than spiritual improvement. They would follow any denomination if they could benefit from hand-outs. Nothing I recorded interrogates this but there was no shortage of places to worship. F.W. Vertue, writing in 1893, recorded that, 'Southwold has one church, one tin Tabernacle, two chapels, one Bethel and a meeting room.'[18] Mr Rogers recalled attending services conducted by the curate in the Bethel on St James's Green.

Whatever their religious affiliations, the Southwold longshore-men – as fishermen around the British coast, indeed around the world – were also ruled by the irrational in the form of superstition. Fundamental was a belief in luck and in those actions, objects, words or people that brought bad luck. Emerson noted a number of these. If a boat or crew-member was thought to be unlucky, each was shunned. They would not move house or sail from a port on a Friday. A new moon should be observed through glass and the first time it was seen, money in the pocket should be turned accompanied by a wish. Whistling at sea was taboo as was mentioning pigs. Flat-footed people were unlucky. It was good luck to attach a horseshoe to a mast. Dreams of jumping or galloping horses, particularly if white were a sure sign of a gale and more reliable than a barometer. If anything the women were more superstitious than the men.

Mr Upcraft recalled others:

'There's hardly any on 'em used t' take a woman in the boat, no! They used t' think it unlucky too, if a woman went on t' the beach t' see a boat go off. They wouldn't have anybody go down an' see 'em. I've known a time, an' been goin' down on t' the beach an' they happened t' pass a nun, they'd turn round an' go home again. You never *bent* a new net on a Friday. You never started fishin' on a Friday. You mustn't talk about a rabbit or a pig when you're off in a boat. A parson or a nun, they always reckoned there'd be a rent net or suthin' go wrong.'

And Mr Winter related this anecdote about Mr Cooper, the Walberswick fisherman. One morning he was trawling close in to the beach when he saw a woman he knew on the shore. Later he came fast and lost his net. He blamed her for his misfortune. Mr Winter also repeated the taboo on mentioning pigs and rabbits by name, though calling them *curly* and *cotton tails* was acceptable. Vicars were to be avoided. He said a person should always turn clockwise with the sun, never against it. And when trawling the longshoremen cast the net to starboard following the example of Christ.

It is interesting that Emerson did not scoff at the superstitions he recorded, except for the belief that being flat-footed was unlucky ('this is really very sad to contemplate!') as we might have expected from a man of science. (He was quite unable to restrain himself when talking about the 'peasants' ' medicinal practices, however.) Reflecting on superstitions to do with trees, as practised on Suffolk farms, George Ewart Evans wrote, 'Superstition would undoubtedly be a very apt word to denote these perennial beliefs, for the reason they stand over (*superstant*) from a more ancient religion or culture.'[19] However he felt that the word now had so many overtones that it was impossible to discuss the beliefs rationally in terms of their origins, place in society or relation to similar beliefs elsewhere.

One writer with fewer reservations was the unorthodox anthropologist, T. C. Lethbridge. *Boats and Boatmen* (1952) contains a chapter on the subject.[20] Simply put, he tried to prove that in Northern Europe a belief arose that the deity of a boat was female and that, by extension, as her shrine, the boat itself was female. This explained, he contended, the superstition against women. The goddess might become jealous of another female in the proximity of her shrine and withdraw her protection. Women, therefore, brought bad luck. (It was certainly a common superstition that if a wife or a loved one saw a fisherman off to sea, it meant he would never be seen again. Thus, when the Southwold women gathered on the cliff to remonstrate with their men before the rescue of the *Sheraton Grange*, they knew exactly what they were doing.) The superstition against clergy could also be explained in the same way. As devotees of a different god they might also arouse jealousy in the goddess with attendant bad luck Nuns, being both female and devotees of a different god, were doubly taboo.

Lethbridge also argued that the superstitions against certain animals such as hares, rabbits could be explained by the fact that these were forms a witch could take. To name them was to summon the witch and thus to expose the fisherman or his boat, nets or gear to her powers. (Shakespeare clearly knew the powers of witches in relation to the sea. When the First Witch in *Macbeth*, aided by her fellows takes revenge on a sailor because his wife refused her chestnuts, she does so by summoning winds that will make him fearful 'He shall live a man forbid…'

and which will make his passage perilous – his bark will become 'tempest-tossed.') Peter Tolhurst has written that in Norfolk it was believed that negating the power of witches could be achieved by breaking eggshells after cracking them for cooking 'to prevent witches setting sail in them and causing havoc.'[21]

Lethbridge adhered to the widely accepted idea that the principle of sympathetic magic explained other superstitions. Thus, to whistle at sea would bring bad luck since, as like produces like, a gale would surely follow. (Sympathetic magic also explains the belief at Southwold recorded by Emerson, that dreams of jumping or galloping horses were a portent of bad weather – white horses being the result of raised winds.)

Though not mentioned by Lethbridge, the superstitions surrounding Friday as a day that would bring bad luck if anything new like a voyage was undertaken, a boat launched, a keel laid down or a net bent, stem from the belief that as Friday was the day of Christ's crucifixion, it was proper not to undertake mundane tasks on such a sacred day. Finally, the nailing of a horseshoe to the mast as noted by Emerson, was explained by Lethbridge as a vestige of tree-worship in which valuable iron was gifted to the tree's spirit.

A colourful maverick, not all of Lethbridge's explanations are accepted and he generally only provides anecdotal evidence for his ideas. It is highly unlikely of course, that the Southwold longshoremen knew the origin of their beliefs, but their belief in luck and its opposite remained stubbornly persistent.

Emerson also recorded that the fishermen believed in ghost stories. He went on to embellish in purplish prose the story of *The Shrieking Woman of Southwold*. This and others were documented by A. Barrett Jenkins in his book *A Selection of Ghost Stories, Smuggling Stories and Poems Connected With Southwold*. Most of them concerning fishermen or mariners relate sightings or dreams of a relative, who having already drowned, appears before the news has reached the wife or parents.

With regard to *Materia Medicia and Medicine*, Emerson observed that longshoremen wore eel-skin garters and applied sting-ray oil extracted from the liver, as cures for rheumatism. Lumbago was a common complaint for which they used pills of "wenus" – turpentine and hot salt externally applied. They drank spruce-beer which they obtained from pilots and used salt-water as a purgative. To remedy whooping cough they used the 'plaice-butt cure', a plaice positioned on the chest where it remained 'till it decays and smells offensive' on the principle of sympathetic magic – that as the plaice decayed the cough went with it. Most longshoremen didn't rely on old cures however, but went to the chemists and in other cases applied to the parson for aid. An occupational hazard was that hooks got caught in their fingers when longlining. Longshoremen also suffered from hernias caused by being urged on by the pilots to row out to vessels requiring their services who promised them quantities of beer as a reward.

Politically 'crassly ignorant' the fishermen voted Blue traditionally because that was the sailor's colour. Nevertheless when a Tory land-lord refused them permission to go eel-picking on his land, they chalked a message up on a boat urging all who read it to vote for the Liberal candidate. The deep-sea fishermen were Liberal voters whose views were beginning to change the longshoremen's.

In their *habits and customs*, longshoremen's lives followed nat-ural rhythms. 'The twenty four hours to them are divided into tides and night and day do not in any way bind them.' Regular meal times did not exist, but they lived well. The fishermen did not take food to sea but 'like savages' ate when they had the opportunity – though little. They did not eat as much fish as might be expected and in hard times resorted to sea-birds, even carrion-crow. They consumed quantities of bread which some of the women baked – but this was the exception – and drank much tea. Butter, treacle, cheese, sausages, salt-pork and roll-pies were staples. Hot coffee could be had in the pubs from as early as four in the morning. Averse to milk, drink in the form of 'large quantities of ale and stout', was a 'curse.' Longshoremen liked to smoke; their wives would 'stint themselves to provide tobacco for their husbands', though they never smoked themselves. Christmas was their festive season when their pockets were 'full from the fishing harvest.' This was the time when many of them married. Longshoremen's morality with money was 'loose', for example in avoiding paying rent. But if one of them was drowned they took out a subscription list to provide for the family. They did not insure their fishing gear and paid a small sum to their companies for the upkeep of their yawls and gigs. Their average annual wage was £20 or £30 if it had been a good year.

At sea the longshoremen could be 'mean and harassing' to each other by means of obstructing each other's nets. Emerson also noted that a 'spirit of rivalry runs high' between the two groups that used the beach. He may have been referring to the beachmen of the two Cliff Companies, though by his time their activities were infrequent. More likely, he meant the two groups of fishermen at the South end and at Kilcock Cliff. The spirit of rivalry was vestigial however, and seems to have transferred itself. It was still there at the start of the new century. Mr Bedingfield fished at California while his father ended up at Klondike:

'The Californians an' the Klondikers, they were rivals. They'd go hammer an' tongs at each other, proper enemies really. Not t' fight, not rear up at each other. But that used t' be like that wuz another town on one side or the other. When they come past, they used t' jeer at each other – but that wuz good-hearted y' know. They used t' take their hats off an' wave to 'em. …I don't know why there wuz this…. My father, in the end went down that way [to Klondike] an' fished that end. There wuz …. more kind o' tauntin'. "Them ol' Californians" or "Them ol' Klondikers. Huh! Don't think much o' them." The Klondikers used t' call us "the posh" 'cos we were at the posh end o' town.'

Mr Barber also remembered it:

'There wuz always rivalry between the Californians an' the Klondikers. The Klondikers always reckoned they were tougher 'n better than the Californians. An' o' course that reversed round th' other way again. "We're better 'n you are," an' all that sorta thing. But …. there wuz a distinction between the two sets o'people in regard t' drinkin' powers for one thing an' smokin'. I don't know why that should be but it wuz. The Klondikers, there wuz more abstinence from liquor an' that sorta thing amongst 'em than there wuz from the others. Heaven knows why but thass true.'

Mr Winter told me that Albert Stannard, *Early and Late*, [because he couldn't keep time], a Californian, was once spratting and had caught so many that he was in danger of sinking. He came ashore safely at Klondike and used *Bull* Smith's crab to winch his boat up the beach. Incensed, Smith threatened to kick him in the rear at which Stannard bent over and said 'Do you do it then.' But when there was real danger, rivalry was forgotten. Mr Barber recalled that 'they wouldn't see anyone in trouble without helpin' on 'em.'

Emerson's chief irritation with the longshoremen stemmed from their contempt of 'professional and scientific men,' which is to say people like him. Thus although he conceded that their knowledge of the weather was 'quite marvellous' for example, he couldn't accept that they summarily dismissed as 'book learning' argument about its patterns. It was an attitude that persisted. Mr Rogers:

'They were pretty good, oh yes. I don't know how they larnt it, they must have larnt it from early childhood. But they used t' tell you. They'd say, "The wind'll be so-and-so." An' that nearly always wuz. When there wuz an easterly wind f'r instance, the ol' man say, "Oh, that 'on't last long." An' that wouldn't as rule.'

During a conversation with Mr Jarvis, he told me:

'Like the weather. They knew the weather from A t' Z. They din't want no television t' tell 'em. I writ to Hunt [An Anglia TV weather man of the 1970s]. I writ t' him twice about different things about the beach but he can't answer me. I writ t' him about these here mock-suns. I said we always call 'em *sun-dogs*. A sure sign o' bad weather – turn round an' go off every time. Funny thing we had a sun-dog day before yesterday an' we've had upside down weather. I've told 'em before, well, every time, I've said t' 'em coast-guards at Low'stoft, "That 'on't be fine: sun-dog." Thass a popular sayin' ever since I remember, a sure sign o' bad weather. I arst him another question. I say could he tell me why the night tide is always higher than the day tides? Say thass high water here at eight this mornin', you go down at eight to-morrer mornin' an' the night tide, you'll see thass been a lot higher. You can see by the weed, the mark. Why is it? I can never make out. O' course it's suthin' t' do with the pull o' the sun an' the moon, but I can't never make that out. I arst him why, years ago, we used t' get, April, May time, froth all on the water. That could be fine for days, there weren't a rough sea or nuthin', but that'd come in an' go all along the back o' the breakers.

Summer-froth we used t' call it. Me an' *Worky* [Upcraft] always say t' each other, "Hello. Summer-froth is here." You never see it now. But Hunt never knew nuthin' about that.'

The TV expert was no expert at all because he was ignorant of local conditions and common knowledge. Mr Jarvis's keen interest in and close observation of the weather, the beach and sea's behaviour were the variables on which so much of the fishing life depended. Incidentally Emerson recorded that the 'peasants' believed that both a moon-dog and a sun-dog meant rain. He also noted that the longshoremen believed the moon controlled both the weather and the tide.

The longshoremen as represented by Emerson's observations and in their own memories were a distinctive sub-group in the town. Poor with hard-working wives, closely related, physically fine, curious of each other, nick-named, occupationally dressed, dirty, living on credit, supported in times of need by public subscription, some fond of drinking and smoking, others coarse in their habits, working from different parts of the beach in a spirit of rivalry, honest but not above trying to foul each other at sea, fearless lifeboatmen, keen observers of their environment, pragmatists, stubborn in their views, religiously diverse but superstitious, living lives according to natural rhythms, using age-old fishing methods. In their own reckoning the kings of their domain, the beach, and of their way of life. 'A right royal lot'.

It is highly unlikely that any of the longshoremen ever set eyes on *Pictures of East Anglian Life*. Emerson was keen to protect his reputation. He achieved this by controlling the market through supply and price.[22] The plates were destroyed. The de-luxe edition of twenty-five copies cost seven guineas, the ordinary edition of 250 copies was five guineas, the latter a quarter of a longshoreman's average annual income if Emerson's estimate is correct.

Emerson lived in Southwold for two years, removing to Chiswick in 1886. Two prints from *Pictures of East Anglian Life* can be seen in the Reading Room. Since their provenance is unknown, it is tempting to think that he might have gifted them. No other trace of him exists in the town nor is there any recognition of his residence, an omission, since the longshoremen contributed a small but inspirational part to the history of photography, though not without having often been coldly anatomised. He left them with as much praise as he could muster in that condescending tone:

'And now we must say goodbye to the longshoremen …. and comfort ourselves with the thought that there may be worse skippers even *than they*, and that after all their hearts are often in the right places.'

Notes

1   For biographical information see: Emerson, P.H. *The English Emersons* and Newhall, Nancy *P.H.Emerson*

2   Emerson, P.H. *Pictures of East Anglian Life* p. 44

3   Taylor, John *The Old Order and The New P.H. Emerson and Photography 1885-1895* p.15

4   Emerson *Pictures of East Anglian Life* p.iii

5   Taylor p.14

6   Ibid p.14

7   Williams, R. *The Country and the City* p.9-12

8   Emerson *Pictures of East Anglian Life* p.135

9   Gooding, D.J. Notebook *Southwold* from the Barrett Jenkins Collection, Southwold Museum Sowdm 2006.14.7 p.14-16

10 This and all following references are in Emerson ibid p. 31-40

11 Logan, Kathryn *Fishing for Ganseys* p.29

12 Tolhurst, Peter *East Anglian Folk Art* (forthcoming)

13 Thompson, Gladys *Guernsey and Jersey Patterns* p.124

14 Tolhurst, Peter *This Hollow Land: Aspects of Norfolk Folklore* p.155

15 The *Victoria* was in East Street formerly the *Pilot Boat*. Now it is a clothes shop from Cornwall, *Sea Salt*; the *Red Lion* remains on South Green

16 See www.soundsurvey.org.uk/index.php/survey/radio_recordings/1930s/1543/

17 See *Blyth Voices* Folk Songs collected in Southwold by Ralph Vaughan Williams in 1910

18 Vertue, F. W. Notebook 2 p.322, Southwold Museum

19 Evans, George Ewart *The Pattern under the Plough* p.64

20 Lethbridge, T. C. *Boats and Boatmen* Chapt.III

21 Tolhurst, Peter *This Hollow Land: Aspects of Norfolk Folklore* p.155

22 Taylor, John *The Old Order* p.49

8

The Rope-Maker's Boy

In 1901, aged twelve and a half, Mr. Rogers left school to work for Goodwins, ironmongers and rope-makers. The shop was in Queen Street, now occupied by Serena Hall's Gallery, though it was a chemist's, Webb's, when Mr. Rogers spoke to me. The rope-walk was on the common by the Baptist chapel at the end of Spinner's Lane. At the top of the walk, a flint-walled building housed the spinning wheels Mr. Rogers was employed to turn. Above was a loft where the hemp was stored and dressed. Originally there were two walks. The 'long' walk for long ropes, ran down to the marshes but was curtailed when the railway was built. The 'short' walk for smaller ropes, ran down to the old gas works. The business was owned by Jasper Goodwin but in Mr. Rogers's day the rope was made by his foreman, George Button. Goodwins closed in 1904 and the business was taken over by Denningtons, a firm from Halesworth. When George died, his brother, William set up on his own and invented a method of spinning and rope-making that didn't require a boy to turn the wheels. William Button continued to make rope by hand until his death in 1935 when he was in his 90th year. He was reputed to be last hand rope-maker in the country.

An older rope-making business run by Henry Oldring situated in Cumberland Road closed in 1880. Its 'short' walk went to Field Stile Road and 'long' walk to North Green via the churchyard wall. Emerson told a ghost story about its premises.

Mr. Rogers's memories are of his time as the boy whose job it was to turn the wheels which helped Mr. Button make threads from the hemp. He also made *norsels* which were short lengths of twine used to attach the *net-rope* [the rope on which the floats were hung] of a drift net to the *oddy* [the first few rows of netting], and *snoods* which were used to attach the hooks to longlines. He spent two years there. Although his memories of the process are accurate it is helpful to explain it as straightforwardly as possible first.

The process was threefold. Hemp was first spun into lengths called *threads*, but elsewhere yarns. The threads were next combined into *strands*. Finally the strands were *laid* into a single rope.

Hemp came to the ground in bales and had to be *dressed* before use by running it through a *hackler board*, upright prongs inserted into a wooden base which made the fibres parallel. When dressed, Mr Button gathered the hemp in a bundle around his waist and the making of threads began. To do this he attached the hemp to *whirls* set in motion by the wheel. Mr Button walked backwards feeding the hemp while Mr Rogers turned. As the thread lengthened, he used a wet cloth to smooth it down. If the rope was to be used under water, the thread was run through a *tar-copper* containing Stockholm tar. Once made, the thread was run along a line of slotted posts on to a bobbin and another spun.

The next stage was to combine the threads into a *strand*. At one end of the walk, the threads were attached to hooks on a machine called a *jack*. The hooks revolved when a wheel, cogged or geared, was turned. At the other end, the threads, supported on posts through the length of the walk, were attached to a *sledge* or *traveller*, a stout wooden structure. When the jack was turned, the threads combined to form a single strand. As the twisting proceeded, the strands became shorter pulling the sledge or traveller towards the jack.

To *lay* a rope of three strands, the strands were attached to a single rotating hook also on the sledge. A conical wooden *top* with three grooves along its length and a wooden handle was inserted between them at the sledge end. When the jack was turned Mr Button walked up with the sledge using the top to ensure the strands combined at the right tension.

'How ol' wuz I when I started at the rope-works? Well, not quite thirteen, twelve an' a half I 'spect, when I started there. How it come about wuz, I say, "I'm thirteen years ol'. I'm goin' t' leave school." Mother say, "You aren't thirteen yit. You aren't ol' enough." "Well," I say, "I am. You can tell 'em I'm thirteen." Anyhow she got away with it! She went across the school here an' told the ol' man – by the way his name wuz Waller, ol' Charlie Waller – an' she say, "All right. You can leave if you go t' night school." I

say, "I aren't goin' t' night school. I in't got much time to go t' night school."
Howsomever, I never went, o' course.

Time went on. I kept goin' down t' the *twine-ground*. I got a job. First
I got a job at the ironmonger's shop where Webb's the chemist's now is –
you don't remember that! – an' I worked there makin' norsels an' various
things. They had an ol' machine up there. Course I wuz interested in
the people that used t' come into the shop. They say, "Can you get us a
farthin'worth o' marbles?" P'raps his [Goodwin's] wife 'ud come an' say,
"What do you boys want?" They say, "Farthin'worth o' marbles." She used
t' look at me an' say, "You might o' got that." I used t' say, "Well, I don't
know anythin' about that." People used t' come round, have a look at me,
say, "What are they?" an' all that sorta thing. I used t' have t' explain t' 'em
what they were.

Mr Button and Mr Rogers as a boy

Norsels were just like a piece o' string but they weren't string though.
They were spun an' made into threads an' then they were put on t' a machine t' *put the turn* into 'em. Then you used t' *lay 'em up* with your knife.
You had an eye in the end where the *net-rope* hung on. The ol' fishermen
used t' buy 'em t' put on their nets. [They had a spliced eye in one end and

were from six to nine inches in length.] I used t' have t' make either a thousand a day or three thousand, I can't remember which, for the princely sum o' a halfpenny an hour. I din't always make as many as that, I know.

Not long after that I got shifted down t' Spinner's Lane. I kept doin' with that. The ol' man say, "Well," he say, "fine day. We'll spin so-an'-so today." Well, this ol' man had this kind o' *stuff* round his waist, this here hemp. I used t' turn this wheel an' supply him with the turn into his thread. When he got the turn regular it wuz all right, but if he got it jerky, the ol' man 'ud give me a pull [on the thread] an' come back again, 'cos he'd got too much turn. Howsomever, he used t' spin these threads an' the more regular you turned the wheel, the better for him. The ol' man used t' go backwards o' course.

I used t' get fed up wi' settin' on this little iron seat, so I used t' stand up an' pull it round. O' course that din't suit the ol' man. He say, "Can't you set there an' turn that wheel?" "No, Button," I say. "That ol' seat is hard!" "That in't hard," he say. "You set down an' turn it. I can't spin wi' you jerkin' the line like that." "All right, Mr Button," I say. Got on all right like that.

The ol' man used t' spin so many o' these threads, then I'd get two an' put 'em on t' some *whirls* an' heave the turn into 'em with the big wheel. [to make a strand]. He used t' *lay 'em up* with a little ol' thing called a *top*. "Ah! Thass how thass done, Mr Button." "Thass done," he say. "You turn that wheel properly!" "All right, Button."

I used t' say, "I wonder what the time is, Mr Button?" We used t' knock off at half-past four. I used t' climb up the boards [that marked the boundary fence of the rope-ground] an' have a look at the time [by the church clock]. I say, "Thass gone four, Button." "Oh, well," he say, "we better be a-packin' up." So by the time th' ol' boy had packed up an' that an' we got outside, the ol' man used t' holler! I say, "What's the matter, Button?" "Look at that," he'd say. "Thass only down about two minutes arter four! An' you a-told me that wuz half-past four!" I never used t' take no notice o' it. "You be here in the mornin'," he say, "a little arter six." "Early i'n'it, Button?" "That in't early," he say, "that'll be daylight." That wuz in the summer time, o' course! So we'd start off again, same procedure every day, till we come t' spinnin' ropes.

He used t' spin so many threads, an' they all used t' be put into one an' laid up an' made into a rope. We used t' make *long ropes* down on the common, back o' where this place is now [Mr Rogers lived in Crick Court]. Used t' go down there t' the Gas-works. He used t' have a *jack-machine* for 'em. We used t' heave it round by hand. That wuz a different thing t' what the little ol' spinnin' wheel wuz. The spinnin' wheel wuz only meant for light work, but this wuz meant for big work.

One time an ol' thread o' hemp got in one o' the cogs o' the jack an' without stoppin' on it, I heaved the end off one o' my fingers. Coh! I yelled! Ol' Button say, "What's up?" I say, "I took my finger off, Mr Button." "Let's have a look at it." Looked at it. "Better go up the doctor's," he say, "see about that." So I went up the doctor's. That wuz a man by the name o' Woolard. I say, "I got the end o' my finger off." Though that wuz only just across the nail. Howsomever, I nursed that up. Thought I wuz goin' t' get clear o' work! "You can turn that wheel," he say, "with the other hand." "I can't," I say. Coh! He wuz a hard ol' feller! "All right, Button," I say. That hurt. Well, Woolard, all he done wuz put a couple o' bits o' plaster on, stuck the end on. That grew. That wuz all right. Howsomever I got over that.

When we'd got a big rope t' make, we used t' employ another ol' man, ol' chap by the name o' Ben Spence. He used t' spin one or two ol' threads along o' Button. The two on 'em used t' go down together. "Coh!" I say, "hard work, Button, two o' you spinnin'!" "That in't hard work," he used t' say. I couldn't get away with it.

The *jack* wuz used for biggish ropes like *wagon-rope*s or *ground-ropes* for trawl nets. That used t' come a nice coil o' rope. That used t' be lovely work, lovely ropes when they were made, with hemp especially. Sometimes the rope 'ud have what they called a *heart* inside it. That wuz a special sort o' thread, p'raps coloured blue for one, p'raps red for another. That used t' go right through the centre.

When you got a wet day, well o' course the ol' boy never used t' be able t' spin. He used t' go up the loft an' *dress* hemp. I thought I'd have a holiday. Not likely! "Get you on that norsel-machine, boy an' make norsels." I used t' go down below on my own an' do what I liked practically. "I don't hear much goin' on," the ol' man used t' say. "Well, I'm makin' on, Button." 'Course I couldn't get away with it then! When he'd done up top, he'd come down an' say, "How many you made?" I'd p'raps made two or three hundred when I oughter have made a thousand. "I thought so," he'd say. "You've earned your money today then!" "Yis, I 'spect I have."

The fishermen used t' buy these norsels. There mustn't be no kinks in 'em or nuthin' like that. If you gave 'em too much turn, you see, you'd get kinks in 'em an' that wouldn't do. There used t' be another boy as well an' he'd have t' chop wood while I used t' work on the norsels. I'd say t' him, "I'm goin' t' chop wood this mornin'." We used t' have fights over it. "No," he say, "thass my turn." Howsomever, we got on all right.

The hemp used t' come from away somewhere. I don't really know where that did come from. That come in bulk in a rough state o' course. That had t' be dressed first before you could do anythin' with it, 'cos that wuz in a bale, you see. The ol' man used t' do that. Up in the loft o' the shed there were rows o' needles like a comb an' the hemp wuz dressed by pullin' it through 'em. If that wuz goin' t' be a coarse rope, that din't get as much dressin' as a fine rope, 'cos the hemp had t' be like fine silk for 'em. I thought t' myself once that I'd have a go one time, but you could soon stab your hands on the needles when you threw the hemp over. That wuz pretty dangerous really.

After it wuz dressed it had t' be spun. The ol' man used t' put so much in a bundle round his waist, what he thought wuz enough, and he used t' feed it as the turn came down t' him. After that, when that wuz done, he used t' have a wet cloth an' walk along it an' smooth it down. If it wuz goin' t' be tarred, that used t' go through a *tar-copper*. Stockholm tar that wuz, for ropes that were goin' t' be used underwater. A press used t' go down on it an' squeeze the tar out an' that used t' come out, not black exactly, but sort o' browny colour. When he'd spun one length o' line, I used t' take it off the wheel an' pin it on t' a post called a *battle-post*. That had slots in it an' you'd put the thread in that an' then start on the next one. The only disadvantage wuz that the ol' man used to have t' come up [to the wheel] after he'd spun one. He din't have a machine at the other end o' the ground t' come back with. So you can see that wuz rather crude. T' make a big rope he'd say, "Put on so-an'-so." An' you'd put on the number o' threads he wanted an' heave the turn into 'em again t' make a strand. He'd then use the top an' the jack, as we called 'em, t' make the strands into the rope with the right amount o' strain an' turn in 'em.

What sort o' rope did the fishermen ask for? Well, that all depended what they wanted! If they wanted a length o' net-rope, that wuz small, but if they wanted a trawl-rope or anythin' like that, o' course that wuz a lot bigger 'n stronger. If they got [long] lines t' fit up, they used t' want *snoods*, what they called snoods. They used t' be longer 'n norsels, you see, made o' different stuff. Thass how we used t' do it. We din't make just for fishermen. Farm workers. They wanted plough-lines – what the hosses used t' have on 'em – t' steer the plough with. They used t' be made o' hemp. Crikey! They were strong! Wagon-ropes an' all that we used t' make. They used t' be a nice job. Made o' hemp. They were coiled up, not just rough-coiled, but wound round a bobbin. So many fathom o' this an' so many fathom o' that somebody would want an' that wuz put down t' 'em.

When I first started there, I got half-a-crown a week an' then I got a raise t' three shillin's. A while later he say, "I think you might have a raise, boy." I say, "A raise? What do you mean, a raise?" "Well," he say, "I'll give you four shillin's a week." Coh! I thought t' myself. Now this is the funny part about it. I got four shillin's an' 'cos my father an' mother always thought I wuz gettin' three, I stopped her the other one! I said to my brother, "I'm gettin' four bob a week now." "Well," he say, "what are you goin' t' do with it? Mother 'on't know, will she? I say, "No. But that 'int right, is it, not t' tell her?" "Well," he say, "Keep it. Get suthin' for yourself." I say, "All right." I did an' that kept on like that for a long while.

O' course, it happened one time that I missed ol' Button. He used t' give the wages out every Saturday afternoon an' for some reason, I missed him. I went down t' Spinner's Lane an' asked the ol' man for 'em. "Oh," he say, "your mother had your money a long while ago. I took it round your house." Coh! I nearly dropped! "Blimey," I thought. "I done it now!" "Fancy tellin' your mother you're only gettin' three shillin's a week, you little varmint," he say. He had t' tell my mother, you see, 'cos she say t' him, "You give me too much. You give me four shillin's." "No, I ain't," he say, "thass the right amount. I know what he get." Well that wuz all right till father come home. "What you done with this shillin' every week?" I say, "Spent it." "Spent it!" he say. "What arter? That'd be better for you t' have saved it, bought your-self a pair o' boots, suthin' like that." I say, "Yes, father, thass what's hap-pened to it."

Durin' the summer months, we used t' have t' go t' work at six o' clock in the mornin'. I used t' say, "I'm not comin' down here at that time in the mornin'!" "Oh yis you are," he say. "That'll be daylight all right." In the winter time we used t' start off at seven. "Coh!" I say, "Button do you fancy

me come right from where I live, down here with snow on the ground?"
"Snow," he say, "make it lighter!"

I used t' torment the ol' man, but you know he give me a good name at
the finish. He got his own back on me once, I remember. One Christmas
time, he an' ol' man Spence got their heads together an' said, "We'll scare
the life outa that boy." I say, "You 'ont frighten me, Button. This place ain't
haunted." He say, "Yis, it is. There's some very odd things happened in that
there shed. We've had Father Christmas come there sometimes." O' course
bein' young an' innocent, I din't know no different. He say "He hid up in
that gret ol' chest." I din't believe that, never thought no more about it.
Somehow or other him or the other chap rigged up a line that ran overhead,
an' as he wuz outside towards the Common, he drew on this line an' that'd
lift this ol' box lid. So he said t' me one afternoon, "Blast!" he say, "I thought
I'd left it! Go into that there shed an' get me my knife. That lay on the shelf
there, over that chest." 'Course, I walked in innocent enough. Blow me!
That lid started t' slam up an' down an' I see a bearded face come out! The
ol' man had rigged it up with hemp! Scared the blinkin' daylights outa me.
So he say, "Ah! Shan't never be scared! But you were scared when you
came outa there weren't you?" I say, "Yis, I wuz, Button." Months arterwards he told me how it wuz done. "I thought that weren't haunted." "Ah!"
he say, "but you din't know."

Well I stuck it there for two years then I runned away. My brother went
down an' Button say t' him, "Where's the boy?" "Don't know," he say. "I
int sin 'im." "Well, he in't bin here." I worn't likely t' be there! I runned
away an' went t' Low'stoft. I kept tellin' the ol' man I wuz goin' t' sea. He
din't believe me. I don't know if you've ever heard o' an ol' man by the
name o' *Pincher* Spence? He used t' run a cargo boat here, coal. I used t'
say, "I'm goin' along o' *Pincher*." I got so the ol' man believed it. "Well, I
want to know," he say, "whether you're a-goin' or not, so I can get another
boy if you don't come." I say, "I'll ask my father." The ol' man cried that
down as soon as I mentioned it. But howsomever one day, I did go. I went
t' Low'stoft, got a berth in one o' the sailin' boats an' went t' sea in that.
When I went an' got my money, he say t' me, "Boy, I think you're a fool t'
yourself. Your got a good job, your gettin' good pay an' now your goin' t'
run away an' leave." I say, "Well, I want t' go t' sea." "Ah!" he say, "I
shouldn't." 'Thass all right," I say, "I'm a-goin'." I don't think the firm

lasted much longer after that. Poor ol' Button, I see him now, sometimes. That wuz about 1904, I 'spect.

Anyhow I left. I went away t' sea an' when I come back, I see the ol' man. Coh! He made a right ol' fuss o' me, goin' up Gun Hill one Sunday mornin'. "Coh, boy," he say, "How you gettin' on?" "Oh, all right, Button," I say. "Do you like it?" "Well," I say, "I got t' make a livin'." "Oh," he say. "I hope you get on all right, boy."

Next thing I know, the ol' man wuz dead when I got back again. Where I wuz at Spinner's Lane, his brother used t' have the garden opposite, William Button. George wuz the ol' man I worked along with. But William rigged up a machine so he done it hisself. He used t' spin his own lines, no boy wanted. He had a couple o' lines come round these little wheels, a pair o' pliers hooked on the line an' fastened t' his belt. He used t' go backwards an' supply his own turn. Soon after, another firm took over from Goodwins, firm by the name o' Dennington, Halesworth.

That wuz interestin', you know. Three shillin's a week. That used t' work out at a halfpenny an hour. They told me I got a good job! I don't know what they'd say now. But you were glad t' get suthin' t' do when you left school.

P'raps he'd send me up Reydon with a coil o' plough-line. "Take this up t' so-and-so's farm," he'd say. I used t' have t' walk, o' course, carryin' this here coil o' rope. I'd get up the farm. The woman used t' come t' the door, say, "What you want, boy?" I say, "I bought the plough-line." "Coh!" she say. "Walked up here?" I say, "Yis, ma'm." "I 'spect you could do with a cup o' tea?" "I say, "Yis, I could, m'am." So she give me a cup o' tea an' a lump o' cake. I used t' do all right. Long time ago, boy!'

Lost Boy

I next saw a boy with his back to me. He turned. I could see he had been sobbing, adding his salt tears to the sea. He said his name was Job. He asked me if I had seen Sam and when I could not answer he begged me to look out for him. We wuz cast together he said an' then I lost him. He said he was sure mother was looking for him. She was thin and had his father's name tattooed on her arm. I would know mother by that name, Billy, Billy, my father.

I told him that I would do as he asked. I would tell them that Job had been looking for them. He thanked me and was gone, disappearing back into the murk from which he came.

9

The Longshoreman's Year

The longshoreman's year at Southwold was seasonal and his day diurnal. These rhythms were dictated seasonally by the arrival of certain species at particular times and daily by the state of the tides. The seasons were centuries old, called *fares* in medieval and early modern documents – the *herring fare*, the *sprat* or *spurling fare*, the *set-nett* fare and so on. A longshoreman on Southwold beach until the First World War was following a way of life his medieval ancestors would easily recognise, a way of life largely unchanged and untouched by industrialisation, worked essentially by wind and hand. The catching of different species demanded different methods so longshoremen needed to know how to *drift*, to *trawl*, to *draw* or *drag* and to *longline*. Success in each of these demanded in turn, knowledge of the habits of the species they were after, the signs of their presence in or on the water, the best times and tides for catching them, the winds that affected them. The longshoreman needed to be not just a master of this side of his calling but also to be a competent seaman, to look after his boat and his gear, to prepare some of his catches for sale as well as to be his own salesman, skills for which he was rarely given credit.

In Southwold the year began in February with smelt fishing in the Blyth or from the beach by *drag-netting*, though this was a specialised option which only a few undertook. The main season started around the end of March or the beginning of April when the longshoremen would *drift* for *spring-herring*, herring without roes or *spents*, which they would use as bait for catching *roker* (thornback ray) or skate on their *longlines*. Alternatively a pair of boats might work together, one drifting and passing the catch to the other to cut up and line for the roker.

When this fishery finished around the end of May, the longshoremen would go *trawling* throughout the summer months for plaice and soles as well as for shrimps. Both were caught with a *beam-trawl*, but the net sizes differed, a shrimp net having a smaller mesh or *shale* and a shorter length.

Towards the end of September or near the beginning of October, the *autumn-herring* season began. These *longshore* or *full herrings*, so-called on account of their roes, were different to the deep-sea herrings and considered to be finer in flavour. They made excellent *bloaters* or *reds*. As in spring, these were caught in drift-nets.

This was followed by the *sprat* season which began at the start of November. Once again these were caught by *drift-net*. The long-shoremen regarded the sprat season as their harvest and relied on it to make sufficient money to pay off the debts accrued during the year and to see them through the winter. A bad sprat season was financially ruinous. Just before or after Christmas, if the season had been a good one, the sprats would disappear but as they began to deplete, the long-shoremen would use them as bait to go *longlining* for cod.

Fishing generally stopped at Christmas and did not recommence until the spring herring returned in April. Thus the darkest and coldest months of the year were those without income. Some would go *deep-sea* fishing. The voyage to the *Westward* from Newlyn and Penzance began after Christmas and could last for six or more weeks. Alternatively they could try to get work on Lowestoft trawlers which involved much shorter voyages. Some of the Walberswick men might be hired to mend the river walls for the local landowners, a back-breaking job called *slubbing*. The Southwold men often sought employment from the Town Council in sea-defence work on the beach. They did whatever they could find to make money. When they had time to spare they would maintain their boats, repairing and repainting them, looking over and mending their nets and gear, so that they would be ready when the season began again. Sometimes in these months the longshoremen would use a *drag-net* on the beach to fish for codling, flounders, dabs or smelts. The latter, they would also follow into the river. One of Emerson's photographs, *Smelting On The River Blythe* (sic), shows three longshoremen examining their catch. It is where we will begin to look in detail at the methods and practices the longshoremen used.

The Revenant

I saw the first man again, and this time, with his gansey unravelled on his arm, that E R was marked there. He told me that he had returned. I asked what he had done.

I shuffled alone up Church Street he replied
An' stood outside the door.
I watched her comin' an' goin'
Where I can cross no more.

I saw her spreadin' washin' out
On green gorse at Whin Hill,
Those sheets so white we slept in once
Would we were in 'em still.

I followed her to the churchyard
Where she stood by our stone,
Raindrops lengthenin' down our names
Her weepin' there alone.

I took her hand an' squeezed it tight
We walked along the shore,
Her warm touch made me want her so,
A shiver set her jaw.

I see her with another man,
A longshoreman like me.
They wuz holding hands together
I died o' jealousy.

When he looked at me his eyes were red-ringed.

10

Smelting On The River Blyth

Smelting On The River Blythe is one of thirty two photogravure prints in P.H. Emerson's *Pictures of East Anglian Life* (1880).The print is characteristic of his subject matter and technique at the time when he was vigorously championing 'naturalistic' photography. Although composed, it is 'naturalistic' in that it attempted to replicate what is seen by the eye. Emerson reproduced it in the book by photogravure, a new, complex and expensive technique by which the original image was etched on to a copper plate enabling it to be printed. Its expense guaranteed exclusivity and suited Emerson in his efforts to establish this kind of photography as art. Emerson was attracted by the superior way photogravure was able to reproduce the tones of the original photograph. The picture was typical also in its subject matter showing three of the 'fisherfolk' at work, in this case examining their catch of smelts on the Southwold side of the River Blyth.

Smelting On The River Blythe, P. H. Emerson

The composition foregrounds the smelters on the mud against the flat bands of the river, the opposite shoreline and the sky. They are grouped in a triangle at right angles to their boat which is drawn up by its bow on the mud, an oar sticking out over the starboard gunwale. The relatively low angle of the shot emphasises the length and expanse of the river and raises the Walberswick shoreline almost to the top of the picture with a small band of sky above it. Sky and river reflect each other, undifferentiated in tone, a flat grey. The smelters and the buildings on the opposite bank also reflect each other tonally in blacks and dull whites as well as in shape, the triangular hats the men wear echoed in the gables of the buildings on the far side. Light glitters on a wavelet in the foreground, on ripples in the river and where it catches the smelters' net. The net also provides texture as do the footprints and weed that break up the flatness of the mud. Contrast is created by the parts of the boat, net and the figures that are not in the light.

The three men, all dressed in tall hats, dirty white slops, and crotch boots stand or crouch. To the right, at the apex of the triangle is a single bearded figure whose profile is in focus. The other two men and the Walberswick shoreline are in 'differential focus', that is slighty out of focus – 'fuzzy' to his critics – a technique based on Emerson's belief that this is the way the eye sees; 'differential focus' was a way to create a hierarchy of seeing as a painting does. The single smelter has gathered some of the net by his left foot and is pulling out a width of what remains. The base of the triangle is formed by the other two figures opposite him, the one nearest the river echoing the first in stance and movement. The third crouches next to him and appears to be pulling the smelts from the net and placing them in a bucket at his right hand. All three figures have their eyes focused intently on the bottom of the net between them. The centre of the net and what it may or may not contain is thus the photograph's focal point. The composition is artistic, its subject is work, its technique 'naturalistic' and its reproduction in photogravure, modern; it is a fine example of Emerson's belief at this time that photography could be considered art.

Emerson provided an accompanying text to the photograph but smelting on the Blyth had been practised by the Southwold and

Walberswick fishermen for at least a century before 1888. The smelt (*Osmerus eperlanus*) was a much-prized fish, valued as a delicacy. Silver, with an elongated body, averaging about five inches and distinguished by its peculiar cucumber-like smell, adult smelts congregated at the mouths of rivers and estuaries in winter and entered them to spawn between February and April before returning to sea while the juveniles remained in the river. In Scotland smelts were called *spirlings* or *sparlings* which are the medieval East Anglian words for the sprat (*Sprattus sprattus*). The *spurling or sparling fare* was the term for the November sprat season. Smelts were often caught in sprat nets and resembled them in size and colour so it is not surprising that the two species were confused.

In the early 19th century the fishery of smelts in the Blyth became the focus of a dispute between a Walberswick fisherman, James Cady and the powerful local landlords whose estates bordered the river. From the mid 18th century the landlords were keen to improve their pasture lands by means of 'sluices, dry walling and drains to contain the estuarial floods which poured over the flat marshes at high tide.'[1] Members of the Blois and Rous families were the chief landowners on the Walberswick and Southwold sides respectively. By 1840 the landlords had appropriated an area of embanked land along the river which amounted to 1,504 acres.[2] A consequence, quite possibly unforeseen,[3] was that the embankments now restricted the volume of water which flowed into the river on a flood tide. This in turn reduced its ability to scour out the mouth at Southwold Harbour on the ebb. The result was that the harbour entrance frequently became silted, inhibiting trade; vessels were at times unable to enter the port or to enter with difficulty.[4] Southwold merchants, frustrated by this state of affairs, were powerless against the landlords. A further twist was that Southwold Harbour was run by a Board of Commissioners comprising the local landed gentry, two of whom were Blois and Rous. The records show that whenever pressed by the merchants to clear the harbour entrance, the Commissioners were tardy in their response and failed to address the root cause, the embankments, preferring instead to pursue options such as dredging. Even when a report on the state of the harbour that they themselves had commissioned from a distinguished engineer, John Rennie, published in 1820, explicitly highlighted that the embankments were the chief cause of the lack of scour, 'an opinion which came to be frequently cited and caused major argument in the first half of the nineteenth century',[5] the Commissioners failed to act.

Cady fell foul of the landlords in such a way as to attract an unnamed advocate to take up his case and present it to a lawyer, Charles Cooper, for his opinion. Whoever he was, the advocate was educated, informed and sufficiently angered to question whether the landlords had a case to answer, a disgruntled merchant perhaps but certainly someone unafraid of their power. The document entitled *Case for Mr Cooper*[6] begins by stating that until 1770, the smelt fishery on the Blyth was conducted 'without any interruption from any person whatever.' Smelts, the writer says, 'were much admired by the gentry in the neighbourhood.' At certain times of the year the fish could command prices of 'sixpence to a shilling each' in the London market. This corroborates a saying that 'a cigar-box full of smelt was enough for one week's wages.'[7]

The original method of catching smelts was called *driving* which involved suspending a sprat net in the water at the correct depth by means of corks and leads and letting it drift with the tide but this was inefficient and the writer states that it was replaced in 1786 by a practice called *drag-netting*, a form of seining by which means 'a considerable quantity of fish have been caught.' Drag-netting involved making a decreasing semi-circle of the net at intervals and dragging it ashore.

In 1817 Cady and others began drag-netting the Blyth for smelts. The document states that the fishermen left the haven on the top of the flood tide and went up river to the Blythburgh Flats to start smelting on the ebb. Two of the landlords – unnamed but presumably Blois and Rous, 'finding the fish in general request and fearing therefore it might become an object of general pursuit…laid their heads together,' the writer alleged, 'in order, if possible, to gain a monopoly of it.' To achieve this they permitted a 'particular person', unnamed, to use their land for all purposes to do with smelt fishing 'on the condition, it is supposed, that they should be supplied with such fish as they might request for their own use at their own price.' The conjectural 'it is supposed' reveals the writer's bias, but he is clearly suggesting that the landlords wanted their own supplies at a rate below the market price and wanted to cut out the local men. Having reached this agreement with their appointed fisherman, the landlords gave notice to Cady and the others not to trespass on their land when pulling the drag-net together. They went so far as to claim that 'the ooze on that part of the river from which the water retires on the ebb and on which the nets are drawn' belonged to them, the smelts being 'generally caught at low water.' Astonishingly, they claimed, in other words, the mud on the river-side of their embankments, which was only revealed at low tide, was their property. The writer emphasised that the landowners did not dispute Cady's right to fish for smelts whilst making it clear that their notice to quit fishing in that part of the Blyth effectively made it impossible. The writer also insisted that 'the fishermen only ever draw their nets on to the mud of the bed of the river from which the water has retired and over which it again flows on the return of the tide'. Never did they venture on to the reclaimed land or even upon 'the wasteland of the banks themselves.'

Cady was untroubled when he received his notice not to trespass. He wondered 'how it could possibly be an offence to draw a net upon the mud of a river from which the tide had fallen and upon which mud a net might legally be drawn when covered in water.' Displaying true longshoreman's stubbornness he only quit after receipt of a third notice and only then because he had gained other employment.

In 1829 however, Cady was once more in need of work and 'having obtained permission of one of the landed proprietors to use his ground' – he had no choice now but to acknowledge the appropriation – Cady invested considerably in a boat and nets. He resumed smelting in early 1830, the right time for the fishery. He did not however confine himself to landing his net on the grounds for which he had permission. He duly received a letter in July from James Cooper, one of Blois's tenants at Westwood Lodge,[8] which told him to cease fishing forthwith 'and if you persist after this notice, you will be considered a wilful trespasser and proceeded against accordingly.' Cady felt this amounted to intimidation and, as before, ignored this and the threats of two further notices.

The writer then stated that the two landlords colluded and the one who originally gave Cady permission to use his grounds, withdrew it, 'with a view, no doubt, of the ultimate attainment of a fishery by the exercise of an exclusive right.'[9] Once again the 'no doubt' makes this conjectural, but the writer clearly felt that, as in 1817, they were pursuing a monopoly even though they did not dispute Cady's right to fish for smelts. Cady, ever the longshoreman, carried on until August 8th.

On that day, whilst fishing, he was confronted by seven men 'who were sent down with a boat to prevent him.' Some were armed with bludgeons 'but on endeavouring to enter his boat, Mr Cady beat them off with an oar, got possession of their bludgeons and ultimately carried away his net safely.' One can imagine this ugly encounter, the threats, the language and the fracas in the wobbling boats. But this was not the end of the matter. Among the seven men were a game-keeper and two underkeepers. In the scuffle one of the underkeepers was injured, either by his own bludgeon or by Cady's oar and he obtained a warrant for the assault. Cady was taken to a sitting of magistrates at Yoxford, the home village of Sir Charles Blois on August 15th. The magistrates, according to the writer, 'appear to have taken for granted what no attempt was made whatever to prove, that is, that there was a private fishery'. Cady was convicted of assault and fined £2.14s.6d with £2.5s.6d. costs. On non-payment of the £5 he was committed to the gaol in nearby Beccles where he remained until the 18th when the money was found. When he returned to Walberswick he discovered that during his incarceration the local constables had seized his nets but had given no satisfactory reason why.

'Your opinion is requested,' on eight counts the advocate wrote to Mr. Cooper. He asked first whether the Lord of any Manor or any other proprietor could have a title to a fishery as to 'justify the exclusion of Mr. Cady or other persons therein.' Cooper was emphatic. In his opinion they had no such title. Second Cooper was asked, given his first opinion, whether 'the proprietors are entitled to prevent Mr. Cady or other persons from drawing a net on the mud between the opposite banks of the River Blyth when the tide has retired therefrom.' Again Cooper was decisive; they are 'not legally authorised' to do this because using the mud 'appertains *necessarily* to the right to fish.' The advocate next asked if the Lord of the Manor 'was justified in employing the force mentioned…for the purpose alluded to.' Cooper's view was that the force was 'unjustifiable' and further, 'that those who *employed* it ought to be indicted either for an assault or a riot.' The fourth question was whether Cady was 'guilty of an assault to warrant his conviction, fine and imprisonment.' Cooper stated that Cady was 'justifiable in using such force' to protect 'his person and his property.' Cooper was further asked whether the magistrates were justified in their summary conviction of Cady. They should not have proceeded in a summary way was the reply. The sixth question was whether Cady had any right of appeal. Cooper stated tellingly that he had none. Penultimately Cooper was asked if Cady could be regarded as a *bona fide* fisherman 'never having been apprenticed,' because he used the same net for the catching of sprats as well as smelts. Cooper was of the opinion that Cady was 'authorised to have and keep the nets for the catching of fish.' The final question was whether the seizure of the nets on Cady's premises could be justified. Cooper's response was that there was no justification for the seizure unless Cady had had a previous conviction for using it unlawfully. The document was signed and dated by Cooper on October 5th, 1830.

While it is always possible to find a sympathetic lawyer, the case itself and Cooper's opinions of it, made without fear or favour, cast the landlords and tenant at the very least as bullying and self-interested. Unfortunately we know nothing more about this incident so what happened is lost but Cady crops up twice in Maggs. On July 9th, 1832 three fishermen from Kirkley in Lowestoft, two brothers named Wyatt and another called Colby, were drowned whilst fishing off Easton. Cady trawled up one of the Wyatt's bodies on the 20th which was interred at Walberswick. And in a tragic echo, Cady lost his own son, William on January 26th, 1850, when he was drowned in a collision between a 'large Bark' and the *Anna Maria* of South Shields, of which he was a crew member, in a 'strong wind'. The force of the collision was so catastrophic that the *Anna Maria* went down 'immediately' with only one survivor.[10] Such were the precarious and difficult lives of seamen and longshoremen trying to make their livings at this time, caught in Cady's case between the unforgiving elements and his self-interested betters.

The Cooper document is also interesting from a technical and historical angle. Smelting on the Blyth by the method of *driving* was practised before 1770 and by *drag-netting* after 1776. A sprat net of about a half inch mesh was used on an ebb tide from Blythburgh Flats, the catches being lucrative in the London Market which could easily be reached.

Emerson's account of smelting on the Blyth in *Pictures of East Anglian Life* corroborates the document in all respects but one, as well as providing more detailed information. The discrepancy lies in which tide to use. Emerson emphatically contradicts the ebb tide option used by Cady:

'The earliest fishermen begin in February', he wrote, 'but March and April are considered the best months here. The net used is locally called here a draw-net, the mesh of which is a sprat mesh. To the top-end are attached corks and to the bottom leads, ropes being attached to either end. These nets are valued at about £4 each.

  Old hands inform us that smelts "always strike one way" and that is from the southward, and that they enter the river to spawn in a flood tide and leave it with the ebb; therefore smelting must be done on a flood as in an ebb "you won't get none."

Two or at most three men work one net. Beginning we will say, at Blackshore, two smelters will get into the boat as the tide is on the turn or while it is still flowing and rowing straight across the river, they will throw out the net as they go, while the third man stays on the shore with one of the end ropes in his hand. When the net is shot, the men in the boat row along the opposite bank, while the man on the shore goes "plouncing" along through the soft mud protected by his tall sea-boots, pulling at the rope which passes over his shoulder, thereby towing one end of the net, while the boat tows the other. Having scoured a portion of the river in this manner, the two in the boat row over to their companion, who again stands still until their boat grounds, then, hastily pulling her up, they jump ashore and all three haul at the ropes of the net. Slowly the semi-circle contracts and nearer each haul come the corks, till at length they lie at the feet of the fishermen. Then with a quick movement, some standing in the water, others in the mud, they draw the net on to the yellow sands and through the dripping mesh of black netting can be seen the glitter of silver fish. The men now open the net and throwing aside the mud and the weeds, they pick out the shining sweet-smelling smelts and place them in a basket or a pail.'

Emerson ends by recording that 'this delicate fish varies in value', the fishermen getting from four to six shillings a score according to season, the average price being half-a-crown a score. On a 'good day' therefore a fisherman can earn a good sum of money.[11]

When Mr English talked to me about smelting in 1978, he agreed with Emerson about the flood-tide. 'We used to pick the slack tide at low water so that we could go with the tide coming in.' But Mr Barber agreed with the evidence of the *Case for Mr Cooper*, 'Say you went up to Blythburgh Flats so you got there at high water or just before, you'd come back with the tide and you had to be pretty smart then 'cos the tide is runnin' with the river.' It seems then that both starting points, low water at Blackshore or high water at Blythburgh, were used depending on preference. Both men however were in accordance about how hard the work was for the *shoreman* pulling the rope on the bank. Mr English, 'That was really hard work if you were on the bank 'cos you had to go through all the mud. You had your long boots on and a jersey and an oilskin but you couldn't help get muddy.' And Mr Barber said:

'We all used t' have long boots on, which were leather in those days, right up t' your thighs, solid leather… You walk along the bank, the shoreman do, up t' his knees in mud sometimes, then he'd get out on a little bit o' stiff mud an' he'll come right along. Then he'll pull the net in at the first opportunity, when there's a bit o' a break, when you come round a corner into a quiet part, an' thass where you'd get your smelts in. The last longshoreman who done that wuz Billy Mayhew, nicknamed *Stork* an' his brother, *Mobbs.*'

Both men's recollections show the continuity of *drag* or *drawnetting* for smelts in the Blyth from the late 18th into the 20th century. But as sometimes happens, when talking about one thing a speaker will reveal another. Mr Barber told a story about an occasion when he and his brother went smelting :

'When us boys used t' go, there used t' be two ol' Mr. Stannards an' these ol' boys, they used t' gut the fish an' they'd never tell you what they got or nuthin'. We were goin' down the harbour one day an' we were goin' acrost Blackshore marshes an' we see a smelt lay on the footpath. We say, "Hello. Somebody got a good lot here, do that wouldn't have fell off the top." That wuz some time after we found out these ol' boys had got a lot o' smelts. So we said we'd be goin' in the mornin' when the tide wuz right. Well the ol' boat lay against the ferry [the location of Emerson's photograph]. We din't want anyone t' know we had gone 'cos we were afraid crowds 'ud go after 'em, you see. We had 'em in the bow o' the little boat covered up with an oilskin over 'em an' we no sooner touched the shore t' step out than an ol' man by the name o' Palmer uncovered the basket an' see all o' these. You can believe the next day on the tide there were dozens up there after 'em. But they'd never go till someone else had gone.'

This reflects the culture of longshoring interestingly. The Barber boys did exactly what they criticised the Stannards for. First they went after someone else had gone and second, they were secretive by hiding their own catch of smelts beneath an oilskin, only discovered by Palmer's brazen nosiness. Secrecy gave the longshoremen a temporary economic advantage over their rivals and they did what they could to preserve it. Indeed, the Barbers themselves only found out 'some time afterwards' that the Stannards had been successful. Suspiciousness, secrecy and trying to capitalise on others' good fortune were among the essential habits of longshore life.

Finally, Mr Tooke remembered an amusing anecdote:

'They used t' get up t' some exploits gettin' smelts. There'd be about a dozen boats up there an' they'd get about a shillin' a score – that's a *score-pair* mind you, forty fish. They'd work up there in the winter time with their beards actually frozen t' their oilskins. I remember one occasion just by Blackshore quay. That used t' be a lovely *draw-ground*. They'd hang there beautiful. This chap stepped outa the boat on t' the shore an' stepped into a soft patch o' mud an' disappeared, just his head stickin' out o' the mud! We got one o' the *lee-boards* an' slid it down t' him so he lay across an' could lean on it. We got a rope in t' him, got ashore an' pulled him out with the leeboard. When he got ashore he say, "Where's my pipe?" I say, "It's in the mud." He say ,"You'd better go an' look for it." I say, "No fear, I aren't. I don't want t' be turned out the same as you." He wouldn't speak t' me for three days! So I said t' him, I say, "About this pipe, what kind o' pipe wuz it?" He say, "It wuz a clay pipe." The stem wuz about as long as my thumb. They used t' smoke 'em bottom up. I went t' *Frosty* Chapman's an' bought him half-a-dozen. I wuz the blue-eyed boy then.'

Emerson recorded seeing longshoremen in winter with ice hanging from their beards.[12]

Notes

1 Lawrence *Southwold River* p.9

2 Ibid p.124/5

3 Ibid p.57

4 Ibid p.94

5 Ibid p.57

6 All Cooper quotes are from *Southwold Borough Collection* 491/15B/5, Lowestoft Records Office

7 Maitland *the status of the smelt…*p.53

8 Lawrence p.56 James Cooper was the father of E.R. Cooper a nice irony given the latter's admiration of the longshoremen

9 There is a possibility that the landlords held a manorial right but I have not been able to ascertain this

10 *The Diaries of James Maggs* Vol 1 p.76 & Vol 2 p.23

11 Emerson *Pictures of East Anglian Life* p.74

12 Ibid p.47

11

Awful Catastrophe At Southwold

On Saturday February 27th, 1858, when there might have been smelting on the Blyth, an incident occurred which divided the town to its core revealing what some really thought of their longshoremen.

This was one of four quarter days chosen annually by the Committee of the Southwold Lifeboat Society for their boat, *Harriett* to go off on exercises. The Committee consisted of many of the town's gentry who lived on or near South Green, the most exclusive part of the town. This group had wrested control of the Town Council earlier in the decade from its incumbents, mainly local builders and tradesmen, whom they had suspected of 'jobbing' (a not inappropriate metaphor) – the practice of awarding themselves contracts for building works around the town from which they had made tidy profits. The Mayor himself, Peter Palmer, had been heavily involved.

Harriett was the second lifeboat of that name. Her predecessor, had been the pride of the Committee who had commissioned her from James Beeching of Great Yarmouth in 1852 to replace the ageing *Solebay*, the town's original boat built in 1840. Beeching had recently won a national competition for the design of a new lifeboat, inaugurated by the Duke of Northumberland, intended to revivify interest in the floundering Royal Institution for the Preservation of Life at Sea, of which he had become President. Over 280 models were submitted to the judging committee chaired by Captain Washington R.N. from as far afield as Germany, Holland and even America. James Beeching's winning self-righting model secured not just the 100 guineas prize but a further 100 to put towards the building of the boat, paid by Northumberland himself. When the Committee approached Beeching to replace *Solebay*, using the prize-winning design, they could not have been more up to date and the Southwold Lifeboat Society more in the vanguard. She was named both for Lady Gooch, the wife of the President and Miss Sherriffe, a wealthy benefactor who had each put up £100 to build her.

Ben Herrington was appointed cox'n. *Harriett's* first service was the rescue of the *Sheraton Grange* on November 29th, 1853 undertaken in defiance of the women gathered on the cliffs who had successfully prevented the launch of the yawl, *John Bull*. For this rescue, Herrington and second cox'n William Waters were awarded Institution medals for bravery at a dinner given in The Old Swan by Miss Sherriffe. Optimism ran high. 'The Southwold Lifeboat is one built by Beeching of Great Yarmouth and it is to be hoped that the present happy result will give that confidence in their noble boat that she so well merits' wrote a correspondent covering the event.

But such feelings for their 'noble boat' were short-lived. Two self-righters had recently capsized at Lytham and Rhyl. The crew had started grumbling. *Harriett* was not safe. Herrington and Waters, summoned to a Committee meeting on December 10th to suggest modifications which would assuage the crew's misgivings, would not co-operate. The problem was the one now being expressed by the beachmen at Lowestoft and even at Yarmouth about Beeching's design. The boat was a 'roly-poly' and would not do. Despite the Committee's decision on December 21st to return *Harriett* to Yarmouth for modifications, Herrington remained obdurate. He informed the secretary, Captain Francis Ellis R.N.(the town's Harbour Master) 'that neither he nor any of the lifeboat crew would go off in Beeching's boat whatever alteration may be made in her.'[1] (His parlance may have been more direct even than this.) And the crew showed their feelings on the day appointed for taking the boat to Yarmouth by going longlining instead. (That same majesty of self-reliance; that certainty that they knew what was right for their own conditions.) Until a replacement was found, they would continue to use *Solebay* which James Critten had declared fit for service.

The preference for *Solebay* was all to do with her design. She was a *Norfolk and Suffolk-type* lifeboat, a *wet-boat* built for these coasts. Wet-boats had relieving valves or plugs placed alongside the keel.[2] When opened they allowed water to flood in, the boat remaining afloat by means of her buoyancy tanks. It thus sat low in the water and, powered by the large foresail, drove *through* the waves. Crucially the wet-boat most resembled the yawls the longshoremen were familiar with and which had proven capabilities in heavy seas.

The Southwold Committee were now in the ironic position of having their new prize-winning self-righter rejected in favour of their old, just serviceable wet-boat. Not having the funds to order a new one, they did the only thing they could and applied to the Institution for advice. After consideration, the reply was duly received. The Institution would provide £200 to contribute to the cost of a new boat provided the Southwold Society wound itself up and found the money locally for any further costs. So it was that on 21st October, 1854 the Southwold Lifeboat Society ceased to exist and became a branch not of the Royal National Institution for the Preservation of Life at Sea but of its rebranded title, the Royal National Lifeboat Institution.

The immediate task of the new branch Committee was to commission the boat. The men remained stubborn. 'I find,' wrote Ellis to Captain J. Ward, the R.N.L.I's Inspector of Lifeboats, 'that nothing will reconcile them … to any other description of boat than that to which they have been hitherto accustomed in Southwold … They argue, and I think justly that Southwold is the most open part of the East Coast [and] that the short seas require a large boat to cross them with safety.'[3] Another reason why they disliked self-righters was not just in principle but also because 'in boarding a wreck the greatest freedom of action is required at the extremities of the boat which is sacrificed by the air-cases.'[4] A new Beeching-built wet-boat was duly commissioned and delivered on December 31st, 1855. She was a 40ft Norfolk and Suffolk-type costing £215. After sea-trials Ellis wrote to R.N.L.I Secretary Richard Lewis, 'The Beachmen and indeed everybody else are in raptures with the Boat and I have no doubt she will realise all our anticipations.'[5] Six days later he wrote to Lewis saying she 'gave the most unbounded satisfaction'.[6] As if to start again and to show respect to Lady Gooch and Miss Sherriffe (the latter once more providing dinner at the Swan) she too was named *Harriett*. Herrington who had resigned as her cox'n in 1857 in a dispute with the Committee was superseded by Francis Cooper.

The day before had been rough which had left a heavy swell on the shoals and on that February Saturday morning in 1858, the wind, calm at first and rising as the morning progressed, was E.N.E. The launch, in an onshore wind like this, by means of the haul-off warp and the sett would be straight in to the breakers but *Harriett* would be head to wind and getting under sail would be relatively straightforward. The beaching, with the wind behind her would have to be more carefully managed. As the wind rose, the sea became rougher but the conditions were well within her capabilities. The breakers over the inner and outer shoals curled white above the sand-filled waves, tawny now rather than their usual grey. Wind and waves combined to make a low roaring mingling with the shingle rattling down the shoreline beneath the hissing foam.

Harriett stood facing the sea on her carriage ahead of the Lifeboat House which was stationed beneath Kilcock Cliff. Her two crews were drawn from the ranks of the Kilcock cliffmen whose yawl, gigs and lookout were nearest to the Lifeboat House. In the event of a call-out they were at hand, nearer than their rivals at Long Island. Cooper was a sound choice as the new cox'n. Just over a year previously he and his crew had saved the brig, *Pensher* of Sunderland on passage to London with a cargo of coal. At that time the R.N.L.I had not yet forgone claims for salvage. £200 was negotiated for the rescue, *Harriett* receiving £38.12s.6d as her share, the highest awarded to any Southwold lifeboat to date. The crew and the floaters doled the remainder between them.[7]

The lifeboat exercises were a spectacle which would draw a crowd. Just after 10 a.m., Thomas White Willingham, the chief Boatman of the Preventive Service, left the Coast Guard House above the cliff on the corner of St James's Green and dropped down the score to the stone-painted Lifeboat House. Willingham made an inspection of the boat and found her, as he put it later, 'in an efficient state in every respect and a credit to those who have the management of her.'[8] Chief among these was William Cress Simmons, the new Branch secretary who had superseded Ellis, one of whose express duties was to ensure the boat was in perfect working order and who had also arrived at the beach some time before the launch. He was joined by fellow committee member, John Leman Ewen. Before long a crowd began to gather. They were a full cross-section of the town: shopkeepers, longshoremen, mariners, publicans, tradesmen, labourers as well as those who lived on South Green and Gun Hill. One who might have been there but who had stayed at home in East Street, was Thomas Henry Jellicoe. Jellicoe's brother-in-law, Francis Palmer, son of the ex-mayor, was also on the beach, as was Ben Herrington.

The crew who had been selected by the Committee soon began to arrive. There were fourteen including Benjamin Spence, the second cox'n, [he who had arrowed *Swiftsure* into *Reliance* in 1855] John Ling, George Upcraft, Foster Bokenham, John Skelton and William Critten, all Kilcock men. In accordance with R.N.L.I. regulations, Cooper issued them with cork lifebelts. Another man, George Welton, a fisherman and not one of the official crewmen, whom Cooper later said had no business to be there, somehow insinuated himself into the boat. He was not issued with a lifebelt.

And it was also at this point that Cooper was approached by three young gentlemen who asked permission to join the exercise. They were led by George Ellis, the seventeen year old only son of Captain Ellis. His companions were John Ord, another seventeen year old, and only son of John Ord Esq of Fornham House near Bury St. Edmunds who was living with the learned Rev J. R. Crowfoot, a Committee member, whose pupil he was. The third gentleman was Rev. Robert Hodges, a 24 year old curate of Rev. French of Wangford. It was not unusual for amateurs, usually gentlemen, to participate in exercises and it would have been particularly difficult for Cooper to refuse the son of the ex-secretary and, as Harbour Master, an important man in the town. Cooper offered them lifebelts but with the bravado of youth they laughed them off. Whether his instincts baulked at allowing clergy aboard we will never know, but there was little he could do.

When all had boarded, *Harriett* was launched. At 12.40 p.m. to three cheers, the sails filled and she began to sheer off. She crossed both shoals, inner and outer without difficulty and reached off about two-and-a-half miles to begin the exercises. There is no evidence as to what was involved in these but we might conjecture that Benjamin Spence would have taken the helm to act as cox'n if Cooper were lost; that they might have tried to sail using one sail only; that they almost certainly dropped both sails at one point and rowed her; that they dropped anchor and practised veering down using the anchor rope; that they would have checked and perhaps used the signals and that they might have practised man overboard routines with a circular life belt. After an hour-and-a-half or so, around two o'clock, they were ready to return. At some point during the exercises Cooper had ordered the plugs to be taken up so that *Harriett* had filled with water.

Before she turned for shore, Cooper ordered the plugs to be put back and the pumping to begin. But not all the water was ejected and some eight inches remained loose in the bottom. Cooper sailed on. He crossed the outer shoal without difficulty. The tide was ebbing north but there was water deep enough this far out. Now he only had to cross the inner shoal and make for the Station where the crowds were assembled once again cheering from shore and cliff. Cooper ordered the three gentlemen to the bow for their safety. On the beach Simmons was talking to William Bokenham and Thomas Spence. Unlike those cheering, he was criticising the custom of sailing over the shoal in a broken sea.

As *Harriett* began to cross, a wave hit her stern and lifted her. She appeared to ground. The water ballast rushed forward depressing her bow and as this happened she broached-to broadside and was struck by a following wave which broke over her into the boat and on to her sails causing her to go over on to her port side. She remained in this position for four or five minutes as the sails, under pressure of the tide, dug the masts into the sand. Finally they snapped and *Harriett* rolled over.

Before she turtled, Cooper called out to the crew to look after themselves. He held fast but when the mizzen mast broke he was trapped beneath the overturned hull, his feet entangled in the rigging. Like most longshoremen he could not swim. George Welton, the unofficial supernumerary who had no lifebelt, held on to him. Cooper begged him to let go as he felt himself near drowning. Welton drifted off. Cooper cried out for help. The crew with their lifebelts on, brown cork and canvas over their blue ganseys were seen from the shore their white faces appearing in and out of the surf. The sea temperature in February is on average between four and five degrees centigrade. Life expectancy is about an hour. As for the gentlemen who were not wearing lifebelts, nothing was clear. What happened to them would become the focus of bitter recrimination which divided the town.

On shore the cheers were rapidly silenced as shock overwhelmed the spectators. The event was unprecedented. News spread through the town as fast as the wind. Thomas Jellicoe heard shrieks as one man ran past his house shouting that the lifeboat was upset. He immediately made for the cliff. Normally when a boat was in distress the cliffmen took to their yawls. The remaining Kilcock men were nearest but seemed paralysed. Fifteen of their men were visibly fighting for their lives but they made no move. The Long Islanders, by contrast, reacted. In half an hour they had launched their yawl, the resurrected *Reliance*, with fifteen hands and rowed off into the surf. They picked up ten of the crew, including Cooper, in some danger of capsize themselves as they leant over the gunwales to haul them in. The other five floundered or drifted to the shore. Simmons, whose forebodings were apparently justified, was now down at the white threshold with Ewen; they both assisted the crew in taking them to their homes.

When Ord was picked up, he was already drowned. Nevertheless he was taken from the beach to Rev. Crowfoot's house where the town surgeon, Mr Vertue attempted resuscitation for three hours. It was no use. Ellis's sister who was on the beach when the boat capsized, fainted; the rest of the family including Ellis's servant, Henry Lanham, having heard the news, immediately made for the beach from Hill House on South Green and arrived after the yawl was launched. Their apprehension rose as Ellis was neither one of the five who swam ashore nor one of the men rescued by the yawl. While Simmons was away assisting the crew, *Harriett* drifted onshore still upturned. There was no sign of Hodges. His fiancée had heard the news and had come down to the beach, wretched with anxiety. By now the boat had remained upturned on the beach for half an hour or more. When Simmons returned, she remonstrated with him. He gave orders to right the boat but could not find enough men. It was said that there was an arm protruding from under the gunwale but Simmons would not allow her bottom to be stove in. When the boat was eventually righted, Hodges was found drowned in the rigging. Some two hours after the yawl had landed, now a lone figure on the beach, Lanham spotted his master's body floating in the breakers beneath Gun Hill. He waded in but could not keep hold of the corpse and even though he felt himself to be in some danger, made a second successful attempt. The body was carried across South Green to the muffled house. As darkness fell and the wind subsided, the grey vault slowly calmed its pulse slackening as the night drew ever on. The pebbles, now rolled shoreward, now seaward, at last came to rest.

Events moved quickly. On Sunday, 1st March, Simmons wrote to the Institution's secretary, Richard Lewis, informing him of the accident. At the Coroner's inquest held in the Town Hall on the Monday and Tuesday, evidence was heard from crew members, a police inspector, Henry Lanham, a helper at the righting of the boat and eye-witnesses who had been on the beach, including Ben Herrington. Several of the crew felt that the water ballast shifting forward when the first wave struck was key in destabilising the boat, others thought the rudder touched bottom, while Herrington and others were of the opinion that the *pads*, the cork fenders that wrapped around the hull, had failed to right the boat as she rolled. They were badly shaped and placed, not airtight and had been complained of several times. The jury took half an hour to reach its verdict: Accidental death caused by the nature or quality of the water ballast and the inefficiency of the pads.

The verdict reflected badly on the Committee and on Simmons particularly since the condition of the boat was his responsibility. A hectic correspondence between him and the Chief Inspector of lifeboats, Capt.Ward R.N., in London ensued. On March 3rd Simmons began to defend himself. 'There was not, nor is there now any defect in the pads as far as being in order goes,' he asserted. He suggested that a survey of the boat should be rapidly undertaken, since 'the prejudice runs very high at the moment.'[9]Accordingly he wrote to Beeching the same day in a more panicky tone urgently requesting his presence,'for your own credit and and for our sake, come to Southwold as soon as you can and make a report on the said pads.'[10] This letter was signed by three other Committee members all of whom were the great and the good of the town. A groundswell of bad feeling against them was growing.

Beeching lost no time and arrived in Southwold on March 5th to make his inspection. He was asked to write up his findings in a report as was the Chief coastguard, Thomas Willingham. On the same day Simmons received two letters from the Institution in London. The first from Lewis, informed him that at a meeting held the previous day the Committee had been exonerated from all blame. He included a letter sent in 1854 in which the Southwold men had insisted on a wet-boat. The second letter was from Ward who also praised Simmons and the Committee. Nevertheless he informed that he and Admiral MacHardy would arrive in Southwold on the 12th to make their own inspection. He added that as far as he was concerned the accident was 'as clear a case of broaching too (sic) from running to (sic) fast before a broken sea in shoal water as ever I heard of.' Among other things he felt Cooper 'had committed a great error of judgement'[11] in not reducing sail before crossing the shoal. These were remarkable opinions given that he had not yet made his inspection nor spoken to anyone and that Cooper had not been criticised at the Inquest. As far as Ward was concerned there was only one person culpable, Cooper, and Lewis blamed the Southwold cliffmen as a whole for preferring the wet-boat.

When Ward arrived on the 12th, he changed his tune after the inspection. Now he stated that in his view the cause was accidental and that the boat should not be condemned but altered and given a fair trial. It was also resolved unanimously that from now on no-one should be allowed to go off who was not a member of the crews without the permission of the secretary or his deputy.

Beeching's report was published in the press the following week. He defended himself vigorously. Regarding the pads he wrote, 'I found her air tanks all in good order and the buoying pads outside in good order – quite as good as when first put on. I paid particular attention to this by ripping the canvas covering in a place that had been chafed so as to expose the cork (of which they are made) and found it to be as above stated. My reason for being particular about ripping the canvas arose from reading the verdict of the coroner's jury, wherein they state "the defective state of the buoying pads to be one of the causes of the accident." This I knew was not the case, as proved on survey…'[12] It seems the Committee and Simmons were off the hook. On this issue the jury had made the wrong decision though the ballasting remained suspect.

On April 1st, Captain Ellis resigned his subscription to the local branch.

On the 2nd, Simmons acknowledged receipt of £7.10s from Lewis on behalf of the R.N.L.I., it being an award of ten shillings for each of the fifteen crew of the *Reliance*. On the 7th he received a further £3.15s.0d, an award of five shillings for each of the lifeboat crew as an extra payment for the exercises.

With the Committee safe, the recriminations began. Following an article published in the March edition of the *Fishermen's Friendly Visitor* magazine, which gave details of the accident, letters started to appear in the local press. The incident had opened old wounds between the South Green gentry and the tradesmen-councillor class. Feelings ran high about the cox'n, the crew, the inaction of the Kilcock cliffmen and the righting of the boat. The payments made by the R.N.L.I also inflamed opinion.

First was AN INHABITANT OF SOUTHWOLD, a craven individual afraid to sign his name but probably of the South Green party. In a stinging letter published in the *Suffolk Chronicle* on April 24th, he asked rhetorically who was deserving of the extra pay handed out by the Institution. In sarcastic and highly emotive flourishes he dismissed in turn the cox'n, the crew, the Kilcock men and those who refused to right the beached boat until they knew what they would be paid. All were by implication unworthy. In an apparent show of even-handedness he excused the cox'n from further blame after he had become entangled in the rigging but the letter succeeded in characterising those involved as insensitive, selfish, cowardly and venal.

Responses on May 1st exacerbated feelings further. A letter in the *Ipswich Journal* signed by NARRATOR took up where AN INHABITANT left off. His first target was the cox'n who, 'either to save trouble or heedless of the consequences, or wholly devoid of nautical skill ordered out nearly the whole of the water ballast.' He asked whether Cooper ordered those without life belts to 'lay hold of one who had not' or whether he pointed out the 'many appurtenances' of the boat by which the gentlemen might have held on to save themselves. The implicit answer, of course, was no. He criticised the crew for following the order to look out for themselves and in a hitherto unreported detail, he singled out one who allegedly refused to help Ellis when he swam towards him. The Kilcock men were lined up next for 'coolly looking on' while their fellows were in trouble and 'refusing to put off to their rescue.' He then turned to the Bible. It was easy to blame God, like one of Jacob's sons, and to believe that 'not even a sparrow falls without the will of our Heavenly Father', moralising that, 'when means provided for our safety are within our grasp and we wilfully stand still and neglect or refuse to use them…then the sin lies at our own door and cannot be charged upon Him…' The Kilcock men and the crew were therefore sinners whose 'heartless selfishness has procured for them a name not soon to be forgotten.'

Another letter was from Francis Palmer, the ex-mayor's son who had been on the beach. He had the decency to name himself and to add that he was builder by trade, thereby reminding readers of the jobbing scandal six years earlier. Palmer took issue with AN INHABITANT defending those whom he had attacked. He suggested that AN INHABITANT had deliberately misconstrued words spoken when the request was made to right the boat on the beach. He defended the cox'n from the accusation that he was 'all self' and the crew from the charge that they had not tried to help the gentlemen. As for the Kilcock men, he said that at the time he had felt that they had dishonoured themselves but had subsequently come to the opinion that with fifteen of their men in the boat, and others assisting those who swam to shore, there was no possibility of mustering a crew to launch their yawl before the Long Islanders. He accused AN INHABITANT of ill-taste and bad feeling in harrowing the feelings of the bereaved if he was not connected with them, and of revenge if he was. He finished by making an extraordinary allegation, which if true, shows how feelings had reached fever pitch. A lady, he said, a relative of one of the deceased (possibly one of Ellis's three sisters) who should have known better, in effect charged one of the crew with murder, and then, in his absence, called on his wife at her house and predicted that her husband would die of drowning. He alluded to her dark complexion implying by her prediction that she had the powers of a gypsy or a witch. Palmer said the wife was so terrified that she was ill for some time.

May 8th saw the controversy continue. This time ANOTHER INHABITANT OF SOUTHWOLD entered the fray in the *Suffolk Chronicle* taking a swipe at the Long Island men for taking too long to get *Reliance* afloat and accusing Palmer of bias towards the beachmen before writing his own biased opinion of them. Although there were some exceptions, he said, the Southwold beachmen were 'a very irreligious and ignorant class of men' who required a 'devoted missionary' to aid them. If such could be found the churches would be better attended on Sundays and the Sunday fishing would cease. Moreover if such a calamity ever occurred again, the beachmen would then make a much more 'generous and praiseworthy' effort to look out for each other than they did. Already labelled sinners, a Sabbatarian had now accused them of being ignorant heathens.

On the same day, the Lifeboat Committee published a face-saving disclaimer in the *Ipswich Journal* stating that the extra payment awarded to the crew was at the recommendation of MacHardy and Ward.

The following week, May 15th bought the correspondence to a close. The principal letter in the *Suffolk Chronicle* was Thomas Jellicoe's in defence of the cliffmen. Jellicoe had a foot in both camps. An in-law of Peter and Francis Palmer, he was neither a builder nor a tradesman, but as the mayor's auditor had stood up for Palmer during the jobbing scandal. While not of the class of the South Green gentry he nevertheless now shared something with the bereaved, for the previous July his son, Edwin, had been drowned on passage to Bombay.

His sensitivity here explains his opening remarks. He thought the anonymous INHABITANTS should have pitied and spared the feelings of the relatives of the deceased instead of misanthropically opening their wounds week after week. He too would have kept silent had he not felt they had libelled the crew of the *Reliance*. He said that he was at home a hundred yards from the cliff when he heard the tumult of the capsize being broadcast through the streets. He immediately ran to the cliff to see *Reliance* afloat and her 'gallant crew of noble hearted fellows using every exertion to reach the men immersed'. Perhaps explaining the delay in getting her off, he said the N. E. wind was so strong the boat had to be carried into the sea. He also said the crew put their own lives in danger of capsize from a broadside wave when leaning over the gunwales to pick up those in the sea. 'I leave your readers to decide if the services of the crew of the *Reliance* were "tardily rendered"' he said in respect of ANOTHER INHABITANT's charge.

Regarding the alleged irreligion of the beachmen he asked why ANOTHER INHABITANT had done nothing about it himself and accused him of being like the Levite, passing on the other side.

His own view of the cliffmen was more generous. 'I have been', he wrote, 'in many sea-ports in England. I never saw a more civil and obliging body of seafaring men than those belonging to South-wold. I have witnessed many hair-breadth escapes from danger and seen men rush to the aid of their brother men to their own peril, but I never saw more prompt and strenuous exertions exercised than by the crew that manned *Reliance*.'

Ted Syer made a painting of the incident, *Fatal Accident at Southwold February 27th 1858* (Plate III). The viewpoint is from the cliff looking down on to the beach and out at the capsized boat. The moment is the approach of *Reliance* as she prepares to rescue the crew who are seen still clinging to the boat or adrift in the waves. It is clear that Syer has carefully chosen crucial details of the catastrophe in his composition. The cork pads are plain to see. The ebb tide is pushing the mizzen sail under, its outligger clear of the waves. The rudder is also shown upturned at the stern. The bow where Hodges was found is submerged. The helmsman of *Reliance* is urging his men on to row as fast as they can while the bowman is pointing to the scene. A large crowd on the beach is looking on, though it has to be said, somewhat undemonstratively. One beachmen pointing out is elevated above the rest in the very centre of the picture standing inside what must be Kilcock's unlaunched yawl. What looks like another of the company's men in a tanned slop has his back to the disaster. The sea is a choppy grey. The message seems clear enough. Like many, Syer appears to think the Kilcock men are failing in their duty as the tragedy unfolds to the horror of all.

Such was one of the ugliest incidents in Southwold's 19th century history which ended in tragedy and exposed some damning views of the longshoremen. Alterations were successfully made to *Harriett* to confine the water ballast. She was trialled on May 19th and passed satisfactorily to all parties: R.N.L.I. chiefs, a Board of Trade inspector, the branch committee, the principal inhabitants of the town and not least, the crew. She was renamed the *London Coal Exchange* and served without further mishap and very creditably until 1893. Ben Herrington was her cox'n from 1860 until 1879.

In October the R.N.L.I issued national instructions in a memorandum about the proper management of a boat when running before a broken sea.

Captain Ellis died several months after his son and was buried beside him in the churchyard. A reredos commemorating the three drowned young men can be seen on the south wall of the church, not far from where, nearly above the main door, Palmer had carved his name in one of the roof-beams repaired by his own contract. Ellis's daughter, Charlotte, some years later, started up a Sunday Bible Class in the by then disused Lifeboat House which became very popular with the cliffmen.

And what of George Ellis? At the time of the accident he had just finished his military training. The following Monday, the day of the Inquest into his death, he was due to join his regiment at Chatham before embarkation to India. Who can say what made him refuse the lifebelt? Was it bravado or impatience to be off or just a youth's unquestioning sense of his own immortality? Perhaps he couldn't wait to see his home town from the sea one last time, to feel the boat riding the waves, to have the salt spray tingle down his face as it crossed the surf, to remember the biting cold of a February day in Southwold before the insufferable heat of the subcontinent became his life, to recall the sound of the wind slicing through the rigging or to tell his fellow officers in the mess that he came from a small sea-port in Suffolk and he took part in the Lifeboat exercises. Not much perhaps, but something to distinguish himself and some image of home to keep in his mind so far away.

His memorial in the churchyard reads:

> The waves of the sea are mighty
> and rage horribly yet the Lord...

The rest has become illegible.

Notes

1 *Minute Book* December 21st, 1853 Southwold Lifeboat Society p.129

2 Lionel Lukin first introduced relieving valves into the Lowestoft Lifeboat *Frances Ann* in 1807

3 *Letter Book* October 31st, 1854 Southwold Lifeboat Society p.13

4 Ibid

5 Ibid January 19th, 1856 p.29-30

6 Ibid January 25th, 1856 p.30

7 *Minute Book* February 9th, 1857 p.170

8 Ibid March 11th, 1858 p.190

9 *Letter Book* March 3rd, 1858 p.68

10 Ibid March 3rd, 1858 p.69

11 Ibid March 5th, 1858 p.71

12 *Minute Book* March 11th, 1858 p.190

12

Sole Bay

'The great and long iron of the wondyrchoun runs so heavily and hardily over the ground when fishing that it destroys the flowers of the land below the water and also the spat of oysters, mussels and other fish upon which the great fish are accustomed to be fed and nourished.' These words, told to a Commission set up by Edward III at Colchester in 1377, reflect a concern about what today is called sustainability. The 'engine' in question, the *wondyrchoun*, the Commission was told, was a net three fathoms long and ten feet wide tied to a ten foot beam which itself was fitted into two iron frames. The beam opened the top of the net while the bottom was weighted down with lead strips and heavy stones. The damage caused by towing this apparatus over the sea bed had caused fishermen from the lower parts of the Thames estuary to petition the King about its effect on their catches which had been in decline for the previous seven years, since its first appearance. In effect a beam trawl, it was the wondyrchoun's indiscriminate destruction of the 'flowers of the land below the water' and 'such quantity of small fish' that the fishermen 'know not what to do with them; and they feed and fat their pigs with them' that led to the petition. The Commission recommended that the 'engine' be used in deep water rather than in estuaries but it did not outlaw the wondrychoun. [1] That was left to private fisheries, such as at Orford Haven where a ban was effected in 1491.[2]

Many subsequent attempts to control trawls and trawling were made over successive centuries without much success. Commercial trawling using beam trawls of up to forty feet seems to have developed more or less simultaneously at Brixham in Devon and Barking in Essex in the 18th century and expanded massively with the discovery of the Silver Pits in the North Sea in the 1830s. Sustainability became and remains an issue for the deep-sea fishery. Longshoremen in Southwold and along the Suffolk coast however, continued to use only slightly larger versions of the wondyrchoun right into the 20th century. Their modest beam trawls in comparison with those used in the North Sea make them appear to be, in hindsight, the more sustainable. The following account was given to me by Mr. English which I took verbatim in his home, Lima Cottage, in Walberswick in 1976:

'We started trawlin' durin' the latter part o' May, beginnin' o' June, an' went right through till September, the end o' September, till the herren started t' arrive. We'd go shrimpin' an' trawlin' throughout the season. We might go two days shrimpin' an' the rest trawlin', that all depended what the merchant wanted. But one thing we wouldn't do wuz go on a Sunday, never went trawlin' on a Sunday. None o' 'em would go. I don't know why that wuz. We weren't Scotch or nuthin', but trawlin', never on a Sunday!

For shrimpin' we used a *beam-trawl*. We never had no *otter-trawls* then. We allus worked an eighteen foot beam 'cos ol' Harry Winter, who braided the nets, allus used t' say, "This is your livin'." In other words that wuzn't worth our while usin' anythin' smaller. Some o' 'em did use a smaller beam just for shrimpin'. They were about thirteen t' sixteen foot long but me an' my uncle allus used the bigger one. The beams used t' come from inland somewhere, from the woods where they'd been cut down, an' they'd bring

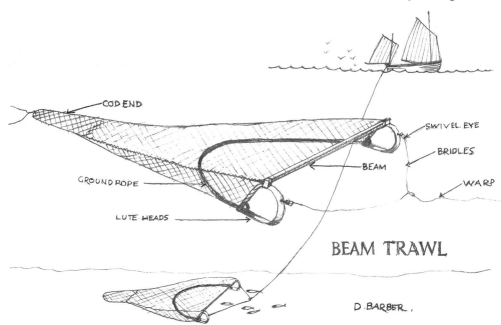

COD END

SWIVEL EYE

BRIDLES

BEAM

GROUND ROPE

WARP

LUTE HEADS

BEAM TRAWL

D. BARBER.

'em down before the season started. We used t' *bark* 'em, shave 'em an' shape 'em; we'd use an *adze* or *draw-knife* on 'em t' do that. They weren't seasoned. We preferred 'em *green* if anythin' 'cos they were heavier, got more weight in 'em, though that din't make much difference. They were mostly ash or elm, though I do remember some oak beams. They were damned heavy, they were!

At each end o' the beam wuz what they called the *lute-heads*. They stood about two foot but some o' 'em had 'em bigger. They were blacksmith-made out o' iron. We got ours from the smith at Bly'burgh, Parkinson I think his name wuz. I expect the Southwold men went t' their smith for theirs. The *lutes* were shaped suthin' like a triangle, if you understand me, three sided but with a rounded top. The bottom wuz called the *shoe* an' wuz about four inches wide so it din't cut up on the mud when you were towin'. On the front edge wuz a *swivel-eye* where the *bridles* went an' at the back on the bottom wuz another eye big enough t' take the *grass ground-rope* which wuz about four inches wide. [This was probably a hemp rope, *softly-laid*, i.e. loosely, also known as a *bass-rope*. As it travelled along the bottom, it gathered sand into itself which helped weigh it down.] On the top wuz a squared hole where the beam wedged in.

The net wuz attached along the length o' the beam by the *top-string*. That wuz a piece o' rope fastened t' the beam with what we called *tie-ers*, bits o' string cut into lengths an' fastened with a reef-knot. The purpose o' that wuz t' hold the top o' the net open an' the ground-rope wuz what held the bottom o' the mouth o' the net open. The ground-rope, as I said, wuz made out o' grass an' wuz weighted with strips o' lead bound round it t' keep it down so it din't jump.

The bridles were attached t' the lute-heads on that swivel-eye. That wuz all one bit o' rope about six fathoms, three fathoms each side. In the middle you put a *thimble* an' that wuz *bent* on the *trawl-warp*, which wuz anything up t' fifty, sixty fathom long. They allus used t' reckon, though I don't quite remember exactly, that for every fathom o' water it wuz two t' three fathom o' warp. In the middle o' the beam wuz another bridle, a single line called the *middle-bridle*, about one fathom o' it. You used that for balancing the whole thing when you swung it over. You attached it t' the *thole* when that wuz across the stern an' when you wanted t' let it go, you just chucked that off an' let out as many fathom o' the trawl warp as you wanted.

147

A shrimp net wuz about sixteen t' twenty foot long from *beam* t' *poke*. The sides o' the net were called *wings* an' on the inside o' 'em a little way up from the poke were the *pockets*. They were bits o' net attached t' the inside that opened at the *poke-end* an' tapered off t' nothin', just like a pocket really. They din't come into use for shrimpin', but when you were trawlin', the soles 'ud get caught in 'em, otherwise they'd go out again. A trawl net wuz bigger, up t' p'raps thirty foot, but designed in the same way. The mesh wuz allus bigger at the beam end than at the poke end. I don't remember how big the meshes were 'cos there wuz no standard size then like there is now but that'd be p'raps big enough t' get a shillin' through at the top end an' p'raps not quite big enough for a sixpence at the bottom. The nets an' ropes were allus tanned in cutch t' preserve the cotton an' make 'em last. We might tan 'em twice durin' the season, an' o' course we had three or four nets. One wuz no good – you might get caught an' rend it on suthin', so you allus had more than one an' you'd change 'em about.

I used t' go shrimpin' on my own. In the sailin' days you'd row an' sail with the tide an' when the motors started comin' in you'd motor with the tide. It din't make no difference whether the tide wuz ebbin' or floodin', just as long as you went with it. If you din't set your gear with the wind an' tide that'd all turn topsy-turvy. You din't go very far off, just on the inner sand shoal, just clear o' the groynes. You might tow p'raps from the pier t' the harbour on that shoal an' on this side [Walberswick] you'd go from the harbour up in t' the *bight*.

The shrimps we caught were brown; they were called *browns*. The Yarmouth people got pink shrimps but these were brown an' they liked a sandy bottom. We used t' think they were best, tasted better. The poke o' the shrimp net wuz allus tied an' they all got in there down the bottom. All you had t' do when you hauled the net wuz untie it an' shake 'em out.

They were sold by the *peck*. There were sixteen pints in a peck an' you'd get about four shillin's a peck, or *thruppence* a pint that worked out at. You din't allus have to cook 'em yourself – that all depended who wanted 'em. We went for Sam Goodwin, who wuz a merchant here an' he did his own boilin'. Others o' 'em used t' do their own though, but as I say, that all depended. You'd get a copper o' salted water an' put the shrimps in a net with a large hoop round it. You'd shoot 'em in there 'till the water boiled up an' out they used t' come again. Then you'd put 'em on a rack t' dry out.

If you rubbed your hand through 'em an' they rattled like nuts you knew they were good 'cos they'd come outa their shells better.

When you went trawlin' you'd go further off, much further off up on t' the Aldeburgh grounds or down below Southwold t' the *Barnard*. If the weather wuz bad you'd go closer in through the bight but generally you'd go right off, two or three miles into the deeper water. You'd tow with the tide, the whole length o' the tide, so you'd be doin' that for about six hours. You'd haul the net once or twice durin' that time but you'd go down on that tide, whichever way it wuz. O' course you had t' get t' wherever you were goin' t' catch the tide an' then you had t' come back in again so you'd be out longer'n six hours.

There were several problems that you could come up against, a wreck, an anchor or a big stone. If you *come fast* you'd come round head on an' try t' pull the beam up that way, try t' *jump it off*, but if you couln't, you *hung* till the tide slacked or come round the other way an' you'd try an' jump it off then. I remember hangin' a good six hours on a wreck once below the Belle Pier an' I just lost a lute-head. Someone come an' tried t' help me get it off but I had t' wait an' eventually I got the net all right when the tide went away.

It wuz also important when you're trawlin' t' use your *lead-line*. That wuz the done thing. You had a lead-line what wuz hollowed out at the bottom an' had *tallow* put in. When you dropped it you'd learn the depth o' the water an' what the ground wuz like because it would stick t' the tallow, mud or stones or whatever it wuz. The line wuz marked every fathom with different coloured rags an' leather that wuz put through the *lay*. Oh yes! You'd allus want t' know where you were an' how many fathom you needed, what depth you were in. If you got fish you'd know for another time at what depth they were an' where t' go. They all had their favourite places, mud for flounders an' roker an' stones for soles – thass why their skin is so rough, so they can get in under the stones.

Another thing we used t' do if there wuz no wind, this is in the sailin' days, we had what we called a *drogue-sail*. That wuz a wooden beam about six t' eight foot long an' about six inches in diameter. Attached t' it wuz a canvas about four foot deep. On the top o' the beam at each corner wuz a *bridle* an' on the bottom o' the canvas, also at each corner wuz another bridle. Well, if there wuz no wind, you'd put it overboard, let it go ahead o'

149

you, let it run about two or three fathom ahead; it'd get pushed out by the tide. When it set right, you'd fix the top bridles t' the *thole-pins* an' the bottom bridles you'd lay until the tide filled into it right. That'd then tow you along at the proper rate for trawlin'. If you come fast or wanted t' haul you let the bottom bridle go an' then pulled it in. It rolled around the beam an' lay in the boat alongside with the leeboard an' the oars.

I went trawlin' on my own, but some often went with two men. We caught soles, plaice, dabs, flounders – they were called *butts, maids* – they were small roker [thornback ray] an' we used t' eat 'em ourselves, just the wings, an' lobsters an' crabs. When I first started, soles were sold in two ways. In the boat you had a board with a nine inch marker on it. Anythin' below nine inches wuz a *slip* an' they were sold by the *score*. Above nine inches they were soles an' sold by the pair. You'd lay 'em out in pairs o' the same size an' the merchant would come along an' say, "I'll give you so much." An' what could you do? You hatta take it. Plaice were sold by the stone, roker also. We sold t' ol' Sam Goodwin. He had a shop here.'

Mr English's account is remarkable when juxtaposed with Emerson's description of the practice in *Pictures of East Anglian Life*. Though separated by 89 years, it's as if Emerson could have been talking to Mr English. The only discrepancy is the species named as *butts*, which Mr English said were flounders and Emerson said were plaice. I am inclined to go with the practitioner and indeed David Butcher in *Fishing Talk* also gives butts as flounders.[3]

The method of avoiding underwater hazards has already been described by Mr English in a previous chapter. The use of *long* and *breast* marks to triangulate a position combined with the use of the *lead-line* to gauge the correct depth was a time-honoured method of navigation used around the coast. When on a holiday in Applecross in Scotland, I asked our elderly neighbour, who had been a fisherman all his life, how he knew where his pots were, he told me he used the same method and added, not quite contemptuously, 'Now they use GPS.'

Mr English's mention of the *otter-trawl* shows how technology affected the longshoremen. The beam-trawl was cumbersome but fit for sailing conditions with the aid of a drogue-sail when required. Once the longshoremen had adapted their boats to the petrol and later to the diesel engine after the First World War, their towing power increased. Mr Cooper put it like this:

'Even us in the small boats, we use what they call otter trawls now; instead o' havin' a beam an' a trawl, you have doors, otter doors. When you tow 'em, you tow a much bigger net than you used t'. You see you started off with sail years ago, then you got the petrol engine an' now you've got your diesel engine with more power, so you're towin' bigger gear altogether.'

Such is 'progress.'

One of the errors I made in my tape recordings was not to have spoken to more women. I did however speak with Doris Duncan (b.1922) in 2012 who remembered her father boiling shrimps:

'We lived in Pinkney's Lane. No 2. We were all born there. I remember my father, when he caught the shrimps, he brought them back home and boiled them in the washhouse. He had a great big board and he'd bring them out, sort them out on the board and salt them. Then he'd fill the basket up and take it to Denny's in Trinity Street [a fishmonger's]. I used to have to take them down to Mr Wright in Queen Street [a shoemaker] at 4½d. a pint. I used to get told not to pick out the big ones! Sometimes there used to be prawns in among them and I wasn't allowed to touch them.'

While flatfish and shrimps were what the longshoremen always hoped to catch in their trawl nets, it wasn't always the case. From the Wild Man of Orford through to the present day, the grey vault has offered up its past in many forms – fossils, gouts of clouded amber, the corpses of drowned sailors (Maggs, July 26th, 1852: The Body of a Man supposed to be a Dutchman – picked up off here and brot on Shore for Internment – No doubt he had been drowned a long time being much decomposed),[4] clothing, ships' timbers, cannons, cannon balls, unexploded bombs, wayward species like the basking shark once paraded round Southwold's streets, parted anchors. These latter were specifically sought by the cliffmen in the 19th century and entered as salvage at the Admiralty Court. The process was called *swiping* and it was another means of getting a living. Emerson described the method which was complex and potentially dangerous:

'In dull times the speculative are induced to go fishing, or as they term it *swiping* for anchors, for which they get 2/- a cwt. from the Admiralty. At times too when a net has got entangled on a sunken anchor the men will go and *swipe* for it to recover their property and get a few extra shillings besides. The method ... is this ... Two boats go out, one that is called the *bully boat*, which is kept for this purpose, being generally an old beach yawl, lug-rigged with a foresail, averaging seven to eight tons tonnage and the other an ordinary rowing boat. The first thing to do, of course, is to find the situation of the anchor and this is done by shooting a line, the swipe which is about sixty fathoms in length, from between the boats. This is always shot on the tide and the boats drive with the tide. If the anchor fishers are successful the line catches in the anchor and *rands* the swipe boat, or in other words pulls it round. The spot is marked by a buoy. The next step is to drag the heavy mass from the depths. The rope which found the anchor is now hauled in short and a big rope, the *weighing rope* is bent on to it and pulled by means of it beneath the anchor into the place of the swipe line, which generally catches beneath a fluke. Both ends of the big rope are now taken on the bully boat which rides at anchor. The position now is that the men have a large cable attached to the sunken anchor, though perhaps very insecurely. To secure the prize, therefore, they use what is called a *salvagee* and a *swipe-lock*. The salvagee is a strong collar made of rope-yarn and the swipe-lock is an old cannon ball, to which is fitted a strong semi-circular iron band, hinged at one end and fitted with a lock at the other, there being just room between the band and the cannon-ball for the passage of the two ends of the weighing rope. The two ends of the weighing rope having been drawn through the lock, the swipe-lock is now put on and locked, and then away goes the cannon-ball down the track of the weighing rope right to the anchor itself. The swipe-lock's use is now apparent. It simply forms a tight clasp to firmly hold the weighing rope round the anchor. The salvagee is now put on so as to *bear two eyes* to which *bousing tackle* is attached. That is, the rope-yarn collar is adjusted tightly to the weighing rope, so that it leaves two loops to which the tackle is fastened, on which the men pull to raise the anchor. A second salvagee is at hand in case one breaks. The bousing tackle consists of two blocks with ropes and is attached firmly to the bully boat. The crew, generally consisting of seven men now pull hard on the tackle and if they have luck, the anchor soon begins to leave its sandy bed.

Two Men by Fishing Sheds and Boat, P. H. Emerson

As it is raised the salvagee is lowered and so the work goes on until the anchor gets up to the boat's stern, when a boating chain is passed beneath it for greater security and two men with hand-spikes lift it over the cheeks of the bully boat as it is drawn into the boat. Exhausted they at last land the iron monster, who is often covered with a colony of barnacles.

This sport is not without its dangers. At times the rope snaps and flying back, thrashes the men cutting them as if with a whip [...]The practice of anchor-fishing is not so common as it was formerly, and it is confined to the slack months, January and February; but if the men are fortunate, the reward is well worth the trouble. A fisherman of our acquaintance was one of a party that recovered nine anchors in one week, each weighing on average 16 cwt.,which meant over £14 to be divided among the crew.'[5]

The bully boat at Kilcock Cliff can be seen in Emerson's photograph *Two Men by Fishing Sheds and Boat.*

The reason why swiping was less common in 1888 was due to the greater safety vessels operated in than formerly. Steam had made shipping more able to avoid being cast on to a lee shore in a storm, improvements made by Trinity House in providing buoys and lights made navigation easier, the introduction of the Plimsoll line stopped the over-lading of vessels all of which contributed to reducing the wrecks that frequently littered this shore after severe weather. Entries in the Southwold Admiralty Court for 1834 and 1835 relate to the retrieval of anchors but swiping went back much further; an undated 17th century entry refers to the *swayping fare*. Although he didn't attend the Court, one Rob pag entered '3 ankers and one of cable'.[6]

Notes

1 Dyson, *Business in Great Waters* p.37-38

2 Arnott, *Alde Estuary* p.49

3 Butcher, *Fishing Talk* p.14

4 *Maggs,* Vol 2 p.55

5 Emerson, *Pictures of East Anglian Life* p.74-76

6 Southwold Borough Council 491/303, Lowestoft Records Office

Dance of Death

Tide pushed me and water lessened so I supposed that I had been taken north. I found myself on the bank of what must once have been a river, a depression filled with mud and overlaid sand, from which I could just make out what looked like the stem of a boat. I could dimly see that the stem-head was elaborately curled like that of furled bracken in spring or the end of a fiddle and that it was a kind of neck, which curved down into the sand.

Another time I was taken south to Dunwich because I entered what seemed to be the ruins of a church, its buttresses like the ribs of a ship. I clearly heard a dull thudding of metal on metal such as is made by the clappers on a bell summoning the faithful and soon some did indeed gather there.

I was never so horrified.

> *I saw them bobbing like dans, hung straight by their sea-boots.*
> *Their faces were skulls,*
> *Grinning.*
> *I saw them waving, arms articulated by the tide.*
> *They pointed all the compass,*
> *Hoping.*
> *I heard their wailings in the waves, babbling through water.*
> *They sounded all the depths,*
> *Sobbing.*
> *I touched their limbs.*
> *They were bone-men, fish-eaten, sea-rolled,*
> *Barnacling.*

And then it seemed to me that the sea in its many waters was Time and that it devoured all things until they became no more than the grains of sand filtering through my fingers and that as it had devoured the past, it would the times to come; and that, ever unsatisfied, it would rise and rise until it whelmed over the whole earth.

13

Long Tail

In existence before Domesday, the herring fishery is the oldest one recorded at Southwold. The Book tells us that prior to the Conquest, the settlement sent 20,000 herrings annually to the Abbot of Bury St Edmunds and that after it the number increased to 25,000. This implies a level of sophistication in catching, preserving and transporting the herring not just at Southwold but at the seventeen other places recorded as yielding herring rents in the hundreds of Blything, Wangford and Lothingland (long since known as Mutford Half-hundred). Used for 'victualling the monks', Dr. Robert Wake in his *Southwold and its Vicinity* calculated facilely that, 'The place then must have been of some importance to *"their Reverences,"* since it afforded them the means of enriching their bill of fare any day in the year, and in the article of fish alone, with no less number than three score and eight.'[1] Sixty eight herrings a day, then, to help them work, rest and pray.[2]

There can be no doubt of the importance of the herring fishery. It probably accounts for the settlement and development of Southwold itself (instead of it being an adjunct of Reydon); merchants who profited from the fishery would have provided funds for the building of its magnificent church, far grander in size than such a town would normally have merited, its stunning perpendicularity similarly echoed at Covehithe, Walberswick and Kessingland; it is recorded in the 16th century Ordnances concerning Regulation of the Fishery which can be found in the Corporation Books both in the time of Henry VIII and Elizabeth. 17th century Admiralty Court Presentments, under the title of the *herringfare* record the *doales* to be paid to the Borough for the right to fish. Southwold even became a place of national importance in the 18th century when it was chosen as the headquarters of the Free British Fishery, a doomed government initiative to compete with the Dutch in the North Sea herring industry. And finally in an attempt to cash in on the golden age of the British herring industry by capitalising on overcrowding at Lowestoft and Yarmouth during the autumn Home Fishing season, the harbour was controversially repaired and dredged, a fish market erected (wryly dubbed the Kipperdrome), stores, sheds and cooperage facilities built, gutting farlanes set up for the itinerant *Scotch girls* who followed the fishing from the Shetlands to East Anglia – girls who who could gut a herring in a second. Opened in 1908, 4,452 cran of herring were landed as well as 1,097 trunks of trawl fish and 122,250 hundreds of mackerel, but overfishing of the herring by the deep-sea fleets made the fishery unsustainable.[3] The outbreak of the First World War ensured the harbour enterprise was a short-lived failure. And yet despite Southwold's persistent inability to profit from the herring, it remained stubbornly iconic in its consciousness, celebrated both in the town's insignia, swimming above, below and between the crossed arrows that martyred St. Edmund, and also on that monument to civic pride, the pump in the Market Place, erected in 1873 by the engineer, George Child where they masquerade, some say, as dolphins.

Longshore herring differ from those caught further out at sea (the latter being bigger) and are in the opinion of many, more flavoursome. We have no records that tell us how they were caught in antiquity but at some point drift-netting became the norm. The adoption of this method would have been the result of close observation of the habits of the species and the knowledge of the best conditions in which to catch them. Herrings are a pelagic species rising in shoals from the bottom of the sea to the surface to feed. Moonlight was thought to be instrumental in causing the rise. At Southwold it was known that the herrings generally struck from the south and so the longshoremen shot their drift nets at a forty five degree angle from the beach on a flood tide, or better still on the slack water at the top of a flood tide. In the latter circumstances the nets hung straight down forming the wall, in the former the outer nets of the fleet were pushed southward by the stronger tide further out, the angle making the wall face north east. This was known as *herring law*. Arthur Grubbe, the gentleman son of the mayor, E.E. Grubbe recorded as much in his diary in July 1889 having been talking to one of the longshoremen:

'The herrings always strike the nets towards the rising day: from this it would seem they are always turned to the north-east; this is the same no matter what time of day or night. Moonlight encourages the herring to rise.'[4]

Mr Jarvis talked of how he remembered *herrenin'* from the beach:

'The season used t' start in the latter part o' March, April. Then you used t' get the herren, which were *spents* with no roes in, an' you used to use a lot for bait for skate. You used t' cut 'em up; one herren 'ud make about five baits – that wuz includin' the whole herren, a piece on the head an' three or four cuts. You used t' put 'em on the hooks an' go out about two mile, three mile sometimes, an' shoot your lines for the skate. You wouldn't leave 'em, as a rule, all night, 'cos if you got a lot o' skate on your lines you'd find no lines there in the mornin'. They were that powerful enough t' take the anchors an' the lines away, which have happened on many occasions, so you used t' haul each day an' then shoot the next day.

After the *spring-herring* which were not so valuable or good in price, came the *full-herring* which came in September, October. They were the full herren, lovely full roes an' o' course weighed a good bit more an' they would make nice *bloaters* or *red herring*. In the winter time when there wuz nuthin' doin', one or two o' the fishermen, if it wuz a fine day, would go an' possibly get a hundred or two o' what we call little *winter-herring*; they were smaller but they used t' be better than nuthin'.

When you go herrenin' you use a net about the same length as a sprat net, about eight fathom [eighteen yards] but *six-score* deep [ten feet]. Thass 'cos they're nearly all an inch mesh. Some o' 'em, especially nowadays 'cos the deep-sea herren fishin' is bad, can buy these deep-sea nets fairly cheap an' split 'em down the middle [i.e. horizontally]. O' course they're longer than an ordinary longshore herren net, an' if they split 'em down the middle an' put corks on the bottom – o' course they've already got corks on the top– they've got the length o' three nets. But, by splittin' 'em down the middle (they've got a *sixteen-score* mesh) they'd end up with an *eight-score* deep net, two meshes longer than an ordinary longshore net. They don't fish like an ol' white longshore net. The softer it is, the better it is every time. You get a nice soft net, even one which we call an *ol' rag*, if there's plenty o' herren, they'll get in this old net, which is full o' holes 'cos it's soft. Another curious fact is this. You join each herren net together by tyin' the *fid*,[5] which is the end o' the net-rope; where the last cork is – there's about two foot o' *double-rope* on the *head-line* which is the fid – well, you tie that together an' that don't entirely close the gap between one net an' another. Well thass a curious fact that if you go t' a net's head, you'll always see more herren there than what you will as you start t' haul. Whether thass 'cos they know that gap is there, can see the gap an' go through it an' get caught in the net's head, thass the only explanation I can find.

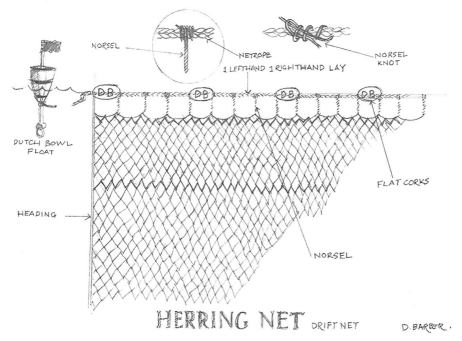

HERRING NET DRIFT NET D. BARBER.

You'd carry about twelve t' fifteen nets – that all depend on the size o' the boat. There used t' be small boats in 'em days which used t' carry eight t' ten nets an' a lone man with a *long-oar* t' *scull* 'em out with. Ol' *Fye* Smith wuz the master hand at that. He'd go, row down, lay his oars in, get his long-oar out over the stern in a cut for scullin' an' he'd scull with one hand an' shoot with the other. There wuz one or two used t' do that; they were boats about fifteen foot. But the number [of nets] depended on the size o' the boat. O' course they wouldn't be all white nets; some o' 'em couln't afford it, or they'd got some white nets that were past their best an' they used t' tan 'em so they were dark-coloured, but you could tell the difference in the fishin'. The only time I ever knew a tanned net t' fish wuz when we bought some from Pakefield. They were very fine cotton nets an' they had never been oiled [in linseed oil] but they'd been straight put in a tan, which wuz made from cutch, from the bark o' a tree, known as *cutch*, an' they turned a reddy colour. Them nets 'ud nearly outfish a white net for some reason. They were soft as silk in your hand.

As I said though, the usual net, the size o' a mesh would be roughly an inch square; the length would be eight fathoms an' the depth would be six-score or eight-score if they'd cut a deep-sea, a *Scotch-net* as they called it. They were bought from Lowestoft from different merchants. They were made up on a machine an' you bought the *lint*, that is cotton net, white, an' that wuz up t' you t' make it up. You set it up on a heading, then you norseled it. You'd go four or five meshes an' hold the *norsel* up t' the *net-rope* an' put it on with a special knot.⁶ You'd have about three or four o' them, then a cork, then another norsel, an' the norsels hold the corks in position. They'd be flat corks. The other corks would be bulky in a small boat an' the nets were always catchin' on 'em, the round corks. Thass the reason they always had flat corks so they'd lay in the boat not in the way, an' when you shot the nets they'd slip over the side without catchin'. The maintenance? They don't know nuthin' about that today! I should think every other day 'em nets would be laid out on the beach t' dry, an' not only that, you'd have t' go along an' *trick* 'em over, that is pick up the lint an' haul it so it lay in a different position an' got dry. You'd also have a pocketful o' norsels, an odd cork or two an' if there wuz a norsel out or a cork out you'd put 'em in. Sometimes the herren nets would heat, but you din't always get that much o' herren t' warrant that. If they got several thousand they might but they were not so particular on that as with the sprat nets.

You get very few herren about here on an ebb tide. You always got t' go on a flowin' tide, every time.⁷ You want t' be shot just before the sun come out o' the water an' the ideal time is high water, slack tide. If you can shoot here [Kilcock cliff] an' drift so's you're just abreast o' the harbour on a slack tide, thass an ideal time. The reason is 'cos your net is hangin' up an' down, perpendicular. If you think t' yourself about a herren net just driftin' along, the lint in't straight up an' down, perpendicular, thass angular 'cos the tide is driftin' it, the tide is hittin' so it in't hangin' straight down, so therefore the slack tide, the top o' the tide is the best. They do get herren on an ebb tide, on the low water, but it's very rare you get many on an ebb tide.

When you go herrenin', if it's calm, you shoot in close, every time, if it's calm. Some o' the fishermen used t' have two or three nets cut down t' about *five-score* or even less than that so they din't *drag the ground* on the inner part o' the net. As they got further from the shore, the amount o' water wuz deeper an' therefore it din't affect 'em. I've seen 'em shoot three nets parallel t' the beach an' then the others off, 'cos the outer ones will gradually drag 'em ones that are inside, off. While they're in the process o' that, you'll find 'em three herren nets will possibly have more herren in than what the others will, 'cos they're in close. If thass a bit choppy, they go out, say half-a-mile or a mile-an'-a-half, sometimes. The favourite trick wuz t' shoot at the pier an' drift across the harbour mouth, which wuz known as the *Hayle*. They've got a conviction that the first one across there always get more herren than the next one. Why that should be, I can't answer it. Nowadays you don't see a herren boat come below the pier.[8] They'll come t' the pier an' go across the harbour an' come back again. The ol' fishermen say, "Oh, they're on the *race-course!*" Years ago, we used t' row down t' the broads [Easton and Benacre], two mile t' the north an' drift up this way t' the pier an' if we hadn't got enough then, there wuzn't much about, I can tell you! If the herren were right in close, what we'd do wuz *split the fleet up*. Say shoot six nets in close then row down before the others an' shoot six more. That counterbalanced losin' the ones that weren't on the outer part.

In herren fishin' the nets were all shot at once, yes. With sprats if you get about fifty or sixty in a net an' you've got t' move it, you've got t' shake 'em out an' fiddle about before you can put it on the other end but with herren, you can soon pick a few out, they'll practically fall out with the weight o' 'em, so it doesn't matter. The best place for 'em would be from Easton Broad up t' above the harbour. In the Dunwich Bight you don't get many. I once shot some nets alone – you have t' go above the huts at Walberswick, otherwise you've got a tide takin' you down t' the harbour pier, even on a flood tide, I shot there an' I don't think I started t' get no herren before I got nearly t' Dunwich cliffs, then they started gettin' in thick. I only had six or eight nets an' that wuz a good haul for me 'cos I got over 1000 herren in 'em few nets.

There weren't no superstitions shootin' the nets, not longshore fishin'. But deep-sea fishin', the drifter I wuz on, the skipper always used to say before we shot – an' that wuz for mackerel, fifty miles west-nor-west o' the *Bishop's Rock* – he'd say, "Heave nets in the name o' the Lord. Please God send 'em." Then there'd be some other rude remarks put in, "Swim up, you little so-an'-sos." He always said, "Please God, send 'em." I don't think he wuz very religious, but I suppose that had gone from family t' family; he wuz the skipper. Round there at that particular time there wuzn't all that many mackerel an' we used t' stay out three or four days till we nearly burnt all our coal up. We used t' ice these mackerel away an' put 'em in the hold. Then when we'd made Land's End, we used t' pull 'em all up on deck ready t' sell when we got t' Newlyn Quay. But no, they didn't do that longshore fishin'. I don't know why. I don't think they were any less religious, p'raps more so religious some o' these ol' fishermen than the deep-sea men. But I've never heard 'em an' I've been with several in my time one way an' another as a boy an' a *full-share man* an' I've never heard that expression said. They'd just say, "Come on then, let's shoot away," an' that wuz that, or, "Pull on 'em oars, boy," or, "Take a mark on the lighthouse," or, "Keep 'em straight off," or, "Edge 'em down," or suthin' like that.

The fishermen could tell if there wuz herren about. They could tell by the colour o' the water. They'd say, "There's a good colour, there'll be herren here." That wuz a nice dark-browny colour an' sometimes oily. In deep-sea fishin', specially mackerel fishin', you've got a tell-tale there. You'll see *gants* [gannets] an' *loons* [red-throated divers] as they used t' call 'em. I used t' have t' sit on the wheelhouse an' the skipper used t' fall asleep an' he'd say, "If you see the gants an' loons a-divin', call me." An' I used t' call him if I see 'em a-divin' an' you'd shoot in that particular spot.

Once you'd shot, you'd drift with them; you'd have a look; you'd go along [this was called *underrunning*]. You'd pull up t' the nets [with the oars]. Supposin' you were driftin' up t' the harbour, you'd approach from the south every time so that you din't drift into 'em. You pulled some o' the lint up t' see whether there wuz any herren gettin' in. Then you'd go row t' the inner end an' have a look there an' pull half a net an' pick one or two out. Then go back t' the outer part an' have a look there. If there wuz a good look on, you'd go t' the inner end an' haul a couple o' nets. If there wuzn't much in 'em you'd tie 'em on t' the outer part. You'd always be busy. Nowadays you just start the motor up an' motor round 'em, but then that wuz

162

rowin' all the time. Then when you'd done, you'd got to row home, that wuz if ther wuzn't no wind, o' course. If there wuz wind, you set your sail an' away you come.

Haulin' depended on the wind a lot. Generally, you hauled from the outer end in. But that all depended on the wind. If there wuz a strong breeze off the land, well if you hauled from the inner end, you'd keep a-blowin' all off. You'd rather haul on the outer end, though you had t' pull harder on the net-ropes 'cos o' the wind. That wuz a question o' wind an' how the nets lay in the water. Sometimes they'd turn right along. Another thing, that depended on which way the herren were striking. Herren generally strike from the south, but not always, sometimes they strike from the north. If you got a lot o' herren, you hauled all the nets into the boat, but if you hadn't got above 5-600, you'd pick 'em out. You'd keep pickin' 'em out an' throw 'em into the *wings* – they had wings in the side o' the boat t' hold the herren. You picked 'em out. There wuz a knack in that. You din't want t' pick a herren out an' pull the head off it, you'd got t' put your finger round the mesh an' clear the gill, then pull it out. 'Cos a herren, as regards smokin' round here in them days, you couldn't put it on the *speet* if you broke the jaw apart.

There always seemed t' be a difference between the type o' herren they got in closer, longshorin', than what they did out on Smith's Knoll or any-where out there. The longshore seemed t' be a smaller type o' herren, better quality. I'd always prefer a longshore herren any day t' a deep-sea herren. But I can't explain why, whether they were shoals o' herren on their own, I can't say.

The herren were sold by the *hundred*, but their 100 wuz 132. That wuz called a *long-tail*. So, if you counted a 100 o' herren out, that wuz thirty-three *warp*. A warp o' herren is four, so that wuz thirty-three fours. If you had half-a-hundred, that wuz the same, so many warp an' two. They mostly weren't sold on the beach. You either had a merchant you'd go for, Denny or Dunton, unless you got a bulk an' they'd go down t' Low'stoft an' you'd get the market price. Pra'ps Denny would want several hundred if they were good condition, t' wash an' salt away t' hang up for *reds* for the winter time, *red-herring*. Nuthin' better! I've had many a one on a grid-iron, snappin' an' crackin', specially with those hard roes; they'd eat like a piece o' ham. They used t' put 'em in the smokehouse right up the top an' they used t' smoke the *bloaters* down below. He'd hang 'em up, like tonight an' he'd sell 'em in the morning with just that sufficient smoke in 'em an' they were lovely. The reds were still there so they were still a-gettin' all that smoke an' they were a golden brown when he got 'em down.'

The method of counting herring by the long-tail (O.E *tellan: to count, estimate, reckon*. French *tailler: to tell or tally*) or long hundred was fixed in the reign of Edward III by *The Statute of Herrings* (1357). Originally a long hundred was thirty warp or six score, 120, but later became 132 perhaps because they became smaller. As with the reference to a barmskin, the use of a 14th century term by 20th century longshoreman working from Southwold beach is persuasive and elegant evidence of a remarkable continuity of practice although it must have been almost its last gasp. Percy Westrup of Thorpeness recalled an old method of tallying which included the warp:

> One is one
> Two is some
> Three is a sort
> Four is a warp
> Five is a good many
> And six is half-a-dozen.

When I was recording in the mid 1970s, the EU instituted a ban on herring fishing in an attempt to preserve fast-dwindling stocks, a measure met with much derision, especially amongst the few longshoremen still working at Southwold who had never fished unsustainably. Although stocks did eventually recover, the herring lost its appeal. Nowadays fresh herring are only available locally in small quantities and a fish so full of goodness is unknown to younger generations. Those silver darlings that first victualled the monks, then the nation ('a plague on those pickled herring' belched Sir Toby in *Twelfth Night*) and created work in the towns and villages where it was caught for a millennium are now almost entirely neglected, and have become instead the subject of well-meaning nostalgia such as that celebrated annually in recent years at the Suffolk Herring Festival in Halesworth.

Notes

1 Wake, Robert *A History of Southwold* p.8

2 'The Bury establishment at Domesday was 32 monks, plus 28 nuns and "poor persons" with 75 servants of one kind or another and 13 reeves.' It is not hard to see why the rents from the eighteen communities were as high as they were. I am indebted to David Butcher for this information.

3 Cooper, E.R. *Notes on Southwold Harbour*

4 Grubbe, Arthur *Diary* July, 1889

5 A curious use of the word. A fid is a tapering spike used to separate the strands of a rope when splicing. Perhaps Mr Jarvis is transferring the separating qualities of the fid to the separation of the nets. On deep-sea drift nets, the warp ropes, when joined, were finished using a fid. So the fid-end could also mean the joined ends of two nets with a gap between them

6 Butcher, David *The Last Haul* p.165 & 168. Headings were, 'the cords which ran down the side of a drift net'; norsels were, 'lengths of twine which joined the meshes to the net-rope on a drift net and held the corks in position'; a net-rope was, 'the double rope on the top of a drift net to which the corks were attached'

7 i.e. drifting in a southerly direction

8 i.e. boats only started fishing at the pier, whereas formerly they started further north

Seabird Man

A young man loomed, talking to himself. He did not speak like a seaman.

A seabird came.
It said,
I am a cross
I will save you.
Reach out to me
Reach out.

But my legs were snaked with ropes.
And grey-green waves whelmed me over.
My lungs were on fire.

We are many
There are many of us.
Reach out.

Its eye was red-ringed.

And when the bird rose from the water
I wanted to rise
To touch that bird,
The cross, my saviour,
To wing away
From this weight of water.

But my legs were snaked with ropes
And grey-green waves whelmed me over
My lungs were on fire ...

He disappeared, simultaneously crossing himself and flapping his arms as if he could somehow take flight.

14

Big Boating

As well as the longshore fishery the records also make clear that Southwold always had some kind of interest in the deep-sea fishery in which the longshoremen took part. A document from 1863 tells us that:

'The other branch of the herring fishery is called the *deep-sea fishing*. It is carried on in decked boats varying from fifteen to twenty tons each, with the addition of one of about thirty-eight tons, which do not go out and return with the tide but are out fishing at distances usually varying from one to three or more days…The first of this description of vessels at South-wold was started in the year 1853, it was speedily followed by others and there are now sixteen or seventeen of them, some belonging to private pro-prietors and the rest to different associations and companies.'[1]

These were the boats known as *half-and-halfers*, so-called because the owner or owners took half the proceeds and the other half was shared between the skipper and the crew. The boats were forty-five foot long, gaff-rigged with a lug mizzen attached to an outligger and carried a crew of eight *peabellies*, some of whom came from the in-land villages where they also worked the land. Henry Ladd built three for the Southwold Fishing Boat Company in 1851, *Andrew, Alfred* and *Henrietta*. The Company's net houses were on the site of Cumberland Terrace and later moved to buildings near the new Lifeboat Shed to-wards the harbour. Maggs tells us of a particularly good season for the three boats in 1854 when 'such a fishing is not remember'd by the oldest Inhabitant living' and that, 'The crews shared upwards of £20 a man.'[2] *Charlie, Beatrice* and *Solebay* followed in 1855 for the same Company. Other half-and-halfers were *Neptune, Julia, Norfolk, Ellen, Union* and *Friendship*.

The work was sometimes dangerous. Maggs recorded that on November 10th, 1857 Henry Page, an eighteen year old, was 'acci-dentally knocked of [sic] the deck of the Fishg Boat *Norfolk* F. Denny Masr and drowned about six miles off Southwold.'[3]

Yet another serious accident is pasted in a cutting dated November 8th, 1863:

'Lowestoft. Fatal accident at sea to Edward Palmer, twenty-three, of the fishing lugger *Union* of Southwold, master Ballantine Brown. Both Palmer and Brown were from Southwold. The *Union* with its crew of six was caught by a sudden squall at half past six on Sunday night as it entered St. Nicholas Gat. Her foremast was broken into three, one piece of which struck Palmer on the head. He never regained consciousness and the boat was raced into Lowestoft to get there at quarter to two, when a surgeon was summoned. Palmer was the master's brother-in-law. Craggy Ashman Hall, William Aldred and William Peck, also of the crew, joined Brown in giving evidence at the inquest.'[4]

Palmer's death was eerily presaged when, on November 8th at about 7 o'clock in the evening, Ballantine Brown's wife was walking to church down Church Street when 'she was startled to find someone walking close beside her. She took particular notice of the figure and saw that it was a man dressed in a long "oily" (oilskin coat) and a peculiarly shaped sou'wester having a peak both in front and behind, of a kind never worn by Southwold or East Coast fishermen.' The figure disappeared at the entrance to the yard of the pub, The *Brickmaker's Arms*, which used to be in the street. The following morning, she went to the cliff and was watching a half-and-halfer she thought was the *Union* beating in to the harbour when she was informed of Palmer's death in the manner described by Maggs. Palmer was her brother and the time of his death 'corresponded exactly with that in which she had seen the figure in Church Street'. In a further twist she was told 'her brother was wearing an oily and sou'wester he had borrowed from Mr Alexander which formerly belonged to a French fisherman.'[5]

E.R. Cooper says that 'scores' of these boats worked until about the 1880s 'when they were out-classed', by which he meant superseded by the Lowestoft drifters which were built to harvest the vast shoals of herring that congregated in the North Sea and were fished round the coast from Devon to Shetland and down the North Sea to Yarmouth and Lowestoft between January and December each year.[6]

The definitive book on the deep-sea herring fishery is David Butcher's *The Driftermen*, an extraordinary piece of oral history. Once the half-and-half fishing dried up, Southwold longshoremen regularly went *big boating* as they called it out of Lowestoft in drifters or trawlers in order to try to make better money than they could longshoring.

Scientific evidence has shown that an earlier belief that the herring shoals appeared off Shetland in May and then circumnavigated the coasts ending up in the Minch early in the following year, is erroneous. According to Butcher, 'The most generally accepted idea now (for there is by no means complete agreement as to the species' behaviour) is that there are half-a-dozen or so individual stocks of herring in the waters round our coasts and it was the spring or autumn spawning pattern of these separate stocks that gave rise to shoal activity in different areas at different times of the year.'[7] This meant that there were a number of voyages that a man could choose to ship for, the three main being the *Westward* to Cornwall in the early part of the year for herring or mackerel, the *Shetland* in summer and the *Home Fishing*, as it was called, carried out off the East Anglian coast between October and December with the catches landed at Yarmouth, Lowestoft and indeed all too briefly, Southwold itself. Of the three, the Home Fishing was the largest. Butcher tells us that the 1913 Home Fishing was the zenith of the North Sea herring boom, 'The 1,006 boats fishing out of Yarmouth (264 local, 742 Scottish) landed a total of 824,213 *crans* of herrings (a cran weighed 28 stones) while the Lowestoft fleet of 770 drifters (350 local, 420 Scottish) brought in nearly 535,000 crans.'[8] A cran was between 800 and 1000 fish. Such figures endorse the etymology of the word herring which may be influenced by Old English *har: grey, hoar* or High German *heri: host or multitude*.

A steam drifter fishing out of Lowestoft was worked in favour of the owners who took 62½% of the boat's net earnings, the remaining 37½% being shared between the skipper and crew [ten in all] in a complex system. The net earnings were the profits made once the expenses had been deducted and these were considerable, consisting of items such as 'coal, lubricating oil and engine stores, food, landing dues, shore labour, baskets, fish salesmen's commission, water charges, salt and ice'.[9] It was thus perfectly possible for the expenses to be greater than the net earnings which meant that the crew would receive no pay off and could even come home in debt. Twenty-four shares covered the net earnings, fifteen going to the owners and nine to the men. For every £100 of net earnings a full share was £4.3s.4d though in practice the owners took a further 10d per share on top. Crew shares were allocated according to rank and calculated in eighths. The skipper took one and a quarter shares down to the cook, usually a boy, who took a half share. If he was good he would customarily be given an extra quarter share at the skipper's discretion.

Regularly drifters shot fleets of up to 100 or more nets that extended about two miles but this depended on certain variables such as the particular voyage they were on, the type of ground, the shoaling pattern and so on. It was the skipper's decision where and when to shoot and he used tell-tale signs such as the colour of the water, the presence of blower whales, porpoises and dolphins, sea birds such as gannets and gulls, and the state of the wind, tide and moon. He decided when to haul having tested the catch in a net or two after which the long process of hauling and shaking out the nets began. This could take as long as eight or nine hours in certain conditions. A wet net weighed a hundredweight and a good haul was considered to be two or three crans per net, a cran weighing twenty-eight stone, so this was tough work carried out sometimes in appalling weather conditions day in, day out.

A number of the men I spoke to went big boating either full time or more often in between spells of longshoring. One of these was Mr. English who went in order to earn enough to buy his own boat. He was able to summarise the experience of going on a Shetland voyage, which itself is a very clear introduction to the experience of going to sea in a steam drifter after the First World War:

'You went down t' Low'stoft an' you walked along the Waveney Road an' looked up on the boards t' see what crew are wanted. You went along there in April or May t' go t' the Shetlands an' Scotland. You'd walk along there an' pick out what boat you wanted or what skipper you thought wuz the best. You went an' see him an' if he'd take you on, well he'd take you on. Perhaps they'd say, 'We're goin' away on the 20th May.' Now a fortnight before they went, you'd go down an' help t' get her all ready – scrape the mast, all the beams, varnish 'em till she wuz all cleaned up. She used t' be in dry dock, ready, an' you'd clean 'em all up so that they went away spick an' span.'

David Butcher tells us that the Shetland voyage started to become popular with the Lowestoft and Yarmouth skippers after 1902 but this itself could cause problems if large catches landed at Lerwick depressed prices and led to dumping. Moreover, the Shetland herring were not particularly good quality, being oily and soft and requiring careful handling once ashore. The east side of Shetland was preferred to the west, the boats heading off up to twenty-five miles off Score Head or twenty miles off Bard. Another favourite was about twelve miles off Sumburgh Head. Mr English:

'You'd leave Low'stoft an' go down there. That'd take you somewhere pr'aps three days. Pr'aps the night before you went in t' Lerwick you'd shoot 100 t' 110 nets. They were *sunk nets*. They'd got a buoy on top, a *buff*, an' on the bottom a big rope, tarred [the *warp*] an' thass what would hold 'em in the straight line. Well, you'd shoot; perhaps you'd be a couple or three hours doin' that, steam 'em out, an' then you'd *hang-on*, bring the boat round t' head-on, set your mizzen an' she'd *keep-to* it all the night, till they'd sing out about four o' clock in the mornin', 'Work-o!' an' you'd all turn out an' then start.

The cook used t' go down in the *rope-room*. He's the one that coiled that big rope [the warp]; an' the cast-off seizin's wuz the one that took the *seizings off*, the ropes off the warp an' the buffs as they come inboard through the *moll-jenny*, a big block. The cook had got t' coil all that – well, 110 nets would be a mile or two o' rope, an' he'd got t' coil all that in there, he'd got t' get it in. Then there'd be the *net-rope man*, an' the *lint-man* t' haul these nets. As they came over the rails there wuz a big roller. The herren come over the rail, they'd give 'em a shake an' they'd all drop into what are called the *coamings*. They were all pieced off by *bank-boards* an' there wuz an openin' what let your herren go down into the *wings*, the hold. The nets went down in the middle part o' the hold. If you had 100 cran, you'd be eight t' ten hours haulin'; that all depended on how they come, how the wind wuz. If the wind come *against the law*, that wuz you couldn't haul head t' wind, you come t' the end o' your net, you *unbent* an' you *chopped* your rope. You had t' go right t' the other end an' pick that up an' haul the other way.

After you hauled 'em all, you went into Lerwick or wherever you fished from. You'd work out o' there; but if you din't do much, you'd come t' the mainland. I used t' like t' come t' the mainland, t' Wick, Aberdeen, Peterhead an' you fished out o' there for so many months. You'd leave in May an' they always used t' reckon t' get back, on the drifters from the Scottish fishin', before the Low'stoft Regatta in late August. That used t' be a thing. You'd gradually work up when you come. You see you left Lerwick, come t' the mainland an' work right along till you come t' the Humber. When you got t' the Humber, the next trip wuz home, you'd come home.

There wuz ten crew. A skipper, a mate, an oarsman [a *hawesman*] – he wuz the man what when you went in, he picked out a dozen or so herren an' put 'em in a little pail an' took them t' the sale, an' they'd be put on the market if they were all right. There was cast-off seizin's, cook, lint-man, net-man, rope-man. The cook got 10/- a week, cast-off seizin's 12/6, then there wuz 15/-, 17/6., £1 an' 25/-. The skipper only got about 25/- a week.

I used t' like goin' driftin'. You din't take it as hard work. You were in every day on the Scotch fishin', an' when you come in on a Saturday mornin' they wouldn't allow you t' go any more till Sunday after twelve so you had a lay in, in Scotland. I wuz in the *Happy Days*, the *Golden Harvest*. I never did do the Home fishing. I always used t' come home for the autumn herrenin' an' the sprattin' 'cos you made more money. I divided my time between the long trips an' longshorin'.'

After Mr Rogers left the rope-works, he also divided his time between big boating and longshoring. He started in sailing drifters going to Scarborough, a short voyage in August sometimes taken between the Shetland voyage and the Home fishing.

'One day I see a boy I knew. I say, "Have you bin t' Low'stoft?" He say, "No." I say, "They tell me you can earn some money when you go big boatin'." They used t' call it big boatin'. He say, "Oh?" "I've got a cousin who go," I say. "I'll ask him." "Well," he say, "thass a bit rough at times but you have to take the rough along o' the smooth."

So one day I say I'm not goin' down t' turn a wheel all day, [at the rope-works] I'm a-goin' t' Low'stoft. There wuz an ol' feller by the name o' Snowden. He had a wooden leg an' he used t' run a horse an' cart down t' Low'stoft. I say, "Will you give me a lift?" He say, "Yis, boy. I'm a-goin' down in the mornin'." He say, "What you goin' arter?" I say, "See if I can get a berth in one o' the drifters." So he give me a lift down. "Coh!" I say. "They look rum boats. They're some size!" I thought they were marvellous things! He say, "See that man there? He want a cook." "Do he?" He say, "Why don't you go an' ask him?" "All right," I say. So I went up t' him. I say, "Skipper, do you want a boy in the boat?" He looked down at me. He say, "Yis. Why?" "Well," I say, "I'm lookin' for a berth." "Well," he say, "yis, all right. You can go. You can start now if you like." "I can't start now," I say. "Why not?" "Well, I must go home an' tell my mother I'm goin'." "Oh," he say, "all right. Get here in the mornin' then. You be aboard the boat about nine o' clock time. Before that if you like." So I walked t' Low'stoft the next mornin'. I say t' my mother, "I got a berth an' I'm goin' t' sea." "I don't know what your father 'll say. He 'ont let you go." "Well," I say, "you get round him an' tell him I'd like t' go." So the ol' man, bein' a gentle sort o' chap, he say, "He can go if he like but he'll be glad t' get outa that." I wished arterwards I'd taken his advice too, I can tell you.

So I stopped at Low'stoft that week, helped t' get the boat ready. I used t' fry steak, that sorta thing for lunchtime. He say, "Boy, we're gettin' the ropes in tomorrer." I say, "Are we?" He say, "Yis. You know the way t' coil ropes don't you?" "Yes, I think so, mister." 'Cos you were down in a little ol' room what they called the rope-room. You had t' keep coilin' these ropes round an' round, layin' them just right so they din't come foul. The illumination down there wuz a little ol' naked oil-lamp, thass all. You used t' come outa there lookin' like a crow! That used t' smoke. Well, I thought t' myself, we shall earn plenty o' money at this game. We shall be all right. So he say, "Boy, are you a-goin' home to day?" "Yis," I say, "Saturday." "Well,' he say, "we shall go t' sea a-Monday. You better come along o' me." He took me up t' ol' Longs in Bevan Street. He say, "You'll want a pair o' short leather boots, on't you? Oilskin. An' you'll want a pair o' boot stockin's t' go with 'em an' you'll want this an' that." I thought he was goin' t' give me all 'em! Howsomever, I went down aboard the boat with all this gear an' an ol' chap, he say t' me, "Do you feel like eatin' strawberries now?" "Yeh," I say, "I had some. Gooseberries an' all."

So we set sail. Nice an' fine when we went outa Low'stoft harbour. Coh! I thought, this is lovely! She was a-layin' over in a nice breeze, goin' through the piers. She wuz the *Springflower*, her number wuz LT 730. By the time we got t' Yarmouth, I began t' feel blinkin' queer! I kept spewin' over the side. O' course the ol' man, he had t' stand at the tiller. "Boy," he say, "you keep lookin' at that water goin' past, you'll feel worse than you do now." I say, "I can't help it." Bloor! Goin' agin "Oh," he say. "You better get down below." One on 'em say to me, "Boy! What about cookin' some dinner?" "Blimey!" I thought. So I went down the cabin. The stove looked t' me as though that were a-jumpin' about, an' there wuz a little ol' steam boiler what used t' be in it too, next t' it. What with the warmth o' that lot, it made me ten times worse. One on 'em say, "Are you cookin' the dinner, boy?" "I can't. No dinner." Ooeer! "I just want t' die!" "Come on," he say. "Get the taters on the way!" I fumbled an' found a few spuds. I was goin' bleerp! "Give me that, boy. Get your head down." "In here?" I say. He say, "Yis, in that bunk." So I crawled into this bunk, just as I wuz, o' course, boots an' all. I never woke up till we got off Scarborough. An' when we got off there, they called me out. "Come on there, boy, see these ropes out. Now goin' t' shoot the nets. Come on, out!" Well, when I got on deck, the blinkin' sea! Looked as if there wuz mountains o' it 'cos there wuz a nasty swell. "Get you down in that hole, boy an' see they come out clear." Down I go. Blinkin' giddy. I kept clutchin' hold o' things. "Don't get hold o' that rope, boy. That'll pull you outa the hole." So that went out all right. That wuz a wonder!

We *come to*. He bought her to after they'd shot the nets. I made a bolt for the cabin. I wuz goin' t' get down again. "Boy," he say, "you want t' get a bit o' grub out here before we go t' work agin." I say, "We won't be goin' t' work agin, will we?" He say, "That 'ont be long." Come haulin' time, they called out all hands t' haul. Coh! I had t' go down the hatch agin, coil the ropes away. They were wet, full o' jellies. Blow me! That wuz punishment! That went on like that till at last we'd hauled. Then I had t' fry breakfast. Coh! I felt queer. "Boy, why don't you eat suthin'?" "I don't want anythin' t' eat." The ol' man say, "Yis you do," he say. "You keep drinkin' water an' before thass down, thass up agin." I say, "Yis, I know. But I thought I wuz goin' t' hold it down." "You'll never hold that down," he say. "Eat a biscuit or suthin'." There wuz one there nobody else wanted. I wondered if I dare try it. Got a little ol' bit. Managed to keep it down. Then I had a mite o' bread. Arter that I worn't so bad. I got all right.

Well, we set sail an' we come t' Scarborough. When we were comin' up the bay, I say t' a bloke, "There's a funny black cloud up there." "Cloud!" he say. "That in't no cloud." "What is it?" "Thass Scarborough Castle what you're a-lookin' at!" 'Cos when we come into the bay, all the visitors were out in little boats, hand fishin' an' that. I wuz busy interested in lookin' at 'em. I weren't thinkin' anythin' about cookin' the dinner. That come nearly one o'clock. They say, "Boy. You got the dinner ready yet?" I say, "No, not yet. The spuds in't quite done." Coh! They weren't in the blinkin' saucepan!

The conditions were blinkin' horrible! There wuz just a little ol' cabin. In that little ol' cabin wuz five or six bunks. Sometimes you had t' sleep two in a bunk. There wuz a steam boiler an' the stove stood [in the middle] with the bunks each side. There weren't room hardly t' move, especially when they all got down there. Crowded! The water tank used t' be down one side but you never saw that really an' there wuz a tap what you used t' get the water out o' it. You used t' have t' cook on this here stove, but fortunately, that first one I went in, she had a little ol' range an' oven t' it what you could put your meat in. You had a gret ol' iron boiler you used t' put on top. You had t' secure that. P'raps when you were fryin' you'd be on one tack, well your pan would be [lopsisded]. "Take your funnel down, boy. We're now goin' about," he'd say. "What? Hold on, I'll take the funnel orf." 'Cos he used t' take the funnel orf the stove, what used t' come up on deck. "When we get round," he say, "you can put it back agin." Somehow we managed. God knows how! We stuck at that, boy, till we come t' Grimsby. I thought, "This is a rum place!" We had a feller there who wuz a little bit religious. He say, "Boy, would you like t' go ashore Sunday mornin'?" "Yis," I say, "I should think I would." "All right then. I'll cook the dinner for you." I din't want any second tellin'! I wuz off! Went along the docks there at Grimsby. See all these big liners. I thought they were lovely ships. I shouldn't mind a voyage on one o' 'em.

Well, when the voyage wuz over, the ol' man say, "Well, we might as well go home." We used t' get home about Yarmouth Races time [in mid September]. So he said, "We might as well pay off now." I thought, "Well, I'm a-goin' t' get some money now." So we paid off an' he say t' me, "Boy, I'm afraid you're goin' t' be a little bit short." I say, "I don't know, Skipper,

I haven't had any money." He used t' give me sometimes a penny, sometimes tuppence. "How are you goin' t' go home, boy?" "Oh. I'm goin' t' walk." "Well," he said, "here's your money. Your had a pair o' boots, your had this an' that an' the other. That gives you ten shillin's." A dozen or fourteen weeks for ten bob!

Well, I come home t' Southwold, swankin' like anythin'. Proper toff! The boy say, "How do you like it, Rogers?" I say, "All right. Ever such a nice life. You oughta go." Then the ol' man say, "How do you like it, Rogers? Thass a rum life in'it?" I say, "If I knew what I now know when I first went, I should never have went!" He say, "I told you you'd soon be glad t' get out of it." I say, "Yes. If I coulda got ashore the first night, I don't think I should ever have went no more." "Ah well," he say, "you'll larn." '

Mr Rogers made another short trip on the Home Fishing, also as cook but fell ill and had to return to Southwold.

'I come home. The ol' man say, "What you doin' home, boy?" I say, "I don't know. I don't feel very well." I bloomin' well din't too! "Ah!" he say, "I thought that'd larn you." Thass all the sympathy I got. "Oh well," he say, "you'd better come along o' us." "What are you doin'?" He say, "We're goin' sprattin' ". "All right," I say. So I went along o' father an' my uncle then, sprattin' an' that sorta thing. My father wuz with the Californians. Used t' lay there opposite *The Inch*.

Well that wuz my experience in a sailin' drifter. So I never went no more, not for the next year. Ol' skipper come over here. Got a couple o' Southwold fellers along with him. He say, "Boy, they tell me you want a berth in a boat. We're goin' round t' the Westward. Do you want t' go?" I say, "I don't know. I'll see what my father have got t' say about it." "You don't want t' ask your father," he say, "but you can if you like." Well he took me down t' the *Southwold Arms* an' say, "What are you goin' t' have t' drink, boy? Do you want a drop o' whisky or suthin'?" "That'd be nice. Yes," I say. So he give me a tot o' whisky. As that got lower, I thought he wuz a better bloke. He say, "We shall get ready so-an'-so. You'll go then?" I say, "Yis." He say, "We're goin' round t' the Westward." I went down [to Lowestoft] an' helped get the boat ready, like the other one. When we were ready we went away. This here boat, particular, where the main sheet used t' come across, travelled across what we used t' call an *iron horse*. O' course that wuz handy. I stood there leanin' up against it after we got outa Low'stoft harbour. Well she come up into the wind, an' the sheet come over an' pinned me t' the side. They rushed arter me! "Boy, are you all right?" I say, "I think I'm all right, skipper." "Are you sure you aren't hurt? Are your ribs all right?" "Well, I feel a bit sore." "If you're hurt," he say, "say so an' we'll go back." Well I thought thass unlucky t' turn back, so I say, "No, I think I'll be all right." Arter a little while I recovered a bit. "Don't stand against that iron horse, boy. If she happen t' gybe, your had it." I learnt by that.

We got over that an' got down t' the Westward, down t' Newlyn. I got on fairly well with 'em. She had an ol' open stove down in the cabin. You used t' put the meat in the tin, put the lid over it, shove it underneath among the ashes, under the gratin'. Used t' cook it all right! One day we got a nasty breeze out there by the Scilly Isles an' o' course the old man shoved her round for some reason or other. Well I hadn't lashed the beef-kettle, an' the whole blinkin' lot come over on the cabin floor – duff, taters, the lot! "Scoop it up," he say, "hull it overboard an' start agin." I had t' blinkin' well start agin! I din't get the dinner up that day till arter three! "That'll larn you," he say, "t' lash your kettle on!" I say, "I never had a chance. I din't know you were a-goin' round." "Oh, well," he say, "get on with it." But the ol' man wuz pretty good, livin' conditions. He'd have anythin'. I used t' cook beef. A-cookin' o' beef every day. Spuds. You din't have dumplin's, you'd have suet puddin' or pr'aps have a rhubarb puddin' or a rice puddin' 'cos that all used t' have t' be boiled bar the meat.

I tell you, I got on well with the ol' man. The first day we shot, ropes come out all right. Next mornin' I got 'em in all right, plenty o' room t' spare. Mornin' arter that, I couldn't get 'em down the room. I hadn't got room enough. Coh! You oughta have heard the ol' man swear! We come in the harbour with half a fleet o' ropes on deck. We pulled 'em all up an' stowed 'em down agin. Thass the sorta life that wuz. But I got on so well with him, that when we paid off, he give me an extra pound. "Boy", he say, "you can go agin, if you like, along o' us. We're goin' on the North Sea." "No, skipper," I say, "I don't think I'm goin' no more." He swore! He say, "Why not? Your gettin' on well. Dinner's up here at twelve o' clock in day time. Never known it. You can go on deck if you like, instead o' goin' cook. You can go next stage up." "No. I don't think so, skipper." '

Mr Rogers did in fact make two more uneventful voyages in drifters and then he went trawling. Not finding it to his liking he took up drifting again, this time in a steam drifter.

' "Yis," he say, "we want a chap, cast-off seizin's that wuz called; you stood forrard there an' took the seizin's off the rope. He say, "You'll be all right." I say, "We in't got no sails t' lug about, thass one thing." O' course she wuz only a cockleshell t' what they had later on. Howsomever, we got on all right. We done a nice little voyage in the North Sea in her. I know I got over £20 share in her. Coh! I din't half swank when I got home t' Southwold, pockets full o' money, all in quids. I went along in her an' stuck it that year. I thought I'd get a bigger boat than this, if I can, so I did next time. That little ol' one, her name wuz called the *Adventure*.

The last one I went in, I went in five or six steam drifters, I wuz down in the engine room then. Went down as *second engineer* as we called ourselves. My ol' chum, he say t' me, "Are you goin' along o' us round t' the Westward?" I say, "Yis." So I went round. I'll tell you this story.

We went round t' the Westward, I should think sometime about the end o' February or start o' March. Her name wuz the *Faithful Friend*. She wuz a lovely big boat. She had what we called a *triple* engine [triple expansion engine] in her. We started off, went round t' the Westward, used t' fish out o' Newlyn. We used t' fish out anythin' up t' forty miles from the Scilly Isles. Carried on like that.

One day we went out, a bloke came down the engine room, say, "The ol' man say, tell somebody t' come up, the hatches keep blowin' off." "Do it?" I say. So I called another fella out. I say, "Come an' put these hatches on. They keep blowin' off for some reason." Couldn't make it out at all, 'cos that weren't too bad weather just then. That wuz before we got t' the *Longships*. So they put it on. Just got down below an' that blew off agin. So they wedged it on an' that carried on an' we got out t' the fishin' grounds, shot the nets. I know we had a devil o' a lot o' nets – mackerel nets, scotch herren nets. A lot o' wind up here, I thought t' myself.

Anyhow, we *dodged* that after we hauled.[10] The ol' man say, "We int got enough mackerel t' go all that way back." It wuz about seventy, eighty mile. "We can't steam all that way back with 'em few mackerel." So we dodged at sea all that day. Well, she dodged it all right. "As long as you keep her goin' dead slow," he say, "just so she hold way, *keep her head to it*." I stuck it all day down in the engine room. About six at night, CRASH! BANG! I thought t' myself, What the deuce is that? I thought the blinkin' propeller had dropped off or suthin'. Then I see a lot of black water down in the engine-room underneath the boiler. Crikey! Before I knew where I wuz, I wuz nearly up t' my knees in water in the engine-room. She'd got a nasty sea. That took away every blinkin' thing, nearly. Mast fell down on the deck, wheelhouse wuz crumpled up like a piece o' cardboard, funnel wuz half-gone an' she wuz full o' water. You talk about a sea, that wuz just like so much smoke!

Well, we din't know what t' do. Little boat wuz gorn an' everything. Thought t' myself, This is a rum do! Get on deck. Nobody seemed t' know where the spare pumps were. "Don't you run on about pumps," the ol' man say. "You keep askin'. Why don't you look for 'em?" I say, "Yis. You tell me where t' look! The steam ones are all messed up. We can't use 'em." So they got, well the mate did, managed t' get a tarpaulin over the hold. Wedged that on. "Well," he say, "now if we do get another one, won't be so much get below." Thought t' myself, If she get another one, she'll sink. My ol' chum say t' me, "Know what that wuz don't you? We'll sink!" I say, "Sure?" He say, "Yis, I am." "Good Lord!" I say. "Keep the engine goin' ". He say, "I can't. Thass stopped goin' " Howsomever, we got a couple o' pails an' we pailed that out. That took us about ten hours, I believe, t' bail that water out on her. We got the water out. I say t' my ol' chum, "Well, she's still afloat." She had four inches o' *freeboard* outa the water. Four inches! If she'd have took that four inches, she'd have sunk. Anyway, she din't. We got t' work on the engine. "Can you get it t' go?" I say. He say, "I don't know. We'll try." After we gathered in the ropes, chains, all that sorta thing that had got washed overboard, I say t' a feller, "Where's the little boat?" He say, "She's gorn along o' the rest." "Crumbs!" I say. "I thought that looked a big deck on, aft." So we got t' work. My ol' chum got t' work on the pumps. He say, "I've cleared all the coal hatches away from the pumps. P'raps they'll work," he say. "I don't know if we'll get any steam," I say, "Why?" he say. "Well, all the tubes are leakin' in the boiler. Open the door an' have a look. God knows if we'll get any steam, but we'll have t' see if the engin'll go round." So we told the ol' man. We rigged up a tiller on the rudder heads somehow or other, so he could steer, 'cos the wheel wuz no good – the wheelhouse had folded down just like a piece o' cardboard. He say, "Will you look arter the fires, or will you look after the engine?" I say, "I don't mind. We'll both have t' be here." We got her t' go round. He say, "Well, we shan't go very fast." I say, "I know that." I think we diddled along somewhere about three knots. The propeller just managed t' go round. The ol' man stood on deck steerin' with the tiller. As regards grub, we made do with what we got, bread or suthin' like that, couldn't do any cookin' or anythin'. We kept joggin' along. I say t' the ol man, "Are you worried?" "That int your fault. We're still here, we're still alive an' we're still afloat." We jogged along all that day from about seven in the mornin' till it come nearly seven at night when we come into Newlyn harbour.

When we come round Mousehole, just before Newlyn, the sea wuz just like this table-top, smooth like a pond. When we rounded into Penzance bay an' come into Newlyn harbour there were swarms o' blinkin' people come aboard. Coh! Blimey! You've never seen so many. "My word! You've bin in the wars!" "Yes, we have!" "Where did that happen? Anybody lost? Anybody hurt?" "No," I say. "I only just got a scratch on one arm where a bit of glass got it. There wuz three people in the wheelhouse an' they all got out on it." You ask me but I can't tell you how they got out. That wuz the only time I got my photo on the front page o' the *Daily Mirror*. That just shew you what a wreck she wuz. We were actually forty five mile from the *Bishop's Rock*.'

When Southwold Harbour eventually opened in 1908 hoping to become a third herring port behind Yarmouth and Lowestoft during the autumn *Home Fishing*, it became the furthest south the *Scotch girls* ever came. Scotch girls was the generic term which referred to the itinerant female work force whose job was to gut and pack the vast catches for export to Germany and Russia. Writing about women from Nairn, Margaret Bochel described their lives before the First World War, in particular time spent in the Shetlands.[11] Aged between fifteen and fifty, they were tight-knit groups who followed the fleets around the British coast. For some women this was their only livelihood; for others it was a temporary release from home, undertaken in the summer or autumn. Either in the spring or after the autumn season in East Anglia, representatives of the curing companies visited the women's home towns and villages recruiting for the next season. A payment called *arles* was given, in effect a two-way binding unwritten contract, if the women accepted. There was no training. Young girls had to learn how to gut and pack from family and friends. Though slower in their first season, they had caught up with the experienced women by the second. The women worked in threes – two gutters and a packer. Only marriage or illness broke their bonds.

The women packed their belongings in wooden trunks called *kists* which contained working and Sunday clothes, sheets and towels as well as housekeeping items for when they looked after themselves in huts such as at Gremista in Shetland, though they also stayed in lodgings in other places. Inside the kist was a *shottle*, a smaller hinged wooden box, used for storing knitting needles, a *wisker*, (a belt tied round the waist with a horse-hair pad at the front used in knitting), bandages for their fingers called *stalls* and their gutting knife. An oilskin with a bib wide enough to wrap round the whole body named a *coat*, was also included. The employers paid to transport the kists from port to port.

Work followed the catches so there were no set times. The women could work from 6 am to10 pm. Before they started, they bandaged their fingers to protect them from cuts and from the salt. The gutters bandaged each finger but the packers just their finger ends. Despite these precautions injuries occurred and in bad cases the women had to stop work with a consequent loss of earnings. As they worked in all weathers outdoors, the women wore headscarves, old skirts and jumpers, knitted stockings, watertight boots, knee-length skirts, and sleeves rolled up to the elbows. The coat was the final all-round covering.

After the herrings were landed and sold, they were put into wooden troughs called *farlanes* to be gutted. Then the work began for the team of three. Three to six tubs or baskets were placed behind the gutters and at their side another called a *coug* held the guts. The gutters sorted the herrings according to quality into the baskets behind them. When these were full they were carried two at a time for *rousing*, a further and more thorough salting than the one they received in the farlanes. Then they were packed in the barrels. A gutter could gut and sort 60-70 herrings a minute, up to 20,000 a day. With one swift movement of her knife, she would remove the gills and gut depositing them in the coug. Milt and roes were left in the fish. Each barrel contained, depending on size, 700-1000 herrings. The packer would aim to fill three an hour. There was both skill and art in the packing. The herrings were laid on their backs round the barrel and a layer of salt thrown in. The next layer had to be at a different angle. Particular attention was paid to the top and bottom layer to make the barrel look attractive on opening. At the bottom the black backs were beautifully arranged while at the top the silver bellies. As the salt drew the moisture out of the fish they settled in the barrels. Then the *filling-up* took place. More herrings were added to the top. The barrel was laid on its side, a bung hole drilled and the pickle poured in. It was then sealed. The barrel was left for a further seven to ten days, the pickle poured out, more herrrings added if necessary, a second pickle poured in to capacity before the barrel was finally sealed by the coopers. Barrels were stacked three high to await shipment. Stacking was done by two girls and two coopers. The second layer was lifted on to the first by means of hooks attached to the rim and the third on to the second by standing on upturned barrels.

For the Nairn women, pay was by piece-work. In the early 20th century £17-£20 per year was regarded as a good wage.

When no catches were in, the women knitted ganseys, stockings and drawers on four or five needles in the round. As the garment grew, the needle being used was stuffed in to the wisker to support it

Scotch girls employed by W. Slater & Sons

and keep it steady. The women would knit standing and were so proficient they hardly needed to look at their work. Sundays were rest days and a time for going to church in Lerwick, or to attend a service in a mission hut at Gremista. After church, it was time to socialise with family, boyfriends and fishermen who came to the huts to enjoy food cooked by the women. Hymns were sung, news exchanged, relationships developed.

1908 was the first time the Scotch girls came to Southwold. Local reports were enthusiastic. Their presence would bring 'notable benefit' to tradesmen and to those who let lodgings. 'Great interest' was shown in them by the locals, many of whom had heard of but never seen them. Before the season began, the women helped to stack the 6-7000 barrels sent by the curers to the harbour with the aid of two or three men, by rolling them down an arrangement of planks.[12] The town showed its hospitality by putting on an entertainment for a hundred of the women given by Mrs Gordon and Miss Aud, two well-known visitors. After tea there was a musical entertainment followed by dancing in which reels played a prominent part. This was followed by musical chairs. Mr W. Eaton Moore, the Mayor, praised the women for showing the townspeople how to work and to play hard. *Auld Lang Syne* ended the evening. Down at the Harbour, opposite the Kipperdrome, The Royal National Mission to Deep Sea Fishermen was opened only for the season. Run by Mr and Mrs Harry Westcott, the women were allowed to use its facilities. The fish-market was happily thought to be unique in that there was no pub near it, thus making the Mission's work that much easier.[13]

A much fuller report appeared in the press for the 1909 season in which the writer described the women at work on the catch landed by the drifter SD 999.[14] Having landed their fifty *crans*, (up to 50,000 herrings) which took 4 hours, the fish were taken to the curing shed, salted and shot 1,000 at a time into the farlanes, which varied from twenty-five feet long, were four to five feet wide and one and three quarter feet deep, where twelve to fourteen women were standing awaiting the call to start. Since their scale of pay, above the weekly wage, (which must have been recently introduced), was calculated on the numbers they processed, starting at the same time was fair.

The women were now regulated by the Factory Act. For a ten hour day, they were allowed three hours off for meals and rest, meaning that in the seven working hours, gutting at a rate of 1,500 per hour, each woman gutted 10,500 per day.

The gutted herrings were then packed, the girl at first disappearing into the barrel so that all that could be seen was a 'vigorous movement of the elbows.' She arranged the bottom layer with 'mathematical precision.' An inspector overlooked the packing process several times. Once packed, the filling process began. Sixty to ninety fish were added after twenty four hours of settling. After the further seven to ten days more herrings were added. Once pickled the barrels were coopered and ready for export. Good for six to eight months, they were sent to Hamburg, Stettin, Konigsberg, St. Petersburg and Libau.

The employers engaged 300 women for the season at Southwold, the majority coming from Invernesshire, Banffshire, the Shetlands, Stornoway, Peterhead, Fraserburgh and Castlebay. Thomas Jenkins of Aberdeen was a principal employer. Others were the Scottish-Russian Fishery Company and variously Messers Woods, Burnett, Mitchell, Slater and Dickson. Wages were between £1.10s-£2.5s a week which included the weekly wage and the additional amount for their output.

'The 'girls' or 'lassies'were 'well-behaved, sturdy, healthy-looking' and 'cheerful in all weathers.' They lodged in the town. Once again they were looked after at the Mission by Mr and Mrs Westcott who provided 'comfortable recreation, reading and refreshment rooms', the Mission having purchased the restaurant at the site previously owned by Marshall. Their presence invested the town with 'a Scottish atmosphere.' Regarding the women in Southwold, I only gleaned this fragment from Mr Barber:

> The Scotch girls were hard workers, nothin' but. A rum race o' people they were. They used t' come every year, well they only come here about two years, before th' harbour began t' block up, but they come t' Low'stoft an' Yarmouth every year then up till the herren fishin' died out. They'd come up there by the hundreds. They all had lodgin's. People used t' take

'em in, two in one house, three in another, all that you know. They used t' get t' work on the herren, boy, fingers tied up in rags, little guttin' knife stickin' out. Head over the trough. They used t' pick 'em up, whip the guts out quick as lightnin'.They used t' throw 'em into a tub, an' when the tub wuz full, they used t' take 'em t' another man, salted, an' he used t' pack 'em all into a barrel, all round, with their belly upwards. All stand on their backs. Used t' look a picture. Then they were all salted down, tops put on, hammered up, rolled away. They all used t' go t' Russia, them days, chiefly t' Russia. These girls used t' work there all afternoon an' into th' night with an oilskin blouse on an' headscarves tied round their head an' rubber boots an' oilskin trousers. You'd see 'em Sundays, walkin' up th' street, two or three, side by side, every one on 'em knittin'. All the while, every one on' 'em knittin'. An' thass all you used t' see at the Shetland Isles, Fair Isle jumpers. Wonderful feel for that, wonderful feel. Thass all gone by the board. Shan't see that no more.'

Notes

1   Source unknown

2   *Maggs Vol.2* p.78

3   Ibid p.92

4   Ibid p.112

5   Jenkins, A.B. *A Selection of Ghost Stories* p.9

6   Cooper, E.R. *Mardles From Suffolk* p.12

7   Butcher, David *The Driftermen* p.197

8   Ibid p.14

9   Ibid p.90

10 *Dodged*: sailing or steaming head to wind

11 See: Bochel, Margaret *The Story of Nairn Fisher Girls at the Gutting*

12 'Scotch Herring Boats at Southwold', newspaper article, October, 1908

13 Cutting from *Toilers of the Deep*, 1908

14 Ife, Harry: 'Southwold Fishing Industry – The Herring in Transition', newspaper article, November 9th, 1909

Tide

I emerged by a huge anchor, to which I attached myself by means of cable. Tide tugged this way then that.

I am flood it seemed to say and I am ebb.
I am spring and I am neap.
I am rise and I am fall.
I measure all.

I am push and I am pull.
I am moon and I am sun.
I am time as old as earth.
Old as when the sea begun.

I am present, never past.
I flow in rhythm, ebb in rhyme.
Round I go and round in time.
I am the eternal dance.

When I'm in, I'm going out
And when I'm out, I'm coming in
Where I am going, where I've been
Is all of me you've ever seen.

I am felt force invisible.

These words or suchlike floated past me as I held place tied between the flukes of that great monster.

One night when the tide had slackened a little and the moon was out, for I could see its light-path winking on the tops, a shoal of herrings came within sight, vast beyond number. They swirled and twisted around each other as I have seen starlings at dusk before roosting. Sometimes they were a dark ball then all flashing silver. As light grew with the coming dawn, they suddenly rose as one, and making a sound like an exhalation, arrowed to the surface and were gone.

Plate IX *Southwold Beach looking towards the town* (detail) (pre-1862) Thomas Smythe

Plate X *Southwold Beach Suffolk* 1921 A. Heaton Cooper

Plate XI *A Study of Sails* 1886 Walter Crane

Plate XII *Fishermen and Boat* 1923 Joseph Southall

Plate XIV *Fisherman Carrying a Sail*
1906-7 Joseph Southall

Plate XIII *The Old Fisherman* 1903 Joseph Southall

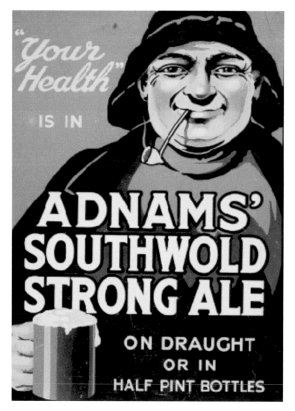

Plate XV *Adnams' advertising poster, mid-20th century*

Plate XVI *A Rough Night Ashore!* copy of print formerly at The Harbour Inn, Southwold

15

Jumping Out Like Sparks

The sprat-fishery, which was practised along the Suffolk coast from Pakefield to Aldeburgh, can be traced with certainty back to the 17th century in Southwold, the 16th century in Aldeburgh and the 15th century in Walberswick and Dunwich but is doubtless much older than that. Presentments to the Southwold Admiralty Court in 1677 for example, show the doales or payments that were made by fishermen in respect of the *sprat-fare*. Over twenty fishermen are named, some of whom, such as Winter, were still associated with fishing into the 20th century. These payments were made to the bailiffs of the town and were in effect a tax on fishing during the different *fares* or seasons.[1] At Aldeburgh 16th century wills detail the owners of 'spurling-botes' and 'sparlyng nets', 'sparling' being another word for the sprat.[2] Similarly at Walberswick, the Churchwardens' accounts between 1450 and 1490 make frequent mention of the 'sperling-fare' and those involved in it.[3] The earliest record though, is from Dunwich. The Bailiffs' Minute Book records the dues from the 'sparling fare' in 1406.[4]

The Southwold documents suggest that one method of catching sprats was the *sette-nette*. This, David Butcher tells us, was 'a wall of netting fixed to the sea-bed with slack in it, which floated up to the surface at high tide and dropped down on the ebb, trapping any fish that came within its area.'[5] Butcher has also recorded a similar kind of net, also called a set-net, in use off Pakefield before 1900. This was suspended at the required depth in the water by means of anchors and floats and worked on the principle of tidal flow thus showing a remarkable continuity of practice even though by then the main method of catching sprats was by drift-netting. Elsewhere in the country, such as in Dorset, sprats were caught by drag-netting, the same method used here to catch smelts.

As we have already noted, there has been a certain amount of species-confusion regarding the sprat, it being mistaken both for smelt and herring. Tobias Gentleman for example, originally from a

Southwold family, but then a Yarmouth mariner and boatbuilder claimed in his pamphlet to encourage fishing, *England's Way to Win Wealth* (1614) that sprats were young herring perhaps intending they should be sold as such and would thus command a higher price. This belief was still extant in the mid-19th century on the streets of London, according to Henry Mayhew.[6] Sprat nets were used in Southwold to catch smelts since both fish were of similar size. In Scotland the word for smelts was *sparlings*, an interesting circularity which merges sprat and smelt in name and mesh size.

The sprat fishery was the most important one of the year for the Southwold longshoremen because, if good, it allowed them to discharge the debts they had accumulated with various shopkeepers during the year. It is perhaps surprising therefore that it has been so little documented. This account from Mr Jarvis is thus welcome for its rarity:

'When we used t' go sprattin' it wuz from November. We allus reckoned t' get sprats on Lord Mayor's Day (I forget the date o' Lord Mayor's Day) an' onward till Christmas in the ol' days or till just after Christmas, then you'd pack up.

The length o' a sprat net is eight fathom an' the depth is *ten-score*. A score is twenty meshes, half inch square or near enough, so with the ten-score an' the piece o' *oddy* or *herren-lint* of nine inches [this was attached to the norsels and the sprat net was attached to the oddy], the depth o' a sprat net would be roughly nine feet deep.[7] Some had deeper nets, *twelve-score* deep for a shoot on the flood. When the tide is a-flowin', you shoot your nets further from the shore, about a mile, as the sprats don't rise on a flood shoot like they do on an ebb shoot.

We used t' go off from the pier with fifteen nets an' go about a quarter-o'-a-mile on the first hour o' the ebb [i.e. north] an' shoot twelve nets an' keep three in the boat. We used t' row for about a quarter-o'-an-hour, then we'd look at the outer part, where we'd done shootin', t' see if there wuz any sprats. If there wuzn't a good shoal, we'd row t' the inner part an' then if they were gettin' in there, 'em three nets we'd kept back, which wuz an ol' trick, we'd tie on the inner part where the sprats were. I've seen the time, I remember once, we shot from the pier driftin' north, ten or twelve nets, an' by the time we put the last net over, we had t' haul straight back as they were sinkin' right away, an' within less than a quarter-o'-a-mile we'd hauled sixty *bushels* o' sprats.[8] On one occasion in two nets, the sprats hit 'em, they turned 'em on the water like a carpet with their heads stickin' out of the water an' makin' a sizzlin' noise. I think if I had a costume on, I think I could have walked on 'em an' they'd have held me up. They were like a mat. If they'd have came, all the nets like that, they'd have eventually died an' sunk an' the nets would've went t' the ground an' we'd have lost 'em. We had t' haul 'em in. One wuz on the corks pullin' the corks in, one wuz on the bottom lint an' I wuz in the middle helpin' t' lift em in, otherwise the nets would have rent t' pieces.

On an ebb shoot, as I say, we'd go about a quarter-o'- a-mile but as the tide fall further away, you shoot further off (well, the length o' the pier, which used t' be say about a half mile off the beach, outside the pier). As the tide fell away, the sprats 'ud work off further from the shore. So if you were late or anythin', you wouldn't shoot quarter-o'-a-mile from the shore, say two hours after high water, you'd shoot from the pier, an' so on. On the flood shoot, [i.e south] you'd turn Lowestoft light red an' white, you'd be out a good way.

By shootin' there, your nets would *lay*. By lay, I mean in a line at an angle from say south t' north. The outer end would be south an' the inner end 'ud be north. If you shot anywhere different t' that position, they'd all curl up an' wouldn't fish at all. You'd get what they called *chittle-nets*; they twiddled 'emselves up into knots, an' you'd have a deuce o' a job when you got ashore too![9] The sprats on a flood shoot never used t' rise very high, very rarely they'd come up more than six or eight inches. They'd be as thick as bees an' all the rest o' the net hadn't got nuthin' in it. So that wuz allus considered the time t' go wuz on the low water, low water for preference. Then you'd patrol above 'em with your boat, [i.e. underrun] only oars, no motor, watchin' out for *lines, dans* [i.e. cod lines and their marker-buoys] which were there, 'cos if they went through your nets, they'd rend 'em.'

It might be worth pausing here to compare Mr Jarvis' account with one David Butcher has written about the practice at Pakefield in the 1950s and 60s. Mr Jarvis makes clear that sprats could be caught on an ebb or a flood tide. If they were taken on the ebb the nets would be shot from a quarter to half a mile off depending on the state of the tide. If taken on the flood, the longshoremen would go much further out, a mile or so, until they could see the Lowestoft lighthouse winking red and white. Here the nets did not become entangled in each other but lay 'true', the outer ones being pushed more south because of the greater strength of the tide further out and the inner ones hanging back more to the north where the tide was less strong. He also tells of the phenomenon of sprats hitting a net in such density that they raised them to the surface and seemed almost to form a 'carpet' that could be walked on. He mentions the curious 'sizzling' noise they made as they swarmed in the nets with their noses out of the water.

'The Pakefield men,' wrote David Butcher, 'always shot their nets on the ebb tide when working inside, taking the last of the flood up to Kessingland and then coming back down on the first of the ebb, or rowing up against the first of the ebb and coming back down on the second half of the tide. It is always said that sprats were only caught on the ebb tide inside the buoys [that marked the Barnard sands], and only on the flood tide outside them. One man put it this way: "That seem as if they went up on the flood to Sowle and then come back down on the ebb."…Sometimes when a good swim of sprats hit the net (the usual number was about twelve or thirteen), the lints hanging where the shoal was densest might have their entire spread brought up onto the surface. When this occurred all that could be seen in fisherman's parlance, was "loads of little ow green snouts stickin' up out o' the water". What had to be done then, and quickly, was for extra buoyancy floats (tin gallon cans were a great favourite) to be secured to the headline before the fish swam down and took the net with them.'[10]

There is therefore a remarkable correlation between the two accounts showing how the practice was much the same in both places.

Mr Jarvis then went on to talk about the nets in more detail:

'These nets were made o' cotton. You'd buy the cotton nets then oil 'em in boiled linseed oil, an' then hang 'em up t' drain in the shed. You had t' be very careful not t' leave 'em in a heap 'cos they'd heat an' burn. We used t' get nice dry weather an' dry 'em an' then they were nice an' soft an' pliable. They outfish any o' these modern nylon nets, 'cos these nylon nets are too brittle. If you shake a nylon net t' shake sprats out, you'll get mostly the heads left in the net; they won't shake out o' a nylon net like they do a cotton net. As the nets began t' get older you would possibly tan 'em, but a white net, oiled net, will outfish a tanned net three times over.

The cotton nets, some are still used today an' they're over thirty and forty year ol'. In 'em days they used t' look after the gear. If there wuz a norsel which hold the net t' the net-ropes, you'd have t' spread all the nets out on the beach t'dry, an' if there wuz a norsel or a cork missin', you'd have t' put 'em in every time you dried 'em. When there wuz sprats about, after you cleaned the nets, you had t' take 'em all down t' the water's edge agin an' wash 'em, haul 'em through the water, tip the barrer near the breakers an' haul 'em back on t' the barrer. You wouldn't leave four or five nets on the barrer, you'd leave about three 'cos they'd heat 'cos o' the oil an' stuff from the sprats.

You don't use round corks on a sprat net or on the local herren nets 'cos they're a darn nuisance. The nets get hooked up around 'em. You used all flat corks an' on the end o' every fisherman's net is his initials. So if you lose some or somebody pinch one, you knew your net. Used t' be C J [Charlie Jarvis] or W H P [Will Herrington Pilot] or J C [John Cragie]. They used t' be what they called the *net's-head cork*. The sides o' the net were called the headin's an' they were o' braidin', thicker than the rest. The rope along the top wuz the net-rope. If there were two ordinary bits o' net-rope, right-handed, they would twist up, so you had t' have left-hand an' right-hand so they would pull against each other, otherwise they would tangle, twist up. The norsels

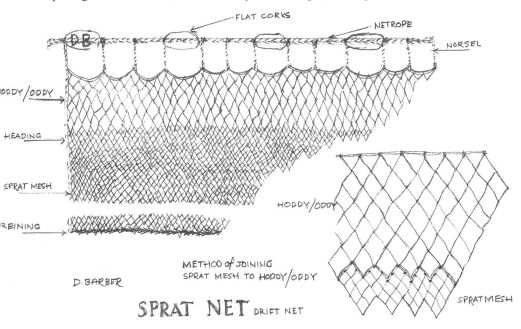

FLAT CORKS

NETROPE

NORSEL

ODDY/ODDY

HEADING

SPRAT MESH

REINING

HODDY/ODDY

D. BARBER

METHOD of JOINING
SPRAT MESH TO HODDY/ODDY

SPRAT NET DRIFT NET

SPRAT MESH

191

were on the oddy, an' put round each side o' each cork t' keep the cork in position. Every six inches, near enough, there wuz a norsel. The oddy wuz a larger mesh an' that attached t' the lint o' the sprat-net. What they used t' do when they got some new nets, rather than go t' too much work, they used t' cut the sprat net off the oddy an' then put the new sprat net on, if the oddy wuz good an' the net-ropes were good, they used t' put the new sprat net on the ol' oddy. The oddy had a herren mesh. If they found they were gettin' herren in the oddy, they'd say, "There's herren about," an' they might put a herren net in. At the bottom wuz the *reining*, about four strands o' thin cotton, laced along the bottom t' form a reinin' or an edgin'.'[11]

Mr Jarvis spoke next about the best conditions for spratting and some of the tricks the longshoremen practised to outdo each other when fishing:

'The best sort o' weather for sprattin' wuz after a south-west wind an' then come off the land from the west so you could nicely get there. I've known it t' blow southerly an' then fly off t' the west, or sou', sou' west so the sea calm down a bit an' away you'd go an' you'd get the sprats. The ol' people used t' say the sprats, they come out o' Dingle marshes, [between Walberswick and Dunwich] an' that proves my sayin' about south-west or south winds. There were exceptions. I can remember one particular day all the fishermen were on the beach an' two fellers, they were fishermen's sons, they pushed off in a little boat an' the ol' boys said they'd be lucky t' see one. The wind had been easterly an' then come off the land, an' the easterly swell wuz still in the water, an' with a few nets they got about ten bushels which wuz sickenin' for the ol' men 'cos they said they'd be lucky t' see one![12] But a white net for your life! two t' one if you got ten bushels out o' ten black nets, you'd get thirty out o' white nets, every time!

There wuz a sayin', "You can't get sprats in the dark". Well my brother, Sid an' m'self, we used t' have a little boat an' we used t' go off with one net, ol' net we got hold o', off the end o' the pier an' we used t' get a bucketful o' sprats in the dark.'

It is interesting to note on both these points how the practice at Pakefield compared. David Butcher once again corroborates Mr Jarvis, thus: 'The best weather for sprats was reckoned to be the mild, muggy sort that sometimes occurs in winter, with a gentle southwesterly or southerly breeze blowing.' And, 'There was a preference for shootin' nets at dawn, but this was subordinate to the dictates of tides and when they were running.'[13]

Mr Jarvis again:

'An' another sayin' too is, an' thass right, I've bin steamin' up Dunwich bight an' they'd bin jumpin' out like sparks, just before daylight, jumpin' everywhere, an' you'd say, "Coh! This is the place t' shoot," an' you'd shoot two nets p'raps an' you wouldn't catch none. When they jump out a lot you'd never get many in your nets for some reason.

It's the same if you go t' Siz'ell sluice an' shoot. If you haven't got no sprats in your net by the time you get t' Dunwich cliff, you might as well haul an' come back 'cos you won't get none driftin' under Dunwich cliffs. In front o' the town from here [East cliff] t' the Ness, Covehithe Ness, yes, but apart from that you don't get many. Why that should be, I can't tell you!

The ol' boys – I'll tell you this trick an' I never knew it, an' I'd been a-sprattin' with my father an' 'em a good while – they would walk up an' down the sea-front near the pier when the high water wuz a-fallin'. The Kessin'land boats used t' come up t' the pier, an' as soon as the tide started t' fall, they would shoot. But the ol' fishermen wouldn't. They'd stand there an' wait an' wait. All o' a sudden they'd make a move. The reason for that wuz, I didn't learn till some time arterwards, the tide had fell enough so that they could see the cross-walin's under the pier. They'd say, "Oh, the sand-bearin's are out," an' I used t' wonder what they meant. Then they'd go. Well, that wuzn't 'cos they were showin' but 'cos the tide had fell that far to show 'em an' they knew that wuz the best time t' go, which wuz p'raps two hours after high water. The Kessin'land boats had drifted away by then. Then they'd go, an' if they didn't get any by the time they got down t' the beginnin' o' Easton cliffs, 'cos the nets set off there, they'd haul an' come back again.

I know another trick they used t' do. I wuz with the Hurrs, a lot o' brothers. They used t' shoot just before daylight, 'cos you reckoned t' go sprattin' in the daylight an' they'd go early t' get a berth, get a place. Well we used t' come just before that wuz daylight, an' the artful ol' boys, they'd come t' some nets, pull 'em up if there wuz sprats in 'em an' over go their nets. When it come t' daylight there wuz such a row! Well, they'd got a good excuse, "We never knew they were there," they'd say. But if there wuzn't any sprats in 'em nets, they'd go along an' look at some more! That wuz rather a dirty trick, but that wuz all in the game.[14]

The shootin' o' the nets wuz very important in sprattin'. You shot as near as you can from west t' south-east. You wouldn't shoot straight off [at right angles to the beach] but more t' the south-east 'cos you know your outer part is goin' t' *turn down*. The more the nets are along the tide, the more the meshes are shut. Once you'd shot, you'd have a look, then you'd row along halfway an' have a look. You'd keep havin' a look, row about. Sometimes you'd see the net-rope go right under all o' a sudden. You'd say, "Hullo! What's that? That's a cod in the net." You'd row gently up an' that'd be a cod rolled up in the net. I've seen sprats get in the nets so quick they'd put extra bowls, wooden bowls they called 'em, or tin cans on if the nets looked like they were goin' t' sink. They'd hurry an' tie some tin cans or even push an oar under the net ropes t' hold 'em up. Sometimes they'd be in four or five nets as thick as bees. The other nets p'raps hadn't got any in. That shoal had struck there.

For haulin', there'd be one on the net-rope, one on the lint an' one on the oars t' keep it open so the stern didn't go into the nets. So there'd allus be three men. I have known two do it, but it's hard work. Allus three. The boy wuz on the oars, the *paddles* as they called 'em, t' keep her *open*, that is t' say, you'd keep her stern clear. They used t' haul in with some sense you know, with all these sprats. I've seen boats get so many in the nets they couldn't get 'em, so they'd leave half the nets an' wave t' somebody ashore – 'cos they were allus watchin' each other like a cat watch a mouse – they'd come out with a boat an' haul your nets what you couldn't take, an' they were entitled t' the fish in 'em, which wuz fair enough. But there is some weight in 'em especially when they turned the net right onto the top o' the water like a *trum-carpet* – you've seen these ol'-fashioned carpets women used t' make, my mother used t' make 'em. They were hissin' all the time. I can guarantee you could walk on 'em. An' thass a remarkable thing, when you're a-sprattin', generally a big, dark gull, he'll hold the nets up for the others! We used t' take stones, rattle, bang, keep frightin' on 'em away. But that din't make no difference, they weren't frightened o' you.

If you'd got a lot o' sprats, you'd come sailin' in – that wuz very rare you rowed – an' you'd pray that when you went across the shoal you wouldn't catch a wave 'cos the punt wuz liable t' broach-to, turn right round. So I used t' get for'ard with a pair o' oars an' my father used t' get a pair o' oars an' we dare not put 'em right in the water if she start t' broach 'cos if you did the oars 'ud snap the thole-pins off like carrots. We'd keep just puttin' 'em in t' keep her straight. That wuz the worst part runnin' across that shoal in a heavy sea 'cos they had a square stern.

When you come ashore there'd be plenty o' help. You'd run up t' the ol'-fashioned crab an' haul the boat out an' then you'd bring a big cover an' lay that over the sand or the shingle. You'd bring your net-barrer t' haul the nets on t' an' stand that about six or eight feet away from the boat. If you got a lot o' sprats, one would be in the boat an' he'd shake 'em an' they'd fall in a space in the boat what they left when they hauled the nets out. There'd be one on the corks an' one on the lints near the net-barrer an' you'd pick the ones out he'd missed. There'd be a lot he missed. They'd land on the cover.

Shaking out sprats. Note the flat corks on the nets. Tom *Kinie* Palmer (back left) Frank *Frenchman* Palmer (front right). The boat is the *Edward Thomas*.

Once you got 'em all out, you'd start carryin' 'em up the beach. I've helped carry as many as sixty bushels at 6d. a bushel. The merchants 'ud measure a bushel every now an' agin which wuz a basket heaped full with a proper measure t' see if they were gettin' their whack. They were measured in a bushel basket level full – that'd be about four stone. The merchants had a proper measure. That wuz like an ol' dustbin, made o' aluminum metal

195

an' that'd got t' be level full. Every now an' then they'd say, "Pour one into here an' see how many you got." They wouldn't do every one. They'd do 'em now an' agin. You'd fill your boxes from the baskets. O' course that wuz hard work carryin'; you'd got t' carry the sprats about fifty yards right across the beach, right t' where they were puttin' 'em in boxes. On your shoulder. A bushel o' sprats, that wuzn't very light. You used t' have t' hold 'em so they din't run off down the back o' your neck. And then you've got all 'em nets t' wash in the sea again. They'd be washed an' put on the barrers, four on a barrer, sometimes three in case they heated. They'd heat up like compost. You could put your hand in an' feel the heat – that wuz all the oil an' scales off the sprats.'

In the summer of 1909, A.H. Patterson, (pseudonymously John Knowlittle), a respected Yarmouth naturalist and a prolific writer of the natural history of Broadland visited Lowestoft, Southwold and Aldeburgh in order to list as many species of fish as he could find, the result being *Rough Notes on the Fish and Fisheries of East Suffolk* (1909). Patterson learnt from one of the Southwold fish merchants, H. J. Sayers that:

'the number of boats working out of that port in Sprat-time is about fifty. Fishing commences at the end of October, and lasts till about the middle of December. Sprats, he assured me, realized from three shillings to eight shillings per bushel, but I might take the average at five shillings. An average catch of some fifty to sixty bushels was the take per boat, with average earnings of from £10 to £15; £20 was reckoned exceptional. None were sold last year for manure; a few were smoked, the majority being sent away fresh.'[15]

The reference to sprats being sold for manure is of interest. Whenever there was a glut, the price fell so much that they would be bought by local farmers who spread them on the land as fertiliser. One occurrence at Kessingland saw a local farmer send his men to the beach to load the catch into tumbrils which he had bought at 6d a bushel. It was then spread on the fields. 'The seagulls watched with interest. By one or two o'clock, the fields of Manor Farm were white, not silver, as the gulls ate every sprat there was. The farmer didn't get any, in the end.'[16]

After the First World war a change took place in the way the

Southwold longshoremen sold their fish. Until then fish were mostly bought on the beach by local merchants and sold on by them, some of which were sent to Billingsgate by rail. Edward (Ted) May (b. 1901) takes up the story:

'We started the fish run after the 1914 war. I can't exactly tell you the time now but that wuz after the 1914 war. Actually what happened wuz, we had some sprats. We had about twelve boxes an' Dunton [a merchant] said there weren't twelve in 'em, there wuz only nine. And ol' 'King' Steadman, he said there wuz twelve. So what we did, we went in for a lorry an' carted our own. Father said if they were going t' do us like that we'd get our own lorry.

We got this Ford. That wuz about £40 then an' we started t' cart our own down to Low'stoft. Dunton had been payin' us about three bob for a bushel – we had ours in a four-stone box – an' o' course the first lot o' sprats made ten shillin's. I said t' the salesman, "Han't you made a mistake?" He said, "No." 'Cos they took their commission an' also the dues an' they gave us the residue. He said, "No. Why?" I said, "We're not used t' this money," I said. "The merchant's only bin givin' us three shillin's." "Coh!" he said. "They've bin robbin' you right an' left."

Well we gradually got more sprats. When people went into a pub they said, "What did you get for your sprats?" They'd say, "We got so much." An' people began t' say, "Would you cart ours?" Father said, "Thass up t' you." So we took theirs as well. We went an' got fifty boxes from Low'stoft, then we got a hundred – as we got the boats we got the boxes. We had two Fords by then an' we were gettin' so many boats as well as cartin' bricks when we weren't fishin', that we got a Bedford, a long wheel-based Bedford so we could cart a hundred boxes at a time. An' later we got a Morris.

As I say, we gradually built up so we had about eighteen or twenty boats; some were from the harbour an' some went off the beach from this side of the pier [Klondike]. What we used t' do, we used t' get so many out o' each boat t' make a load up. We din't wait t' take 'em all out – but if they were all out we took 'em – but we'd take so many out o' each boat an' we'd take 'em down. We used t' say t' the salesman, "There'll be some more." So what they did they averaged the price right up. Sometimes your first lot o' sprats 'ud make a shillin' or sixpence more 'n the last lot; or sometimes you could go down an' your last lot could make p'raps two or three bob more than your first lot, so they averaged 'em all out, so they all got the same. That wuz the same for herren an' trawl fish as well. We used t' cart for Denny [another merchant who had longshoremen fishing for him], used t' go down an' cart his stuff an' bring his stuff home. Make a bit o' a journey o' it. If anybody like the butchers wanted any ice, we used to bring a cut or two o' ice for 'em.'

A letter entitled 'The Sprat-Fisher's Remuneration' published in the local press on December 4th, 1918 complained of the 'inordinate profiteering' of the retailers who bought sprats at two shillings a bushel and sold at 4d. a lb, thereby netting 18s. 8d per bushel for their two shillings outlay. "Is this just? The writer, SOUTHWOLDER asked rhetorically. This treatment, perhaps the immediate cause of the Mays carting to Lowestoft, is indicative of the difficulties the longshoremen faced in selling their catches.

At the start of his conversation with me, Mr Jarvis said he couldn't remember the date of Lord Mayor's Day. The Lord Mayor in question is London's and until 1959, the date was November 9th. Sprats were traditionally part of the banquet held in his honour and we can imagine him and the dignitaries feasting on those caught at South-wold. A broadside ballad of 1851 references the banquet as follows:

> At night so grand, so gay and fine,
> What numbers will sit down to dine,
> On pig and mutton, beef and wine,
> With the Lord Mayor of London.
> Rolls and butter, bacon fat,
> Eels and herrings, this & that
> Ginger pop and pickled sprats
> With the Lord Mayor of London.

Henry Mayhew gave a vivid account of the selling of sprats on the streets of London in *London Labour and the London Poor* (1850) which began on Lord Mayor's Day, also known as 'sprat day'. They were bought at Billingsgate by the *toss* or *chuck*, a half bushel measure, which Mayhew gives as between forty to fifty lbs and were then were sold in the streets by the pennyworth at fixed points or 'pitches'. According to Mayhew, the costermongers took

£10,000 between them over a ten week season. Sprats were regarded as a 'blessing to the poor'.

In the case of the Southwold men, the sprat season was the one they relied on to get them off *living on tick*. In the two years before 1880, the fishing was so bad that the Church set up a scheme of net-making to employ the men through the winter. By contrast the 1913 sprat season was the best in living memory (this year also saw the highest number of deep-sea herring ever caught in the *Home Fishing*).[17] It was reported that 'The sprats made the nets look like silver' and that in the week of December 12th the longshoremen took 5,500 bushels, approximately ten million fish. 'This is the best harvest that the longshoremen have had for many years and is particularly acceptable as the fates have been very unkind throughout the year, the trawl and herring fishing being failures.'[18]

Mr Jarvis put it like this:

'Sometimes durin' the sprattin' season we got so many sprats that there wuz no real market for 'em, only for manure for the land at 6d. a bushel, sometimes less. But we still used t' go 'cos every penny counted an' the reason wuz this. Durin' the year we had some very understandin' grocers an' different shopkeepers about Southwold who would let you have things on trust an' you'd pay when the sprattin' season came round, which wuz honoured, mostly, by the fishermen. If not then, possibly they might get a good herren fishin', then pay up. I can remember the doctors about here, they always used t' come, as there wuz no National Health. Sometimes you'd get some money an' sometimes you paid it off, the bill, if you got a good herren or sprattin' fishin' so that prove how hard things were at that particular time.'

Notes

1   *Southwold Borough Collection* 491/3/4/2/8, Lowestoft Records Office

2   Arnott, W.G. *Alde Estuary* p.50

3   Lewis, Rev. R.W. M. *Walberswick Churchwardens' Accounts 1450-1499*

4   Bailey, Mark, ed. *The Bailiff's Minute Book of Dunwich 1404-1430*

5   Butcher, David *Rigged for River and Sea* p.172

6   Mayhew, Henry *Life and Labour of the London Poor Vol 1* p.69-70

7   Oddy/oddie/hoddy: 'the reinforced meshes at the top and bottom of a drift-net.'
Butcher, David *Fishing Talk* p.55. In this case the oddy was made from a herring net

8   A bushel weighed about 4 stone

9   'a term used of drift-nets when the lint rolled up around the head-rope...there may be a reference to pigs' intestines here, in that a chittled net might be supposed to have resembled twisted guts.' *Fishing Talk* p.16

10   Butcher, David *From The Catcher's Angle* p.68

11   'strips of old net fastened to the bottom of longshore drift-nets, which served to weight them down and make them hang better in the water.' *Fishing Talk* p.64

12   The longshoremen hated easterly winds because the fish were dragged further out to sea by counter-currents beneath the surface. Flatfish also buried themselves into the sea-bed. The swell, which was also present with a north or north-west wind, was called a *logie-swell*. Butcher, David *The Last Haul* p.68n, 74

13   *From the Catcher's Angle* p.68

14   This is the kind of practice Emerson was referring to when he wrote that the 'fisherfolk' could be 'mean and harrassing' of each other

15   Patterson, A.H. *Rough Notes on the Fish and Fisheries of East Suffolk* p.6

16   Anonymous author self-styled as *West Wind Give Time, Time Songs and Tales of A Longshoreman* Author's collection

17   Butcher, David *The Driftermen* p.14

18   Allen Collection, Southwold Museum 2006.62

16

Baiting The Lines

'For cod we used t' get up about five o'clock in the mornin', have a cup o' tea an' a piece o' bread an' butter, walk down t' the harbour, pull your boots on, wait for the daylight, put all the lines in the boat already baited up from the night before, row two-an'-a-half t' three mile off an' shoot the lines, drop anchor. You'd *lay the tide* for six hours an' then haul, get fish from one end o' the boat t' the other, enormous cods (the Al'bro' boys used t' call 'em *man-cods*) they were about as big as a man. Then you'd have t' sit down, row the three mile back home, start packin' up about nine o'clock, get back home at about ten, eleven o'clock at night an' sit in the back kitchen some-times an' bait up the lines at the back o' the house for the next mornin'. They were hard times. An' for the biggest cod you'd be lucky if he offered you a shillin' each for 'em. The fishermen were definitely exploited in 'em days. You'd never see a fishmonger with his coat off.'

Rory Tooke's condensed memories of the practice of longlining recall the hard work for little reward he experienced. The longshore-men went longlining for cod after the sprat season had finished in late November or December. If the fishery was good, they would extend into January before stopping altogether until March when the spring-herring season began. These were used as longlining bait for *roker* [thornback ray] and the yearly round began again. Longlining was thus the last fishery of the year.

The method, in principle, was straightforward enough, as Mr. Tooke's account makes clear. Baited hooks on short lengths of twine called *snoods* (pronounced *snuds*) were attached to lines which were shot from the boat and anchored. They were allowed to *lay* for the duration of a tide before being hauled and the fish, cod in the winter, roker in the spring, manhandled aboard, often with the aid of a gaff. Once back home the lines had to be baited again before the next day's fishing could commence. This longshore version of lining was the scaled down practice of a fishery that was ancient and had taken men from this coast far away to Iceland in the Middle Ages.

Mr Tooke's brief account is the only one I recorded in Southwold, a real gap, but Emerson captured it both in words and in an extraordinary print, *Baiting the line.*

'The cod-lines are forty fathoms long and have thirty-five hooks to the line. Each boat has a crew of four men, and the lines, anchors and buoys are by them taken out to sea and set. The lines are sunk with small anchors, two anchors being attached to eighty fathoms of line, or one anchor to each line. The position of the line marked with buoys, four being placed for every forty lines and anchored with eight-pound anchors, while the lines themselves are sunk with pound-and-a-half anchors; and, to make things secure, two twelve-pound anchors called "end-anchors" placed at the end of each system of lines. The lines, once sunk, are left to be revisited later. When they have to be examined, the buoy is first hauled in; then anchors weighed, the cod-line unbent and passed aft to a man whose duty is to coil the line as it comes in to a basket and to unbend the anchors. Two other men hold the oars whilst the fourth man stands forward with a *cod-pick* in his hand (a weapon fashioned like a shepherd crook with a handle three feet long, and the steel crook very sharp). He pulls in the line and picks or gaffs the cod with his pick as they come up, landing them in the boat and twisting the hooks out of their mouths with the same implement. The boat is then rowed ashore, and the cod immediately packed in regulation boxes. Four good-sized fish of the average size of twelve pounds the fish, will fill a box. The men get from five to twenty shillings a box... In the middle of November the sprats arrive, and from that day herrings are no longer used as bait, but only sprats. The Southwold fishermen do not think much of the cod taken before the sprats are in. Before that time these fish are called by them *herring-cod*, and afterwards *sprat-cod*. The first fish caught with herring-bait are called *November starches*, because they say there is no flesh in them. But the sprat-cod, they say are *the* fish, and are looked for in the middle of November. The best fish, we are informed is a sprat-cod weighing at most ten pounds and having a round black back – the blacker the better.'[1]

Baiting the line is a tremendous composition taken on the beach at the bottom of South Green. The Reading Room is mistily visible at Long Island with the look-out below jutting out of the cliff. What appears to be snow or sleet on the beach indicates the time of year.

Four bearded longshoremen, one white-slopped, two ganseyed, one in a duffel jacket, each with different headgear, two with their Dunwich clays, sit side by side looking down baiting the lines and coiling them into baskets.[2] As before, work is the focal point of the composition. A line-anchor can be seen in front of them, three barrels and a buff. Behind the men is a punt, apparently belonging to another longshoreman, seaward, who is looking at his nets on a *net-barrow*, posed by Emerson there to provide depth. The beach stretches back in differential focus behind the foregrounded sitters beyond Long Island to Kilcock where punts stand facing the sea. Its length is magnificently echoed in the skyscape above creating a long perspective. This is the beach as workplace.

Baiting the line P. H. Emerson c.1886

Tony Warner from Kessingland gave me a much fuller account of lining at Kessingland, having picked up the practice from his grandfather.

'They would start longlinin' about now, after the sprats, late November, December an' go through the winter. They'd leave a barrow-load o' nets so they could get some sprats for bait t' begin with. They'd go linin' for cod in the winter until about March, if they could get enough bait. Then they'd have the *spring-herren* an' they'd use 'em as bait for roker, as well as send the herren down t' Low'stoft market for sale. Ol' Benji Saywack would go herrenin' on his own in his small boat (about thirteen foot) with twelve nets an' use the spring-herren for bait 'cos he always said, "If I can get enough herren, I'll get a good week's work." They'd go for roker till May, June an' send 'em down t' the market at Low'stoft. They'd sell one or two here, if people wanted 'em, but most they'd send down. In those days a couple o' quid wuz a good day's work. They'd have only got about thirty bob a week on the farms, I s'pose. An' also Harold Brown, he used t' go after dogs, dog-fish. I remember when I wuz about twelve, I'd see him come here. He'd be full up! Poor ol' Harold. Character!

A longline wuz forty fathom. Thass normal. Some o' 'em were a bit longer 'n that, but forty fathom. You'd put an eye in each end o' the line. You'd use one eye t' join the line t' the next one. You'd do that with a *sheet-bend*. You'd put a hook on the line every fathom an' a foot. You'd use a snud for that. A snud wuz a length o' twine about fifteen t' eighteen inches long, which in 'em days wuz two bits o' twine rolled over each other. That formed an eye at the end an' the eye wuz put through the hook an' over the back t' secure it. The hooks were size number six, galvanized in 'em days. They'd come from Stuart's or Bridport in Low'stoft. The other end o' the snud wuz attached t' the longline in the same way as a norsel wuz attached t' net, t' stop it slippin'. A line wuz forty fathom so that worked out at thirty-one or thirty-two hooks.

When we baited, we had a galvanised bath an' you had t' keep the lines in the bath. We'd bait with sprats, mackerel, spring-herren (nowadays they use squid) an' in 'em days we'd use whelks. You'd smash the whelks with a bit o' hardwood. The whelks came from up Wells. They used t' come t' Low'stoft an' you'd pick 'em up there. They say that roker could crush a whelk but I've never seen it! Mind you, they've got a hard ol' mouth. You could feel it when you gut 'em sometimes. If you used a herren [for bait] you'd slice 'em right across in six or seven places, dependin' on the size. You'd put the hook through the top o' the herren and hitch it back round the bone t' make it hold better. You'd use a whole sprat. It would take roughly an hour t' do a whole bath which had nine or ten lines in it. Some-times you'd be a bit slower 'cos you had t' put a few hooks on or another snud. I have baited on lugworm. That got so expensive you couldn't afford it. The baths were galvanised, about two-an'-a-half t' three foot long an' eighteen inches or so wide an' tapered at the bottom. You'd put the first eye through the handle o' the bath. You'd use that eye for the *big-anchor* when you were shootin' away. You had t' remember t' take it out o' the handle or you'd shoot the bath as well! That happened! You'd put that first eye through the handle an' start t' coil the line around the bath, clockwise. You'd come t' your first hook, bait that an' coil the line over it two or three times then come t' the next hook an' do the same thing an' keep followin' like that. You'd aim to keep the line level as you went round 'till you fill the bath up. You did it that way t' stop it gettin' snagged up. When you'd finish one line you'd join it t' the next with the sheet-bend at the eye. The eyes were all placed over the edge o' the bath consecutively. That allowed you t' put the *line-anchor* on t' the eye as you were shootin' away. The line-anchors kept the line on the bottom o' the sea-bed. They'd have three or four baths in the boat but no more than thirty-five lines 'cos you've got t' hand – haul all o' 'em an' that wuz hard work!

In the punts they shot by rowin' across the tide, just after slack water. You went across 'cos if you shot down the tide the lines wouldn't lie right; they'd spin round an' round in the tide an' wind up. Across the tide would push out the hooks an' raise 'em up a bit. You'd aim t' shoot east t' west as best as you could. If you were on an ebb you'd get a bit more north an' on a flood you'd be a bit south.

First you'd shoot the *dan* away which wuz called the *dan-tow* an' about a fathom or so behind that you'd tie a little *buff* on which would take the force o' the tide off the dan an' allow it t' stand up. Even so, on the top o' the tide that buff'd be under water sometimes, the tide wuz so strong. Then you'd have your *dan-anchor*,[3] about three foot high with big flukes (it'd hold the punt) which had a cord on it an' you'd attach the first line to that cord. Then you'd pull [row] away, let go o' the big dan-anchor an' you'd start shootin' away. You'd flick the lines out with a stick; sometimes you'd use the other end o' the gaff. You'd got t' make sure you didn't get a hook in your fingers. I wuz with Dick Turrell once an' he got one. I said, "I'll have t' get you t' hospital." He said, "No. That on't be in there when I get ashore." We cut the snud an' he wriggled it out. The barb wuz right in his finger. Blood wuz a-going every-where! You wouldn't feel it so much in the cold, would you?

When you got t' the end o' a line, you put the *little-anchor* into the eye at the end, but you had t' tie it on before you shot it out. The little-anchors lay on the rail o' the boat so they were all ready. You'd hold the eye with the anchor in t' your body, shoot a couple o' hooks o' the next line an' then let go. You'd carry on like that till you come t' the end o' the bath. The last line had already been joined t' the top line in the next bath an' away you'd go again. If you had three baths – thirty lines – the last line in the bottom o' the last bath, you'd attach t' the other dan-anchor. You'd let it come tight an' then cast it off. There wuz also a buff with that. So there's a dan one end an' a dan the other. There'd be about nine hundred hooks in the water. It'd take about fifteen to twenty minutes t' shoot that lot.

You'd lay the tide. You could be out there for five t' six hours or more. That'd be really cold this time o' year. My feet always got cold. In the punts the ol' boys didn't even have rubber gloves, only mittens their wives had knitted. If they'd sailed up t' Cove [hithe] say, they've got t' get back an' that'd take about an hour. So they would start haulin' just before the slack water, half-an-hour or so before. Then once they'd hauled, the tide 'ud help 'em back. It wuz best t' haul over the slack part o' the tide 'cos that wuz easier than if a tide wuz runnin'. You'd aim t' have it all hauled on the slack. On the top o' the tide you'd start a bit earlier when you saw the buff come up. Then you'd get t' work. You'd go into the bow an' pull in the tow-anchor first. You'd really feel that as it came up. As soon as you'd got the dan-tow

LONG LINES (SET)

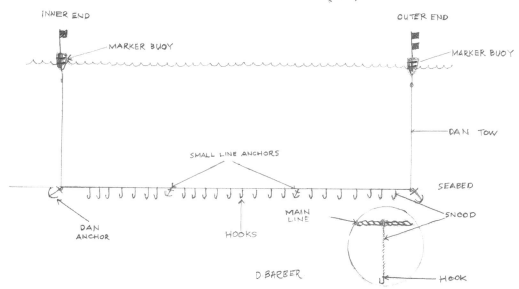

206

Packing the cod for the London Market, Southwold c.1886, P.H. Emerson

out then you were all right. Then you'd haul. The first part o' the line wuz quite easy but the second half that wuz attached t' the little-anchor wuz harder 'cos the boat would come up t' it. You'd got t' get the fish off at the same time o' course. If that wuz a big fish that hadn't hooked much, you'd use the gaff, yank the fish off with a flick o' the wrist. You'd chuck the fish into the *wing*.

Dependin' what you got that could take an hour, sometimes an hour-an'-a-half. Sailin' an' rowin' back could take an hour or so, so you could be out there seven or eight hours at least. An' o' course you'd got t' gut the fish as you're comin' back as well, one lookin' after the boat, the other guttin' an' washin' the fish. You've got t' land the boat, pull it up the beach, then box the fish, get the baths out. Those days you could leave the dans an' anchors in the boat – no-one would touch 'em but you couldn't do that now.

In the old days the carters here would take the boxes t' Low'stoft. The fishermen had so many boxes. They called 'em *pool boxes*. They put so much money in an' they were in common. They were stamped on the sides *Kessingland Pool Box*. Dependin' on the weather you'd then bait for the next day or wait till you could go again. Wooden ships, iron men!'

By its very nature longshoring was local, adapted to the particular conditions offshore by particular fishing communities. While the deep-sea fleets necessarily attracted migratory labour, following the herring down the North Sea for example, it was very unusual for longshoremen to fish anywhere other than from home. During my recordings I was told that for some years in the 1920s longshoremen from Cromer travelled to Southwold to go lining for cod during the season. I went to Cromer and spoke to John (Jack) Davies, (b.1909) a member of a famous Cromer fishing family who told me:

'I went down in 1922, that wuz in the *Boy Jack*, an' I think the *Q, J & J* wuz there an' the *Admiral Jellicoe* an' the *Morning Star*, but there wuz three *hovellers* at one period, the *Puffing Billy* wuz the other one.[4] We went t' fish – longlinin'. There wuz more fish that way than there wuz this way. In fact there wuz more liners from Cromer than there wuz Southwold so we had room t' spread out a bit. We went into lodgin's. Mr Stimson, I wuz with, his sister put us up, but the others in the *Q, J & J* an' that, went into different lodgin's, only about three or four houses at Blackshore. One chap, we called him *Cock-a-doodle*, his wife went down an' looked after the others in a empty house. Thass how they done. We kept the boats at Blackshore, up the river: no, the only time we went t' the beach wuz when the *Morning Star* turned over goin' ashore. That wuz Billy Davies an' Acy Davies. Acy Davies come from Overstrand.

We'd spend the day at sea. Get up an' go out, haul the lines. Then we used t' take so many lines again t' *lay in*, so they laid all night. Used t' then come home an' you'd be a-baitin' in this ol' place next t' the pub. They used t' have little ol' flares, *duck-lamps* they called 'em, for light; no electricity, just all ol' duck-lamps for a flare. Used t' have t' bait with 'em, get ready for the next procedure, next day.

A hoveller wuz bigger than a crab-boat – used t' go longshorin' in 'em, mostly. They used t' have what they call a *cuddy* on – little stove, three bunks. Well they din't have 'em on when we went linin', used t' take 'em off; you'd got t' have plenty o' room t' stow the buoys an' that. We used t' lay about twelve *packs*, we called 'em packs, but they put 'em in baths nowadays. There wuz about 200-250 hooks on a pack. We used t' have an anchor an' a buoy each pack, then go from there, anchor an' buoy.

We used t' go away four in a hoveller, three in a crab-boat. Occasionally they'd leave someone ashore t' be a-baitin', if that wuz a nice fine day. O' course, they used t' lay more lines in a hoveller than in the crab-boat. Used t' get 120, 130, 140 stone o' fish up there. Used t' get a nice lot o' fish 'em days. Once laid-off t' the *Barnard*. One boat, we wuz partners then, I wuz in the *Morning Star*, one laid from the Barnard off, we laid inside. We had forty stone o' roker with the sprats an' twenty stone o' cod; an' the other boat wuz just the opposite, had more cod an' just a few roker, layin' off. Thass how we used t' work, thass how we used t' find the fish, two boats, partners, you see.

O' course the Southwold boats... hardly any o' 'em went linin'. They used t' lay the odd few lines, but they wuz more sprats, more their job sprat-tin' or herren' catchin', shrimpin', trawlin'. They were dab hands at sprattin', all that. Well, we used t' get a bit o' bait, sprats, off 'em if we couldn't get whelks. Oh, we used t' use cuttle-fish, used t' come from Low'stoft. Chiefly we baited with whelks. The whelks used t' have t' come from Sheringham by train, by train t' Low'stoft, an' the man who used t' buy the fish, Osborne his name wuz, used t' buy the fish, take it t' Low'stoft an' sell – he used t' give us a price for 'em at Southwold – then he used t' bring the bait back for us, 'cos we in't got no lorries or no motors 'em days. Well, the Frenchmen used t' go in. We used t' be able t' buy the ol' *squibs* [squid] as we called 'em, cut 'em up for bait; they used t' lay in Low'stoft 'em days. When we got the cod, we used t' *lum* 'em up, put a piece o' rope through the gills, so many cod on a string an' hang 'em on the steelyards. He din't get the weight o' the basket then, did he? There wuz no takin' weight off the basket; that wuz dead-weights all the time. Then they'd reckon 'em up.

We used t' come home two or three days for Christmas 'cos there wuz nuthin' doin' on the sale market at Low'soft, so we used t' come home for Christmas an' then go back for about two or three weeks. We'd come home by train; left the boats there – well someone t' look arter 'em while the boats were there. Cock-a-doodle, we used t' call him Cock-a-doodle, (he used t' crow like an ol' cockerel, thass how he got his nickname) he looked arter the boats till we got back. He lived there all over Christmas till we got back two or three days arter. I know one time they hired a car out o' the garage t' come home, well there wuz only one driver, that wuz Bob Davies, an' they come home. They come Norwich way, Hevingham *Fox*, an' they had the *dole* there, had t' square up with the money, an' they had t' keep puttin' a penny in the wheels t' keep the tyres on, in the rims. O' course the man who hired the motor out t' 'em said, "You'll definitely be back two or three days arter Christmas, I got a man comin' arter this motor." But it wuz later than that before they got back. We paid out on a share system. My father owned the boat but the chap who worked with him, Mr Stimson, he had a share o' course, an' me, bein' a boy, I had half a share.

They thought we wuz a bit rougher perhaps. Perhaps we wuz more hard up an' had t' go rougher! The lifeboat came out after us once. I wuz in the *Boy John*. We wouldn't take no help. We said we'd sail into the harbour. That wuz the day they went ashore an' turned over. I liked Southwold myself. Used t' go t' the pictures now an' agin, walk up through the golf course t' the pictures. Only, if the air wuz a bit thick when you come home, you had t' be careful not t' go in the dykes! I think they got on well with the Southwold fishermen. Ol' Harry Winter made us a shrimp net. If that got a bit rough an' they din't go t' sea, ol' Cock-a-doodle got the accordion out an' they'd go in the pub an' have a little sing-song. The Southwold fisher-men would come an' all, all join in. Sung a lot o' rum things at times! I shouldn't have bin in a pub, but I wuz there!

You'd start gettin' the [crab] pots ready by the time you got back home. There wuz more work in 'em days gettin' the pots ready than there is now 'cos they last a lot longer now. All our crabs used t' go away live, never had t' cook anything, not 'til the last few years. Now everybody want 'em cooked. I think they want us to catch 'em in the tin!'

Winter was always a hard time for the longshoremen and they had to make whatever money they could, particularly in the days before the Welfare state. It seems the Cromer men saw a gap in the market, their perception being that the Southwold men were not longliners and being hard up during those years, they made this very unusual voyage. The Lifeboat books do not record the incident referred to by Mr Davies but I found the following account in the Parish Magazine. Though not named, the boat must have been the *Morning Star*:

'Early in the morning of 26th Nov, 1924 three motor fishing boats of Cromer left Southwold to lay cod-lines. A gale got up from the South East with a very heavy sea and as they had not returned by noon a look-out for them was kept. It was close on one o' clock when one of the three was seen lying off the harbour, apparently not daring to attempt the entrance. The Life-boat was launched to stand by, and first one then another of the fishing boats ran in under her own power. The third was less fortunate. Her crew could not make the harbour but beached her about three-quarters of a mile to the north. At this point there are two shoals lying off the beach, one about forty, the other between sixty and seventy yards from it, with deep gullies separating them from the shore and from one another Over these shoals a very heavy sea was running. As the boat crossed the outer one she was struck by a wave and broached to. The shock threw two of her crew of three men out of her. One kept hold and managed to struggle back on board. The other was flung clear into the deep water between the two shoals. He was encumbered by his heavy oilskins and in grave danger.

A number of people had gathered on the beach to help if help were needed, and one of them, Mr J.H. Gillings, rushed at once into the sea, fully clothed. He struggled through the first gully, crossed the inner shoal, and went on in to the deep water beyond. He was at least forty yards out and up to his neck in water, when the waves receded, but they still continued to break far above his head.

Between the two shoals he seized the fisherman, by now utterly exhausted, and after a hard struggle, brought him safely ashore. Mr. Gillings' prompt and courageous action undoubtedly saved the fisherman's life. He said himself that when Mr. Gillings reached him he was "completely done." In recognition of his gallantry the Institution has awarded Mr Gillings its Bronze Medal...'[5]

Notes

1 Emerson, P.H. *Pictures of East Anglian Life* p.126

2 Shooting lines from baskets was the old method. It was very hazardous as the hooks were likely to snag on the basket or the shooter. They were later replaced by galvanised baths whose smooth sides were safer

3 Butcher, David *Fishing Talk – Dan*: 'a type of buoy used by trawlers and longliners to mark the area being fished by the former and to show the exact position of the lines by the latter. It consisted of a pole on the floating section bearing a flag by day and a lamp at night ...p. 21
Dan-tow: 'the cord that secured the dan buoy to the seabed anchor [or *dan-anchor*] on longlines p. 21
Buffs: 'large spherical inflatable canvas floats...' p.13

4 *Q, J & J, Admiral Jellicoe* and *Puffing Billy* were hovellers 'a sturdy, broad-beamed beach boat used in salvage work and longshore fishing' Ibid p.38

5 *Southwold Magazine* April 6th 1925

17

The Fish Merchant

In this chapter we hear the voice of Noel Denny, a (reluctant) fish merchant, who recalled his father's business.¹ Of all those with whom the fishermen dealt – boat-builder, rope-maker, sail-maker for example, none was more important than the merchant who bought the produce of his labour. Mr. Barber said that in his father's day fish was sold on the beach direct, the merchants competing with each other, but that this changed when merchants took on three or four fishermen to work exclusively for them. At the end of the First World War, as we have heard, some of the fishermen felt they were not being paid fairly and the May brothers began to take the fish to Lowestoft where it was sold on the market, the fishermen only having to pay auction and cartage fees. Noel Denny's father had fishermen working for him and he explains the risk involved from his father's point of view:

'My grandfather actually started the business an' my father went in with him in 1903. That wuz in Trinity Street an' known as 4,Trinity Street, though it wuzn't really, it wuz 6, but it wuz known as 4! When he opened the business, he wuz simply a retail fishmonger, no wholesale at all, sellin' just simply from the shop, you see.

Originally most o' the fish wuz bought from local boats. An' o' course that wuz all a gamble really 'cos he had t' buy from the fishermen when they bought stuff up t' him. He had t' buy from 'em an' take a chance on sellin' what he'd got. Anythin' that wuz left over had t' be marketed down at Low'stoft, an' o' course he had t' chance whether he lost or not. That wuz just a gamble t' an extent at the start, but a little later on, once he'd really been in the business an' got an idea o' the markets, he knew roughly how much he could buy. But it wuz always a chancy business even in the early days 'cos the snag o' it wuz, say you had about three or four boats goin' for you, well if they struck on a good bit o' fish, you bought perhaps three times more than you really wanted an' could dispose of, so you had t' take a chance an' send t' Low'stoft an' hope for the best on the market.

I can't remember how the fish wuz sent there before May brothers started. They had a lorry an' their business wuz simply cartin' fish for all the fishermen who weren't allocated t' shops. They used t' oblige us by takin' it down. But there must have been somebody else before 'em 'cos, you see, we had t' get crushed ice from Low'stoft for keepin' everythin' we had, 'cos in those days the fish wuz kept in ice. We used t' have t' get crushed ice every day an' box our fish away in it every night.

I can remember when I wuz quite a youngster – I wuz born in 1908, I'm not afraid t' tell you me age! – an' durin' the First World War, as early as 1915 an' '16, I used t' have t' go with my father an' we had a long flat truck about six foot by eight a big two-wheeled truck, an' we used t' have t' go down t' the Gun Hill, 'cos May brothers were fishin' there, from the actual Gun Hill, an' we used t' go an' get cod from 'em. My uncle wuz in the business with my father t' an extent, an' we had a man workin' for us, an' we had t' go down with this truck, an' two or three other schoolboys would come along. We'd have a load o' cod on there which we had t' go an' get when they'd been longlinin'. We used t' have t' stagger up Queen's Road, pull it right up there t' the shop. We had no other form o' transport, only just the horse an' trap that we used mainly for the cartin' o' sprats. You see, when it came t' sprat-cartin', as far as I can remember, most o' our sprats were landed near the pier. We used t' have t' cart 'em along Pier Avenue into the ol' Station yard an' thass where they were boxed up ready t' go t' Billingsgate. Thass how we got the cod an' the sprats but the rest o' the fish, mainly the fishermen used t' bring 'em up 'emselves. The shrimps they used t' have t' take home an' boil, you see. We din't buy 'em till they boiled 'em, but the fish they'd bring, perhaps three or four baskets o' fish. They used t' have an ol' truck; sometimes they used t' have three or four journeys. They'd have t' push 'em up. Those days o'course, there wuz no fishin' worth talkin' about out o' the harbour. That wuz all beach fishin'. As you probably know, originally there wuz boats right along from the Gun Hill t' the Lifeboat sheds, an' o' course they used t' fish from the pier as well. Each one had their own special allocated place where they went from. They were called Californians an' Klondikers. California wuz the Gun Hill, Klondike wuz the pier end.

Though we got most o' our fish locally, we had t' buy from Low'stoft certain times o' the year. As you know, fishin' is seasonal an' in Southwold trawl fish, for example, we were limited t' sole an' plaice, an' then we got herren, sprats an' occasionally mackerel, but very seldom were mackerel caught here. An' o' course shellfish in the early days wuzn't really worth the candle. There wuz always the theory you wanted rocks for good lobsters an' crabs an' o'course there's no rocks here, this is purely sandy, perfect for the brown shrimp but no good for lobsters an' crabs. There were very few pink shrimps. When I first started with my father, a pink shrimp wuz a big event! In fact I used t' go through 'em an' pick 'em out myself, nobody got the chance t' buy 'em! Well, they're not really shrimps at all. What they call a pink shrimp is really an *Aesop's Prawn*. Dr. Collings told me that. I wuz talkin' t' him on one occasion an' he told me: "Of course they're not shrimps you know, Mr Denny, that's an *Aesop's Prawn*." You used t' get the bigger prawns, the king prawns 'cos there wuz a time before this Second War when Roger Smith wuz shrimpin' for us regularly, there wuz quite a glut o' good big prawns. We used t' get several pints o' 'em. The fishermen used t' pick 'em out an' we used t' have 'em separately an' they used t' get a good price for 'em. While we're talkin' about delicacies, in the winter time they used t' go *drawin'*. The Mayhew brothers used t' go for us somewhere in the river an' they used t' get a tremendous lot o' smelts. They also used t' go *eelin'*, an', at the right time o' the season, there wuz quite a bit o' sea-trout. They did that in the warmer weather; you'd get that mainly in June, July, the summer months. They'd go drawin' for 'em too, a style o' ring net. There wuz no groynes t' worry about those days; the only obstruction wuz the ol' wreck o' the *Seahawk*, up there near the pier. But, you see, if anybody wuz choosy, turbot or brill an' any o' the better class o' fish, we had t' get that in from Low'stoft. Occasionally you'd get a spate, sometimes we'd get half-a-dozen nice brill come in with the plaice but you wouldn't get enough t' call 'em a commodity. But that wuz very seldom. You might go a month an' never see one.

The people who fished for us, well, we used t' have Joe *Satan* Palmer; there wuz *Mobbs* Mayhew an' his brother, *Stork*; Albert Stannard, *Early an' Late* wuz his nickname – he wuz always one o' the first t' go fishin' an' one o' the last ones ashore; then we had *Winner*, *Bull* Smith, Willie *Fye* Smith, Roger Smith; *Bunny* Simpson, he went fishin' for us; Wally Upcraft used t' fish for us an' *Brushy* Watson. There were one or two others we bought off but they were more or less the regulars, the ones we relied on. They would bring the fish up an' most o' 'em would bring up a pail full o' what they called *dust*. That wuz what you might call a *latch-lifter*. It wuz what they called *hovel money* or dust.[2] Short soles, small plaice, that sort o' thing, they used to bring a pail full o' 'em up 'cos they wanted enough money t' go an' see the local publican t' get the first pint. O' course you know once they got in the pubs they could tell a tall story t' some ol' *freak*, as they called any visitor that wuz about. *Dusso* an' *Jarvo*, they were good boys for freaks; so wuz ol' *Mobbs* Mayhew an' *Stork*, they used t' be able t' tell a good tall story an' o' course, "Have another drink,". 'Cos once they'd got an opener or latch-lifter from this dust-money, they'd be away. Thass where my father used t' look after a lot o' the local poor people o' Southwold. I've seen my father on more than one occasion pay a shillin' for a pail o' fish an' turn round an' sell it t' some real poor person for about 9d., which wuzn't good business, but then my father din't have all that much money when he died. I mean if he'd been a good businessman I shouldn't want t' work no more! He had the opportunity but he wuz too good-natured, that wuz the trouble with him!

They kept irregular times. That might be 11 o'clock at night, that might be 3 o'clock in the mornin' when they'd come hollerin', rattlin' on the door. That wuz seven days a week, twenty-four hours a day. You never did know when. You see, they had t' fish by the tides. More often than not, when they were trawlin', twelve o'clock, midday t' two or three they used t' come along an' o' course Albert Stannard would be along about five! You'd know Albert would be about an hour behind everybody else! With the herren an' that, when they were about, they were always after 'em. They never used t' rest. They would go sprattin' four or five times a day an' once they hit anythin' like that, they would really keep after 'em. I've seen sprats dumped at Old Hall Farm. Sometimes o' a night when the moon wuz out, you could come along the Halesworth Road an' you'd be struck by a phosphorescent glow on the fields. The whole field would be covered by sprats that had gone down t' Low'stoft an' hadn't even made the cartage. I think May's cartage fee at the time would be roughly 9d. a box. I've known 'em cart 'em for 6d., so the fishermen got some returns. I have known 'em t' go down t' Low'stoft an' nobody would look at 'em an' they'd come back here an' the only answer wuz t' go an' dump 'em on the fields an' they were ploughed in for manure.

You used t' buy herren by the *hundred*, which wuz a hundred an' thirty-two, thirty-three *warp*; sprats by the *bushel*; they used t' measure 'em in bushel baskets or *skips*, a two-handled basket, one each side, for carryin', an' o' course they'd carry 'em on their shoulder an' then tip 'em into boxes. You used t' reckon a box o' sprats weighed four stone an' there used t' be a good bushel t' a basket. Herren were boxed in *margarines* which were roughly three-an'-a-half [stone]. You see, if the herren were goin' t' Low'stoft, they used t' go up by the box. They'd count 'em into the baskets so they knew how many hundreds they'd got 'emselves, but then they were put in boxes an' they were sold by weight at Low'stoft. They were what they called margarines, margarine boxes, an' a sprat box wuz a lower, flatter box that'd be about a four-stone box. Cod goin' to Low'stoft were the same. They used t' reverse the cod head t' tail an' they would go in four-stone boxes when we sent 'em. They were sold by the weight or box. But there wuz never the demand for long-shore fish. That never used t' make the price unless there wuz a real shortage. For some reason or other, the merchants used t' get together, there used t' be, more or less, a ring. The snag o' it wuz they'd always sell the Low'stoft fish first an' the longshore fish last o' all, an' the fish never made the money it wuz really worth, well, not what we considered it wuz worth, 'cos I mean, it wuz always fresher than the Low'stoft stuff. Shrimps were sold by the *peck*. What we used t' do wuz measure a peck out an' put 'em in an ol' kipper box, little ol' square boxes, they used t' hold a stone o' kippers, an' we used t' have t' get 'em from Low'stoft. We used t' save 'em or send 'em back with shrimps in 'em. Plaice an' soles we used t' weigh 'em an' box 'em an' send 'em down. We used t' have t' supply our own boxes, o' course; every merchant had t' supply their own boxes.

We used t' send 'em down with Mays or whoever wuz cartin'. Occasionally there wuz times when Mitchell Brothers o' Low'stoft, they were big auctioneers on the market, they used t' run their own fleet o' lorries, if they really wanted anythin', they'd ring through t' my father or Mays – they'd contact one o' us – an' they'd give a certain price, say for herren, if we could make a load up. That meant panickin', rushin' t' the beach t' see the fishermen as they were comin' in. Perhaps they'd want 100, 150 boxes an' they used t' come an' fetch their own stuff if necessary. Mind you, they'd have t' be under pressure, they'd have t' be pushed for that, tryin' t' get ahead o' somebody else. That wuz when stuff wuz on the scarce side. We always did a certain amount o' wholesalin' you see, but that wuzn't the original intention o' the business.

The shop itself wuz open-fronted. In the winter that used t' be freezin'. No winders only right in the middle o' winter we had wooden slatted shutters an' if that got really bad, we'd have t' put 'em on the front o' the shop an' the side would have t' be open. One or the other had t' be open. There wuz a big white slab that we displayed the fish on, with drainage right along the front. As you washed your fish, plenty o' times I've had a pailfull o'

Edward (Ted) Denny, Noel's father, outside the shop in Trinity Street c.1920s.

water, an' you weren't allowed warm water, naturally enough, you'd spoil fish straight away with warm water. You had t' take the water, wash the ice off, that the fish had been stored in an' put 'em on the slab wherever you wanted 'em. You could start p'raps at the bottom o' the slab. There'd be a run o' ice right the way down [the slab] t' the bottom. Plenty o' times there's been live fish wobblin' about there – soles, eels used t' crawl about there for hours! Beyond the shop, up the alleyway wuz the cleanin' house an' beyond that wuz just the toilets from our house, next door's, the two or three houses up there. Then there were outhouses, the ol' stables, an' the big smokehouse right up the top o' the yard. In the cleanin' house we'd do the filletin' an' that as people came along. An' we were very modern! Our till wuz composed o' two puddin' basins! Never did have anythin' else.

I wuz an errand boy at the shop in the summer months an' naturally enough, when we knew a house wuz let – you see, in those days people used t' have six week lets – an' as soon as we got the wheeze – the different errand boys used t' tell each other, "Lady Oliver's comin' t' Stone House for six weeks." Well, o'course you'd be on the doorstep a-waitin' for 'em t' come there, or push your business card through or have a nice talk, try an' soft-talk the cook or housekeeper. I started in 1916. I wuz at school still then but any holiday I had t' work for my father. O'course in the summer weather, when that wuz light enough, we used t' have t' come straight home from school an' there would be a bicycle loaded up with fish, about twelve or fourteen pound o' fish, an' we used t' have t' go t' Henham Hall, t' the Army Hospital over at Henham Hall,'cos we supplied 'em. That wuz one o' my jobs. But, t' be quite honest, I din't want t' go in the fish business. I'd had more or less enough o' it by the time I wuz ready t' leave school. I had two years at Leiston Secondary, which my mother paid for, after ordinary school. Then I tried t' get into newspaper work, but I couldn't get a job as a reporter, which I wuz really keen on, so I went in the printin' trade. Just previous t' that I tried t' get in the Air Force as a boy entrant, but I wuz unlucky 'cos I'd got a perforated ear-drum an' in those days they could be choosy, so they wouldn't have me. I wuz ten years in Ipswich, 'cos I wuz in Ipswich when the General Strike wuz on, the big strike, 1926, an' I wuz about twenty-five when I had t' come out o' work durin' the slump, an' I had t' come back into the fish business 'cos there wuz nothin' doin' in the printin' trade whatsoever. I couldn't get a job anywhere so I came back.

It wuz a rum job t' get a livin' in those days durin' the winter months once the season had stopped. The season used t' start here you could say, more or less in April an' that would go through t' the end o' October. That would be a six month season an' thass what we had t' rely on. As long as the longshore herren lasted, I used t' have an ol' motorbike an' sidecar an' I used t' take perhaps a couple o' boxes o' herren an' a margarine o' bloaters an' go round the country, Westleton, Wenhaston, within say a six or seven mile area, well as far as I could go till I sold out. They used t' be about a dozen herren for 6d. an' nine bloaters for 6d. They were the only thing I *hawked* an' sprats. When sprats came in, I would go out an' sell 'em so much the pound. I never used t' take anythin' else. Well, cod you couldn't really sell. The ordinary country people would buy. You never went t' the landed gentry's houses 'cos we knew very well they'd got their regular fish merchant. What you used t' have t' look for wuz somebody who wuz lookin' for a bargain. The trouble wuz after you'd been t' two or three houses, "Oh! Mr So-an'-so's just been round an' he's got ten for 6d." "Oh well, you can have twelve o' these for 6d." O' course these other people would be ahead o' you, but by the time you got a little way out, you could start t' get rid o' 'em. But o' course when you got a little bit further, Mr So-an'-so had upped his an' he wuz sellin' twelve. It wuz a cut-throat job all the time. You used t' have a small basket, a little tiny delivery basket, an' you used t' divide the bloaters one end an' the herren the other an' just go tap on the door an' ask, "Do you want any longshore herren or bloaters today?" They'd either say yes or no an' that wuz all there wuz t' it. You wouldn't go the same way every time, you'd vary it. You used t' hope t' sell out near enough within the hour, with the motor bike.

A lot o' my time in the winter wuz spent cuttin' up trees. Mr Henry Raven who used t' be about here, lived in York Road. He used t' be a *carter*, had horses an' carts. Well, he used t' go round the country an' as soon as he heard someone wuz gettin' rid o' a dozen or so oak trees, he would go an' buy the tops. The tree wuz felled an' the only thing the timber merchant wanted wuz the trunk. All the boughs were simply hacked off an' left. Well, I used t' have t' g' round with a saw an' *beetle*, a big ol' wooden mallet an' wedges – the head used t' be about a foot long with an iron hoop each end – well, I used t' go an' spend days an' days cuttin' that up. We've had as much as seventy ton o' oak layin' up the top o' our yard in the ol' sheds an' places. When you were *smokin'* you see, you wanted ol' oak. That wanted t' be kept at least four t' six years, even longer if necessary. You'd have t' get it really dry so you could get it t' start. Mr Henry Raven would go an' buy 'em for us. He'd just come along an' say, "There's half-a-dozen trees, so-an'-so's Johnson's farm at the Smere", or even Mrs Girlin' when she had the ol' bullock sheds at Frostenden, I've been there an' cut as many as thirty trees on one occasion. I used t' cut it up in the necessary lengths so that it wuz easily moveable, on the farms, an' he'd come up with his horse an' cart an' bring it an' then dump it.

My father used t' get up at half-past-four or five o' clock. Directly he wuz ready, he'd start openin' bloaters. He'd give me a little while an' then he'd come an' call me an' I'd start about six o'clock. I would be the first errand boy on the rounds an' that wuz deliverin' bloaters from half-past-six until sometimes it wuz quarter-past-eight even before we finished deliverin' *breakfast bloaters*, an' o'course gettin' sworn at by several o' the cooks 'cos they wanted theirs for breakfast at a certain time, but everybody couldn't be first. When I first started as a kid at school, we used t' do anythin' from three t' four margarines o' bloaters per day right through the season when it wuz possible t' get herren. Ninety-five per cent o' those had t' be split an' boned 'cos they had t' go into the houses ready for the pan. That wuz my father's job an' my uncle would turn up a bit later on an' help as well. Half-past eight used t' be p'raps ten minutes for breakfast. Then the first job I would get would be washin' the fish on the slab, get 'em out o' the ice an' lay 'em on the slab for display. That would take about half-an-hour. Then nine o'clock time, you'd have t' go out. We would have a round. I would do South Green an' the common an' the other one who used t' work with me, he would do all North Parade an' all round that way t' the High Street. Well, at nine o'clock I would go out round certain calls down the South Green which were regular customers, just see if there wuz anythin' they wanted, get orders, goin' by bike, an' then I'd go back t' the shop an' leave the orders. The boardin' houses were the ones we mainly had t' get an' if there wuz anythin' special we wanted from Low'stoft, that would have t' be got in. You always tried t' get a day in advance on that so you made sure an' had the stuff. That would be the idea, get the boardin' house stuff in. That used t' take p'raps three-quarters-of-an-hour t' get round the main ones down the South Green an' then directly I got back, I'd hand the order book in t' my father. Then him an' my mother would start gettin' orders ready for lunch. In the meantime I'd be round the common doin' the same thing there. Up till lunch time that wuz a mad rush. We'd go back, clean fish up an' help get the orders ready.

P'raps an hour for lunch, which we never did get really 'cos my father never did close the shop – that always used t' be open. Directly you sat down someone would come along. Well, he'd serve the first two or three, then he'd say, "Go on, boy. You'd better go an' see what Mrs so-an'-so want." 'Cos there wuz always somebody comin'. Our house door wuz an ol' stable-door, double-door an' my father used t' sit at the table an' he could see through. Originally that house wuz a pub, the ol' *Rising Sun*, well not a pub, an off-licence. In the room facin' Trinity Street there were special guards, iron bars across the window, chair height. That wuz a *pilots' room* one time. The ol' Harbour pilots, that wuz their own room, an' naturally enough nobody else wuz allowed t' go in the pilots' room; they were the cream.

We used t' reopen again at two o'clock which meant flyin' about gettin' all the evenin' orders out. The ol' chap 'ud have t' keep goin' up the yard, t' a place up the yard with an open roof an' a concrete floor where he used t' do all the fish buyin'. We had scales an' used t' have t' keep the tubs o' ice an' boxes there, an' as the fishermen used t' bring the stuff, everythin' wuz gutted you see, we only bought gutted stuff, we'd ice an' box it up. That wuz the same place where we did all the picklin', an' there wuz a copper up the corner for boilin' lobsters an' crabs, which we had t' do when we could get 'em. If we were lucky we'd finish at six an' I don't mind tellin' you, you were tired after that, you din't want much.

There were two smokehouses in the yard, a big one at the top that we din't use an' a smaller one. I should say it [the smaller one] wuz about ten foot by just over eight by sixteen foot high. There wuz some open tiles in the roof t' make a draught an' the roof itself wuz pantiled. There wuz a big double door, only one side o' which would open. Inside the smokehouse we had what we called *loughs*.[3] They were like parallel bars runnin' all the way up about a foot apart. They only had t' be just deep enough for a herren t' hang between. We had eighteen loughs at the wall side, a framework across the middle with a lough each side an' the other side wall had eighteen loughs again. We had a ladder in there so we would be able t' get t' the top. The lowest lough would hang five foot from ground level an' we had eighteen up. For our own shop work, we only used half o' one side an' only go up three or four loughs. The idea wuz you used t' stagger. You'd put the bloaters in so that the smoke would get between the lot. We used to *speet* eighteen herren t' a speet an' do roughly 600 at a time.[4] The floor wuz earth, but orig-inally that wuz brick an' through constant heat the bricks more or less dete-riorated an' that finished up so there wuz a hole in the floor.

You used t' start a fire with shavin's. You used t' work it so that you al-ways finish up with so many pieces o' oak that had already been partly smoked t' make sure you got a start. Our main commodity wuz oak dust. We used t' buy the oak dust an' my father had an arrangement with Latten's, the timber merchants. Ol' Henry Raven, he used t' go down t' Latten's every so often an' he used t' bring p'raps twelve or twenty bags, terrific great bags o' oak dust. If you used new wood, that weren't no good; you never got no smell with it an' you never got the oak flavourin'. We used t' make a little cone o' shavin's just t' start things off, an', as I say, kept three or four *billets* o' oak t' start. As soon as they caught, they would catch the others an' once you'd got a good glow, you'd throw your dust on. You'd have t' visit the smoke house every three-quarters-of-an-hour an' keep your sawdust goin'. You had a big container o' sawdust t' keep it goin'.

T' smoke a bloater, we used t' have *picklin' tubs*. They were originally ol' barrels, big barrels cut down, open-topped tubs. We used t' make a *brine* an' for the purpose o' smokin' bloaters, kippers or haddock, though we din't do much kippers or haddock; our main wuz bloaterin'. T' do that we had t' mix a pickle which wuz made o' special coarse salt which we had t' get through the merchants at Low'stoft. We used t' get coarse salt t' make a brine in which we pickled the herren. If ever you wanted t' test your brine, you'd peel a potato an' put a piece in. If that floated your brine wuz strong enough. But you see, the trouble o' it wuz, if you made your brine really heavy t' start with, that'd float the potato but that wuz a lot saltier than you needed. So you had t' be careful an' we used t' rely on a measure. We used t' know exactly. Say we'd use two pails o' water – we had a certain pail that we'd keep for picklin' purposes only – an' we put, say, a pail o' salt, could be a pail-an'-a-half in the water. We used t' reckon t' use a pickle about four times, that wuz all. What we'd do when we put a fresh batch o' herren in, we'd sprinkle salt over the top an' then about every half hour somebody'd have t' go an' push 'em about so that they all had an even chance. We had t' do that by hand. We would leave 'em three t' four hours in the pickle. That would be part o' your routine work, you see. The ol' man would say, "You can go an' speet 'em herren." You used t' do eighteen on a speet. You put the pointed end o' the speet on the pickle tub, put your hand in [the pickle], whip the gill out [of the bloater] an' shove it on the speet. Eighteen o' 'em. We had a special nail in the wall that supported the end o' the speet an' then you used t' run through 'em with finger an' thumb an' space 'em out so they were evenly spaced. Then they would be laid outside across boxes or on trestles on the speet an' washed down with about three or four pails o' fresh water. Then they would be left t' dry. As soon as they were dry enough they would go in the smokehouse. But the smokehouse would never be lit. My father used t' do that at roughly half-past five, six o'clock at night.

Occasionally you'd do sprats the same, or you'd *dry-salt* 'em. T' dry-salt sprats you'd have 'em in a bowl or basket an' throw a handful o' salt on 'em, ruffle 'em up with your hand, keep addin' salt till you'd got 'em done evenly. They would lay about a couple o' hours. Being a small thing there'd be no salt really adhere t' 'em so you used t' wash 'em, get the salt off an' speet 'em on special little speets. We had a special contraption rigged up underneath the bloaters t' take the sprats. Thass all there wuz t' sprats, either dry-salted or pickled, but we preferred t' dry-salt 'em if possible.

Now *red-herren*, thass an entirely different thing. We had this concrete floor an' that had a back an' two sides which we had t' use. You would throw rough salt on the floor. You would tip two boxes of herren on t' that an' all the time you were tippin' them on, somebody would stand there dry-saltin' 'em. All the time dry-salt. Then they would lay three or four hours. We used t' have these special wooden shovels; they were made o' one piece o' wood, handle an' everythin'. The handle wuz about two-an'-a-half foot long an' the blade wuz curved so it wuz slightly edged, a good eighteen inches long by well over a foot across. Every so many hours somebody would have t' go an' *roust* 'em, we called it *roustin'*. That meant t' say you had t' turn 'em over, turn 'em over with the shovel 'till every herren got more or less the same amount o' salt as wuz possible. The idea o' the concrete floor wuz so that you could run these shovels under an' they wouldn't damage the herren in any way. Well that would go on for p'raps four days, turnin' 'em over an' sprinklin' fresh salt on t' 'em. At the end o' that time you'd have t' put 'em in some water, wash the salt off 'em an' speet 'em. They would have t' go right t' the top o' the smokehouse 'cos that would be a month, six weeks before they even began t' reach anythin' like maturity. When you first put 'em in, if it wuz possible, you'd keep a fire goin' night an' day an' you'd have t' leave your bloaters outside until you wanted t' put 'em in. After that they'd smoke each day when the bloaters were doin'. I don't mind tellin' you thass a pretty grim job goin' into an ol' smokehouse thass been puffin' away smoke. The only ventilation you'd got wuz the door. You'd put about two speets up an' you'd have t' come out. Your eyes would water, you'd be coughin' an' spittin'. We used t' do a double lot o' *reds*. We used t' salt one lot – they would only be done, mind you, with the prime herren, the real October prime herren, they would have t' be *full*, spents were useless. Our first lot we put down we would give six days saltin', make sure they got an extra bit o' salt. They would go in right at the top, say on the left-hand side an' then we would do a four-day saltin' an' they would go on the other side. They would even hang all winter. Sometimes instead o' the golden, reddy colour, they'd be nearly black by the time they came out but they were per-fectly good. After my father died I found three or four speets o' red-herren right in the top o' the smokehouse that I never even knew were in there an' they'd been there, I should think eighteen t' twenty years an' they were still fit t' eat! Mind you they were all salt, not very tasty, but they were fit t' eat after all that time!

When you split a herren you split down the back but haddock an' whitin' an' cod they split down the front. We used t' do ours the same as the bloaters. We had a pickle that they would go in, then washed down an' hung out. They had special speets, so did the kippers. I don't know if you've ever seen a kipper speet, well, thass a square *baulk*, piece o' timber. A bloater speet is round. We used t' get 'em from people around, basket makers an' that. There wuz an ol' boy the other side o' Wangford, he used t' do our baskets an' cut the speets. Four foot lengths, cut out o' the hedges, round. O'course you got t' trim all the knots. But these others [kipper speets] were a timber baulk an' at intervals there used t' be a special hook, a *game hook*, like an L-shaped nail that you would drive in an' hang the kipper on 'em. A kipper you could smoke the same time as you did a bloater an' they would be all night, but a haddock you had t' hang two nights.

A bloater, say you'd start at six o'clock in the evenin', that would smoke 'till about three or four o'clock in the mornin', ten hours, suthin' like that.

224

The reds, there would have t' be a continual fire for so many days an' then once you saw they were gettin' a certain colour on 'em it wouldn't matter so much 'cos they were always ready weeks before you wanted 'em. They were a standby. Nobody wanted reds 'till they got really hard up an' there wuz no other food about. Sprats, the same as a bloater. The art o' smokin', more than anythin', is not t' get too much heat. If you do, you do what they call *fire* 'em. If you get a bloater that has been *fired*, if you just touch above the tail, that 'll be soft. The idea used t' be t' get the smoke without the heat.

Durin' the winter time, early spring, once we'd done reds, we used t' do hams for people, hams an' bacon. They would have t' pickle 'em 'emselves; all we used t' do wuz hang 'em up an' smoke 'em. They used t' get the smoke as the fish wuz done. They'd probably go a month but that all depend when the customer come after 'em. Some o' 'em liked 'em lightly smoked, some o' 'em would rather have 'em heavier smoked – if they'd pickled 'em strongly they'd let 'em go a good while. Lady Hamlyn had a lot done. Horrie Ladd, the butcher, we used t' do a lot o' bacon smokin' for him at one time. We used t' do for butchers, one at Wangford, two at Halesworth, you know, they used t' bring their stuff in. Ol' E. G. Clarke, originally from Framling-ham, he'd bring his own; Mr. Leguen de la Croix, his father used t' do his own picklin' an' bring it in. O' course, instead o' payin', they used t' give me a piece o' bacon, a piece o' the pig.

In the season, October, November, my father an' I used t' send hundreds o' boxes o' dozens o' bloaters t' customers. We used t' have these tiny boxes, we'd get sections from Latten's an' that'd be part o' my winter evenin's, ham-merin' these boxes up – used t' make 'em. There used t' be different size. They'd take eight bloaters, twelve bloaters, up t' two dozen. Plenty o' times I've been down the Post Office with thirty boxes a day for days on end. That wuz only bloaters. Some o' 'em would come down an' leave orders. A Mr. Sam Smith o' Tottenham, had a brickworks in Tottenham, he used t' come down an' when he went away he used t' leave us a list o' addresses t' send a dozen, a dozen-an'-a-half t' Mr. Fox, Nancy Fox's uncle. He wuz a big man in the Scouts. He would leave thirty, forty even, addresses an' before you got that lot away, there'd be a letter come through the post, a dozen more addresses t' send t'. We had customers like that all over. The furthest they went I know o', I can't remember the name o' the man, but Judge Swan, used t' live on the common at *Armargh*, well, he had a friend that wuz somethin' t' do with the Hope Brewery at Weymouth, an' I think that wuz about the furthest. He used t' get three-dozen boxes, bigger boxes. We used t' send him one or two boxes a week an' he used t' distribute 'em among the employees o' this brewery. Every year we used t' get a dozen bottles o' Hope Brewery strong Old, an' my word, that wuz a real drink; Adnams can't touch anythin' they used t' turn out. I used t' have one o' those an' that used t' send me t' sleep for three or four hours! That wuz real beer! We used t' send t' the editor o' *The Field*; we used t' send t' the editor o' *The Lady*. As long as longshore herren lasted we used t' send these quantities o' bloaters t' these different people. We used t' have t' buy extra herren for that. We'd know roughly in advance how many we'd want. A bloater would last four or five days, no longer. But the Post Office used t' know what they were an' they used t' put 'em through. We used t' always make a point o' gettin' 'em t' the Southwold Post Office by four o'clock t' get 'em away.

Our book keepin' wuz very haphazard! We had a slate. You've heard o' *puttin' things on the slate*. Well, Denny's put everythin' on the slate! All orders were put on that so it wuz covered an' quite often overwritten too. The slate wuz only used for orders taken in the shop. Then we had the boys' errand-books, we used t' take orders in 'em. The thing o' it wuz that half the time we never had a chance t' really enter everythin', we just used our own shorthand for the weight o' fish that wuz supplied. At six o' clock the shop would close an' then my father would prop himself up at the desk an' we would have a list o' the houses that we used t' serve that we'd booked an' we used t' take it in rotation. We'd start say, along the Station Road or along the Pier Avenue, Hotson Road, North Parade an' we used t' gradually go round all the town an' book everythin' that'd gone out durin' the day. A lot o' stuff din't matter about weight at all. Kippers, you see, were so much a pair, bloaters were sold individually an' so on. Some o' it wuz memory, so it wuz a more or less haphazard, happy-go-lucky affair an' with the two puddin' basins, one for silver an' one for copper, that wuz how it went.

My father used t' go t' church every Sunday an' come home just after half-past seven an' he would sit there t' half-past ten, eleven o'clock makin' out his weekly account books. When the month came around, he'd have t' do a bit o' time Sunday afternoon p'raps, an' then evenin's just sendin' out the weekly accounts which were sent out every Monday mornin', not always paid, I don't mind tellin' you. They were pretty regular though, an' there's one thing about it, the class o' visitor that came to Southwold, they weren't like the person who came an' bought at the auction here the other day, there weren't no stolen cheques in those days. The people that came in those days were very, very fussy. They would warn you. "We will be off tomorrow. Will you be sure the bill is made up?" Well, you'd just go down the house, say they were goin' off at one, you'd be down the house at twelve o'clock with the bill an' there would be the cheque within a few minutes. There were no twisters in those days.

My father started his pipe up about half-past six when he'd finished handlin' fish. He'd never touch a smoke all day long till then. His pipe would never go out until he went t' bed at eleven or quarter-past. He wuz a very regular member o' the Constitution Club. I never did know how much he used t' drink there but he always had a pint, pint-an'-a-half o' beer for his *elevensies*. He used t' have an ol' brown mug an' he used t' go across the back way o' the *Nelson* – that din't matter how many customers were there, they'd have t' wait if he wuz in the mood for his beer – he'd just slip across an' get his pint or pint-an'-a-half o' mild an' bitter an' he'd drink that as he could, snatched in odd lots. That wuz all he'd ever have. I don't know if he ever touched spirits at all, unless o' course just at Christmas time. In the ol' days there used t' be a custom, this is when I was quite a youngster, the fishermen who used t' fish for us, would come round on Christmas day an' he used to give 'em occasionally a Christmas box or they'd have a smoke an' he'd give 'em a drink, whisky, that sort o' thing.

My father died in 1946. I wuz in the Air Force durin' the Second World War. I started in the Royal Observer Corps then I volunteered an' went in the Air Force in 1942. My father had a heart attack followed by a stroke an' he lay from October 1944 until '46 an' I had compassionate release from the Air Force an' then I got discharged. I carried on from then an' finished in April 1951. I'd started in 1916 an' except for ten years in Ipswich in the printin' trade, I served my life there.'

Notes

1 For more information on the business see the excellent southwoldandson.co.uk

2 In the sense of 'of lesser value'. The pail was made up of fish that were not worth much

3 Also known as loves: 'The wooden racks/frames on the inside walls of smokehouses which supported the speets and baulks of fish to be cured.' *Fishing Talk* David Butcher p.47

4 Speets were wooden rods on which the fish to be smoked were suspended

The Distracted Mother

A woman appeared. My boy she said my boy. Ha' you sin my boy? He wuz with his father when the boat cast goin' off. They say one minute the boat wuz there an' then that weren't. An' when I come t' the cliff, I see it taken by the tide, upturned, goin' away up the beach. I ran down. I went in. They tried t'stop me, but I shook 'em off. I went in. I had t'. But since I've bin here I 'int sin 'em nowhere. Job, my boy, and his friend Sam. Ha' you sin 'em, Job an' Sam?

The night before, when I wuz in bed, I heard suthin' splashin' in the water-butt outside the house. That wuz makin' a right racket. An' there wuz strange noises an' all, moanin', like suthin' was breathin' right heavy. I went down, opened the back door into the yard an' that splashin' wuz still a-goin' an' that moanin' wuz still a-goin', but there weren't nuthin' there. I wuz right scairt. An' then, I don't know how t' tell it, that suddenly went quiet. An' I thought that musta bin me, that weren't nuthin', that I'd just bin dreamin' or suthin'. But when I wuz just about t' close the door, two birds, thass the only way I can describe it, these two birds rose outa the butt an' flew at me a-walin', like o' which I int never heard nor niver want t'. I slammed the door quick and fell t' th' floor on the other side an' there wuz this drummin' an' drummin' on th' door. But I couldn't do nuthin' I couldn't open it agin. I think I musta fainted, suthin', gone out anyhow, 'cos th' next thing I remember, Job an' Billy found me there by the door when they come down t' go off. They told me t' go back t' bed an' that on their way t' the beach they'd call on mother t' come. An' she did come. But that wind began a-risin' an' risin', shriekin' an' rattlin' the winders so the both on us went straight t' the cliff t' make sure they wuz all right, that they han't gone off.

An' you know the rest. An' I still int sin 'em. Look out for 'em mister. Tell 'em I'm a-comin' for 'em, that I'll find 'em an' that I'm here. Tell 'em…

I saw her arm with its name marked in blue and wanted to tell her, but already she had pushed on raising sand clouds till I could see her no more.

18

Raising The Wind

When the longshoremen finished longlining in January, the hardest part of their year began since they would not begin fishing again until the spring-herring arrived in late March or April. The coldest and darkest time of the year thus coincided with a major loss of earnings. We have already heard about the difficulties this caused. Fathers would steal swedes from Easton Bavents, the families would live *on tick* again, having paid off the previous year's debts if there had been a good spratting. The fishermen would try to find other work locally or they might decide to go deep-sea fishing for mackarel on the *Westward* which started at the end of February or wait a bit to go on the *Scotch-fishing* starting in the Shetlands. If they stayed at home, this would also be the time for maintenance of their boats and gear. Mr English told me how he spent the winters:

'We used t' reckon t' finish fishin' Christmas time. We'd *make up* the nets – the nets had t' be dried an' then folded an' then stored – an' we wouldn't start again until round about May when we'd start trawlin'. But if there wuz a few spring-herren about, we'd start earlier, in April. So it wuz necessary for the fishermen t' do whatever they could over those months t' make 'emselves a few shillin's. If the weather wuz fine, we would go on the beach so we could *draw*. There'd be three men doin' that, two in the boat an' one on the beach. The net we used wuz about sixty yards long with a bridle at each end an' a long rope attached t' each bridle. One man stayed on the beach with one end o' the rope an' the other two stayed in the boat. One o' 'em would shoot the net *straight off* an' the other one would row. When they done that, they'd make their end o' the net fast t' the thwart an' would gradually pull so they came round in a semi-circle t' make the net into a bow shape. At the same time, the man on the beach would be walkin' slowly so when they met they'd be a few yards apart. Then they'd pull the net ashore an' see what they'd got – codlin', flounders, smelts, dabs or whatever. Each *drag* would take about half-an-hour an' you'd work right along the beach accordin' t' which way the tide wuz.

229

The same sort o' thing happened up the river, only there you went drawin' for smelts. It wuz harder work up there. We used t' have two sizes o' nets, one *herren shale* an' one *sprat shale* an' the rope along the bottom had bits o' lead on it t' keep it down when you pulled it. It wuz the same method. You went with the tide an' there'd be two in the boat an' one on the bank pullin' along. That wuz really hard work if you were the one on the bank 'cos you had t' go through all the mud. You'd have your long boots on an' an oil-skin an' a jersey but you couldn't help gettin' muddy. We used t' pick the slack tide at low water so that we could go with the tide comin' in. When you'd finished a drag, the two men would row t' the shore; one would stop in it an' the other'd get out an' pull the net an' see what you'd got. We used t' get a shillin' a score for smelts. They're lovely little fish, four, five inches long in the river an' they smelled like cucumbers; they'd have a strong smell o' cucumber. They were a delicacy, they were. Very tasty. We used t' get bigger ones on the beach with roes in but they were smaller in the river. They'd be sold t' the merchants.

Another thing we'd do winter time wuz *eel-pickin'* when the eels buried theirselves in the mud in the ditches or dykes; we called 'em *ditches*. You'd have an *eel-pick* which wuz triangular or fan-shaped an' which had two metal prongs, one on each side, flat like knife-blades an' between 'em would be two other barbed prongs. That wuz springy. That'd have t' be for the kind o' work it did. The blacksmith would make 'em for you. I had two or three, different shapes an' sizes an' I gave one t' the Rural Life Museum at Stow-market. Attached t' the pick wuz a pole twelve t' sixteen foot long made out o' ash. You'd go t' the ditches on the marshes with this pick an' if it wuz a wide ditch you'd pick each side o' it, plungin' it in under the banks. Thass where the eels would congregate, you see, under the edge. You'd see the blowholes the eels made sometimes an' you'd know they were there. If that wuz a smaller ditch, your staff wuz long enough for you t' pick all over it. The eels would get caught in the prongs, you see, between the barbs. You had a canvas bag thing round your neck an' as you picked 'em out you'd slip 'em in this bag. If you put 'em in a bucket they'd be outa there in no time. You'd keep 'em alive. They'd even get sent alive t' London but they had t' be kept damp. You'd get a shillin' a pound for 'em but o' course, the merchant would make more.

I'll tell you some more things about eels though. In the summer time

Eel-picking in Suffolk Waters c. 1886, P.H. Emerson

we'd go what they called *eel-babbing* an' *night-lining*. For eel-babbin' you had a long pole with a long string on it an' you tied *worsted* or wool on t' the string with worms all threaded on the wool so you might have a dozen or so worms in a big clump. You sat there on the bank an' dangled the worms in the water so the eels got their teeth entangled in the wool or worsted an' then you'd swing 'em out on the bank or marsh. If that wuz long grass you had a job t' find 'em sometimes! We used t' reckon that when that wuz cloudy that wuz better. Perhaps with the sunlight they could see you.

Night-linin' you had a piece o' string about a yard long with one hook which you'd bait with a garden worm an' a little piece o' lead t' sink it. You'd attach this t' a stick an' you'd have maybe a dozen o' these; stick 'em in the bank an' leave 'em overnight an' back next mornin' an' see what you got. You did that in the summer time when the eels were *out*. When it got warmer they'd *come out*.

Gettin' back t' winter work another thing we used t' do wuz what wuz called *slubbing* or *mudding*. That wuz puttin' mud o' the river an' dyke walls t' fill all the cracks an' holes up an' t' strengthen 'em as well. Occasionally we topped 'em with sods from the side o' the river. The maintenance o' the river banks wuz the responsibility o' the various farmers an'

231

landowners whose land went down t' the river. T' get the work they might say they wanted so many men t' do the job an' you'd hear they wanted so many men an' you'd go an' see if you could get a job. On this side [Walberswick] you'd work for the Parish, Charity Trust, or the local farmers. Flick o' Saxmundham had some marshes at Tinker's House an' Overland on the Southwold side had some o' the marshes above the bridge.

You worked from seven in the mornin' till three in the afternoon. There'd be five or six o' you work together. One would be cuttin' the sods with the *muddin'-shovel* – it wuz iron or steel – an' very narrow an' long, about five inches wide an' a good foot long. I'd cut out the sods with that an' a man with a two-pronged fork, on a long handle, a *muddin'-fork*, he'd just stick it in the sods an' heave 'em into the barrow. The barrow wuz wooden bar the wheel which wuz iron, an' would run along wooden planks placed where you were workin'. You had t' have those planks, you see, otherwise you'd never push 'em over the marshes. Perhaps there may be a quarter-t'-a-half-a-mile o' 'em 'cos the men would know which mud they wanted an' which wuz best. You'd never use mud that had *crab-weed* growin' in it because that'd go all flaky. Every so often there'd be a *turn-off* so you could pass each other with the barrows on the way. T' move the planks you had a *plank-hook* so you din't pick 'em up with your hands. That wuz a shaft with a bar on the top an' the bottom part wuz a long straight piece o' iron with a spike on so you slipped it under, jerked it up an' pulled the plank along. The planks were twelve t' fourteen foot long, about two inches thick an' a foot wide, so that wuz quite hard work movin' 'em. There would be each man t' his job, as the sayin' goes, but you would change over t' vary the work an' perhaps if you were young an' strong, you'd be on the barrow a fair bit. There'd be two barrows goin' all the time an' the sods would be taken t' the wall. At the wall there'd be another man t' lay 'em.

Say there'd been a break in the wall after a flood or suthin'. We used t' go t' the woods o' the landowner an' cut all the small trees into small lengths with a sharp point at one end. They'd be driven into the breach with a mallet or a *bell* vertically on each side o' the breach. Along each side wuz put a *walin'-piece*, a long tree, an' at right angles t' the walin'-pieces at each end o' the breach, were put two ties so that the whole structure wuz held an' slotted together in a rectangular shape. We also went t' the common an' cut ling an' heather an' we used t' cart that t' the site an' for every layer o' sods we put a layer o' ling or heather an' that worked just like wire an' held it together. You started at the bottom layin' every sod level right through an' then worked the angles as you went up so you kept the shape o' the wall. That may have been ten or twelve foot wide at the bottom but only four foot at the top, so you had t' work the angle. That wuz for wall makin'.

Slubbers repairing walls on the Blyth

Once you'd built the wall the landowners would run sheep on 'em in the summer time t' stamp 'em down an' make 'em really firm. The last wall I worked on wuz in 1928 an' that lasted till 1977 so that tell you how strong that were, all done by hand-power, nuthin' like they've got today!

If there wuz no walls t' do you might go *bottom-fying* – that wuz cleanin' out the ditches. You dammed 'em with wood an' you had a short-bladed scythe about two foot long on a very long handle t' cut the reeds an' rushes right down in the bottom o' the ditch. You'd dam it so you could get at 'em, you see. You'd have a *crome* which you pulled all the roots out with. After that you got in the ditch between the dams with your *scuppet* – that wuz like a wooden spade, narrow an' rounded, scooped out with copper fastened at the bottom an' a leather guard at the top where the blade joined the handle t' stop the mud goin' up your arm. You scooped an' threw the mud about on t' the marsh so that wuz spread out well. You had t' spread it out, the grass wouldn't grow through it agin. You kept workin' along the dyke, movin' one dam at a time so it would fill up agin t' the back of you.

We started on the walls in January an' finished in May. If you were lucky you see, you could get regular work at that. The wages were thirty shillings a week; that wuz a good wage then. After that I used t' go t' Low'stoft an' get a berth t' go on the Scotch-fishin' but you earned more on the wall than what you got on the Scotch-fishin', though sometimes you might make £2 a week.

Whenever they got the chance the longshoremen would spend time makin' repairs t' their boats an' gear so that it'd be all ready when the fishin' started agin. After Christmas the boats used t' be pulled up on t' the beach or on t' the *flats* here in Walberswick. They would scrape the bottoms an' on the inside o' the boats the *bottom-boards* were taken out an' scrubbed down. Along the *sand-streaks* the runs were all cleared o' sand an' washed down the plughole. In fact all the boat wuz scrubbed, scale cleaned off, sprat scales, herren scales so that it wuz all clean an' dried out ready t' be painted agin. Most o' 'em round here were painted black an' white an' all numbered o' course, LT so-an'-so, whatever it wuz.

Nets, lines an' all that sorta thing all used t' be looked over as well. If the weather wuz nice, you done 'em down the sheds by the quay, but if that wuz bad you took 'em home by the fire an' hung 'em from the *hank*, the peg or ring that you had on the wall near the fire. All the fishermen's cottages had those, an' you can still see 'em in some o' 'em today. If your net had a hole in, you'd *cut out* an' *beat back*. You'd cut out the bit that wuz torn an' *beat* it, or mend it, startin' on a *half-mesh* an' finishin' on a half-mesh. A *sprank-mesh* wuz called a *crowsfoot*. A mesh is like a diamond shape an' if one side o' it wuz broken, it wuz shaped like a crow's foot; an' when you hung your net up, you'd hang it so it wuz straight an' you'd beat the meshes in a line straight across. If not, that wouldn't pull right. You mended the nets with *beating needles*. The old chaps used t' cut 'em theirselves an' they were made out o' bone or wood with their initials cut on 'em. Oh yes, they made their own tools – they had t'! The needle would be made t' different sizes for each type o' net, *sprat-shale, herren-shale, trawl-shale* an' so on.

You *tricked over* your lines, pullin' 'em out an' coilin' 'em agin in another place, lookin' t' see where hooks were missin'. If there were, you'd put a *snud* on. That wuz a length o' line twenty-seven inches long with a hook which wuz bound on with a wax thread. The snud had a loop in it the other end an' that wuz attached t' the line by threadin' the hook through the loop an' puttin' a half-hitch on the line t' stop it pullin' along. I've got some snuds here that were made by ol' Button over at Southwold. [quite possibly by Mr Rogers].

If your sails needed repairin', you'd take 'em home as well. They were made o' calico, I think, or treated cotton. Jeckells used t' make 'em. We used t' mend 'em where they had got chafed along the edges an' where the *thimbles* were that the sheets went through. You'd also check the *reef-points* an' replace 'em if they needed it. You'd patch up the sails with a needle an' *palm* an', o'course , you used t' tan 'em as well if they needed it. You'd tan 'em in *cutch* like you would the nets an' the ropes. Here, on this side, there were two great coppers down on the flats. You'd fill 'em with water, boil 'em up, put the cutch in an' tan 'em in that. You see when you first got the sails they would be white but after a year or two you'd need t' tan 'em t' preserve 'em. When they were dried they were put away for the winter up in the loft in the shed.

Another thing they'd do is make *thole-pins*. You'd want a good hard wood for that, apple or pear or suthin', holly, nuthin' short-grained any way. Talkin' o' 'em ol' *Crikey* Rogers used t' say they were *as poult as a carrot*, meanin' they would break or snap like a carrot. We used t' like 'em t' break. I mean, if you were towin' an' you got caught on suthin' say, you'd get in t' some trouble if they din't snap.

All through the winter an' durin' the blows o' the sprat season when it wuz impossible t' *get off* we'd go duckin' an' rabbit shootin', snarin' an' ferretin' on the marshes an' on the common. We've got about fifty-four acres o' common land here, you know so it's quite a large area.

When you went duckin' the conditions were all-important. If the tide wuz ebbin', goin' down t' Lowestoft an' the wind southerly, we'd go an' *take the flight* about four o'clock or at dusk. The ducks always spent the night feedin' in the *Lodge marshes*, so if the tide wuz ebbin' – they'd spend the day out at sea – they'd have t' fly into the wind south or south-west t' get back an' of course then they'd always fly right low, hedge-hoppin' almost. You could allus hear 'em comin' an' you'd be able t' shoot a few. Not only duck but wigeon, teal, that sorta thing.

When that blew an' we couldn't get off, we'd be down on the quay an' sometimes we might decide t' go an' get some pheasants. We'd say, "Well, we'll go after dinner." An' three o' us used t' go. One would walk up on the river wall an' the other two took the boat. The one on the wall would walk as far as the end o' the wall till he came t' the flats, as he allus knew the ol' gamekeeper would come that way t' go t' the farm t' get his milk. After he'd gone [the gamekeeper] he'd go back an' tell the others in the boat t' come along. We'd all get in the boat together an' go up t' the island in the middle o' the river. Well, then we'd start our shoot, brushin' 'em up an' shootin' 'em down, mostly pheasants or whatever. The keeper would come an' watch but o' course he couldn't get near you! I remember one time we went up there an' got thirty-two. A day or so after – 'cos we sold 'em locally at half-a-crown each – when the wind had eased an' we could get off, as I came down the road the local copper wuz talkin' t' a gentleman. I heard this gentleman say he'd bought pheasants off one o' us. When I got down t' the river, I asked my mate if he had sold any t' this man an' he said, "Yis." "Well," I said, "he's just told the copper." But we never heard no more. He weren't a bad ol' stick, the ol' copper.

After Christmas an' the weather wuz bad – cold, snowy an' icy – two of us would go away early mornin' about seven an' walk all the dykes puttin' all the fowl up an' shootin' 'em. O' course in the evenin' we would go back t' the reedland between Dingle an' Dunwich where there's a big stretch o' open water an' we'd stand either side o' this t' see the fowl come *down t' light*. Even if that wuz frozen they'd still come an' slide about on the ice an' we'd shoot 'em as they came down. Dogs? Some used t' take 'em but I had a sheepdog but I didn't allus take him because it wuz often so cold that it wuz cruel. I mean, I've seen him covered in icicles that rattled when he

236

walked! I remember one shoot up there when I knocked eleven shovellers down in one shot! That wuz a-snowin' an' I only had one barrel too but I could hear 'em patterin' down on the ice an' I got eleven o' 'em.

When the thaw set in, we would walk the rushes an' reeds at the back o' the beach as the ducks used t' like t' get there. One day me an' a mate were *walking these up*; one o' us wuz by the side o' the dyke an' the other wuz away in the rushes when he said t' me, "There's lots of ducks swimmin' up the dyke. You go round t' the front o' where they're swimmin', I'll shoot along, an' whatever get up you can shoot at." He had a double along the dyke, but nuthin' got up. Well, when I went t' look t' find out why, he'd shot somebody's tame ducks! We had t' scrab these up, stuff 'em in our bags an' come away directly. He'd shot the lot but we never heard nuthin' about it.

I use t' snare all the common an' the fields up the back here. I mean you weren't allowed t' snare on the fields but I used t'. You'd set 'em at the close [of day] an' go round agin first thing as it come daylight t' take the rabbits an' hares out. Then you could leave your snares, lay 'em down in the run an' set them up agin at night. I've had a dozen a night an' I used t' set forty or fifty snares, set 'em all about.

Sometimes we might go nettin' on the local marshes. That wuz all right but on Blois's an' the landowners' land that wuzn't. You would stake the net out across the marsh gate 'cos the rabbits had t' go through that t' get on the marsh. Then we'd get the dogs out t' drive the rabbits an' hares through the gate. The net wuz about three foot high an' thirty t' forty foot long. You'd stake it in the ground an' it would bag an' the rabbits would roll up when they hit it. We used t' make the nets ourselves but they had a pretty big shale, a four inch mesh, much bigger 'n anythin' you'd use fishin'. Two o' us would also go after rabbits with a torch an' gun. The light shone on the rabbit would mesmerise it an' o' course all you'd got t' do then wuz shoot it. Most o' the rabbits we sold t' the local butcher who gave us about sixpence each for 'em an' three shillin's for a hare.

Some o' the fishermen kept ferrets an' we'd go on the common an' find all the holes an' put a *purse-net* over 'em, leavin' the hole t' put the ferret in. The rabbits would start then an' get up in the nets an' you'd get 'em that way.'

Guy Barber remembered working for Southwold Corporation on one occasion doing coastal defence work in the days before the seawall was built and high tides could be very damaging:

'Do you know, some years ago now, they decided t' put some faggots along from the Gun Hill t' the Lifeboat shed along that bank, 'cos the bank worn't so high then. They put the contract out t' the unemployed. You'rd got t' put a price in, how much you could do it for. There wuz t' be a double row o' faggots from the foot o' the Gun Hill t' down opposite the Dutch Barn. Your'd got t' put a price in, how much you reckoned you could do this contract for. The faggots would be found for you an' brought down t' the beach an' your'd got t' put 'em in. Me, my cousin Ernie, poor ol' *Brushy* Watson, an' ol' Bob Deadman put in a contract for it an' we got it. We put these here faggots in. Ol' Bob used t' dig the trench, Ernie wuz older 'n us, he used t' wire 'em up an' cut the heads orf, I used t' take 'em away from him up on the bank an' I had t' set 'em in the holes in the trench. When we finished this contract, 'cos a lot o' 'em said we wouldn't pay our way, we had £10 in pocket. So ol' Alf Baggott, he wuz the Mayor, he come down one day. He say, "You together have made such a good job o' this, we had a Council Meetin' the other night, an' want t' know if you'll continue on as far as the Yacht Pond." So we did, an' I should think when we finished up, we'd got £7 apiece after we paid off.'

Finally Mr Jarvis remembered two ways his father tried to make ends meet:

'There wuz so many ways o' *raisin' the wind*. You'd go along the beach pick up wood, all sorts o' things. I can remember my father, two o' 'em, pickin' up a sail, mast an' a sail. They knew they couldn't get it into the town without the customs people seein' it, so they went right up Easton, round Reydon an' come in the back somewhere, the back o' the common. Carted this thing miles so they shouldn't be caught. Oh yes! Another thing they told me about, in a shed down there somebody had picked up a barrel o' rum an' people couldn't make it out, middle o' the mornin' some o' 'em were rollin' about. They were a long time before they found out about this. Customs din't find out but people used t' wonder, always keep a-goin' t' this shed, havin' a tipple or two now an' then!... Through the winter time my father used t' pick up cornelians or what he could an' he'd keep 'em till the visitors come. Then while they were lookin', he'd say, "Well I've got some here." Perhaps he'd get a bob for 'em. They were all full o' little tricks t' raise the wind, you know.'

19

The Doom Of The Sea

On July 1st, 1845 an incident occurred by now all too familiar in these pages. Several punts had gone off before daybreak to trawl for soles when a sudden violent storm arose from the south-west which forced them to make immediately for the shore, where it soon became obvious by the turbulence of the sea that beaching would be impossible.

At around 11 a.m. Robert English, whose two sons were with him, nevertheless attempted to beach but the punt, having struck on the shoal, capsized and the boys drowned. In the confusion of the capsize, English grabbed hold of the oars and was swept out to sea on the tide. His plight was witnessed by many visitors and townspeople watching from the cliffs as he appeared and disappeared at intervals.

Two fishermen off in the punt *Dart*, themselves making for shore, seeing English in peril of his life, with great skill managed to get close enough to haul him aboard. They then headed towards the Pilot Cutter, *Providence* riding out the storm at anchor in the bay in an attempt to shelter under her lee, but to no avail. Their only hope now was to drop anchor and wait.

Meanwhile, the Lifeboat, *Solebay* was successfully launched. As it was not possible to come alongside *Dart*, the crew manoeuvred into a direct line astern of her and signalled to the fishermen to slip anchor. *Dart* duly drove down towards *Solebay* and through skilful work the crew got a line aboard and the three men were saved.

Generous persons in the Town subsequently raised a subscription of £21.19s.6d. for the benefit of the Lifeboat crew and the two fishermen for their efforts in saving English. William Cragie further proposed that English himself should be a sharer in the subscription to compensate for the loss of his boat. The incident was duly written up in The Lifeboat Society Minute Book which rightly praised the crew for their efforts, skill and bravery.

Maggs also recorded the incident giving more details. English's two sons were William, seventeen and James, fifteen. English managed to stay afloat with the assistance of the oars for nearly an hour before Jo B Hurr and James May in Ben Herrington's *Dart* went to his aid. With the wind still increasing, the Lifeboat was launched, the general opinion being that had it not done so, English too would have drowned. On Sunday July 6th, William was picked up at Easton and on the 8th, James at nearly the same place. Both were interred at Walberswick.[1]

In his *Diary* Maggs then inserts a ballad on the tragedy written by Mary Smith of Wangford whom he identifies as the daughter of the late John Lowsey of Southwold. The Lowseys were an ancient family in the town with a strong maritime background.

Smith's ballad gives unfolding details of the incident. According to her, another boat (presumably *Dart*) is close by when English's boat capsizes. After English surfaces, Smith adds a new and astonishing detail:

> The father arose to the surface again,
> But who knows the anguish he feels,
> When attempting to swim, is prevented by one
> Of his sons, that held fast to his heels.

With the boat near, English now faces a terrible choice:

> The boat it is nigh, and if he is saved,
> His son from his heels he must shake.

Did English deliberately kick his son from his heels to save his own life? And if he did how did the knowledge emerge to be made into a ballad and circulated in the surrounding district? If English volunteered it himself, as the ballad later suggests, what then of his relations with his wife? Would she ever be able to forgive him? How could they to live together again? And in the community, how would English be regarded? What would his fellow fishermen think of him? What thoughts would enter minds as he went about his business? What was said to his face? No wonder Smith suggests at the end of the ballad that the only aid that can come is from on high. And perhaps this explains why the account in the Lifeboat Minute Book states cryptically that 'the circumstances attending the occurance (sic) require no inflated language…yet it is deemed advisable that the simple facts be stated.'[2] Stick to the facts, in other words, and do not indulge in speculation.

When E. R. Cooper wrote about the incident in *Seventy Years' Work of the Southwold Lifeboats* (1912) he furnished more detail still. Contradicting Maggs, he says English's sons were twins about ten years old both of whom 'it is said hung on to their father's legs and nearly drowned him' and that 'in his struggles [English] kicked them off for which involuntary act report says the mother never forgave him.'

Next Cooper says that, according to tradition, when John Bedingfield Hurr and James May were crossing South Green about 2 a.m. to board *Dart* early that morning, they saw:

'…a tall woman approaching, who just before they met, turned up the path to the Casino; they remarked upon this unusual occurrence but thought she was the wife of some master mariner who was going to sea that tide, and been down to see him off; as they passed the path they stopped to look after her but she had disappeared and no one was to be seen, and on thinking the matter over they came to the conclusion that she had no head, and were firmly convinced that it was a warning, it is needless to add that they were absolutely confirmed in that opinion by the subsequent events of that morning.'[3]

A possible filicide now presaged by the unlucky sighting of a headless woman has further inflated the incident and was bound to lodge itself in the collective memory. It next appears in a novel by Neil Bell, *Forgive Us Our Trespasses* (1943) who misleadingly claimed that the incident took place in his lifetime and was the reason he wrote it.[4] This darker novel, like *Bredon And Sons* also set in Southwold, explores the weakness in the character of Tom Bokenham, a longshoreman's son who becomes an apprentice in the boatbuilding firm of Welton. To my mind, Bell's descriptions of the beach and the beachmen's lives surpass those in *Bredon and Sons* for accuracy and atmosphere. Here he describes how the character, Jaunty Crickmore, became the owner of the nameboard, *Nyl-Ghau*:

'She was found on the Barnard Sand by the yawl *Reliance*...*Reliance* stood by through an icy February night with half a gale blowing, and the following morning, the wind dropping and the sea falling away, four of *Reliance*'s crew, Jaunty one of them, got aboard her, and at high tide, helped by *Reliance* warped her off and brought her to anchor off Senwich. Here was a rich prize and a good night's work: salvage wouldn't be less than twenty pounds a head. And then the gale got up again (*Nyl-Ghau* leaking all the time like a riddle) and she pulled her anchor, drove on to the Kaneway and went to pieces before any of the yawls could get out to take the men off. Jaunty and two others reached the shore safely, battered and half drowned; but the fourth man, Will Jellicoe, failed to reach the shore alive. And not a penny piece for salvage from the owners. Most of the wreckage came ashore and the nameboard became Jaunty's.'[5]

Nyl-Ghau, a Persian word meaning Blue Cow, was attached to a shed on Ferry Road belonging to one of the Rogers, (see p 264). Bell is faithful to the beachmen's experience here; sometimes they profited from salvage, sometimes their efforts gained them nothing and even cost them their lives.

Tom's flaw first manifests itself as a child in an inexplicable crisis of confidence when he loses a diving competition at the Town's Regatta, having been expected to win a prize on previous form. When asked to explain by his father he can only say:

' "I felt – I felt not frightened, but – but O, I dorn't *knaw* Father." Again he was silent for a moment or so, and then he added, "But I did knaw sutthin: that I weren't gewin to be no good." '[6]

The poverty of his life, as the son of a longshoreman and a parsimonious, resentful mother, makes Tom a solitary brooding character. After his father's loss at sea, Tom is apprenticed to Arthur Welton who takes pity on him. Bell includes an initiation ceremony, an 'indecent ceremonial' (perpetrated I am afraid to say by Harry Jellicoe – my son's name) which re-enacts his own real-life experience at Chatham to which Tom reacts 'with passionate fury'. He confronts Welton who admits to it being 'a dom silly monkey trick and dirty tew'[7] and says he will stop it in future. Tom remains silent, let down and humiliated.

As time goes by, Tom proves a first-class boat builder but rejects Welton's offer to take his indentures early, preferring to follow his father into longshoring, to the incredulity of his master. Once again, he cannot explain his decision, but he is sure of it. Separated from his childhood friends, the son of the wealthy local builder and Welton's own now privately educated children, and following the death of his mother, Tom's solitary life continues though he can never stop loving Hetty Welton. Two further episodes of funk occur, first when Tom loses a punt race to Dick Welton at the Regatta by sailing wide round a buoy instead of holding his course and second when, just after winning a wrestling contest at the annual Trinity Fair, he freezes and does nothing as a dog threatens to attack a child. 'I was petrified for the moment' is all he can say.[8]

Prevailing against all opposition however, Tom overcomes class prejudice and eventually marries Hetty. They have a daughter, Sally followed by twins, Jon and David. Then Bell uses the English incident.

Tom decides to take his new punt, *Sally* on her maiden voyage with the boys, joining others going off. Warned by Jack Craigie (sic) that a Friday and the 13th is 'no daay to wet a new bort. Bor'[9] the wind backs and a north-east storm suddenly erupts. The longshoremen are shepherded home by the lifeboat, Tom, with the twins aboard, the last to arrive near the shore. A crowd, including Hetty, has gathered on the cliff watching the drama. As *Sally* approaches the Kaneway she:

'…was hidden in a trough; rose and came on as straight as an arrow. And now she was into it; was hidden by the breakers and a sheet of spray. She reappeared for a moment and then suddenly was gone. A great groan rose up suddenly from the crowd. But Hetty heard nothing, was conscious of nothing for a moment; and then hardly aware of her action, she was scrambling down the cliff and hurrying over the shingle, ankle-deep in spume. They made way for her, and presently she stood among a scattered line of men and stared out to the Kaneway and saw what they saw: a head bobbing; someone swimming; or a dead man; or a dead child; coming in on the breakers.'

A living chain was formed which rushed into the sea. The first man clutched the swimmer or the body and held fast. It was Tom Bokenham, battered but conscious. Ashore, he struggled to his feet.

' "Where are the boys?" he gasped. No one answered. He made as if to plunge into the sea, but they closed about him. Hetty dragged at his arm as he stared out towards the sea. "Jon and Davie!" she cried distraught, "Jon and Davie! Where are they?" He stared down at her, "God knows," he said.'[10]

And though he is restrained from going back into the sea, it later emerges from two eye-witnesses that after the boat capsized the boys were seen clinging to Tom's legs and that he kicked them off. When Hetty confronts him, he neither confirms nor denies it. The inevitable split occurs and Tom removes himself, returning to a solitary life on the cliff at Easton. A pariah, he is eventually forgiven by Sally who nurses him but when she dies suddenly in shocking circumstances, only a brief reconciliation with Hetty takes places before their own dramatic end.

As in *Bredon And Sons* (in which Bell also includes the incident), the doom of the sea is ever present in the novel, but Bell's real interest is in dysfunction, a theme he knew would deter some readers. Tom's inexplicable cowardice is the cause of his undoing and a further version of the unreliable father, the source of Bell's own angst.

It is not really surprising that catastrophe at sea would preoc-cupy a fishing and sea-faring community. It occurs twice in what is perhaps the longshoremen's first appearance in fiction, Susanna Moodie's *Flora Lyndsay; or Passages in an Eventful Life* (1854). Moodie was one of the five Strickland sisters who lived at Reydon Hall. Brought up to be independent women, all became writers. Agnes achieved fame for her romanticised histories of the Queens of England and Scotland, her elder sister, Elizabeth her amanuensis. The two younger girls, Susanna and Catharine, married and with no hope of inheritances on their own or their husbands' sides, decided to emigrate to Canada to improve their prospects. They settled to the north of Lake Ontario where they wrote about their experi-ences. Susanna Moodie's *Roughing it in the Bush* and Catharine Parr Traill's *Canadian Crusoes* both published in 1852 have be-come foundation texts of Canadian Literature, Moodie referenced for example by Margaret Atwood in her poem, *The Journals of Susanna Moodie* (1970). Such is the sisters' status in Canada that stamps were issued in 2003 commemorating them both while Trent University's downtown campus and its Graduate College are named for Catharine.

Flora Lyndsay is a prequel to *Roughing it in the Bush*, a barely disguised fiction which tells of the sisters' preparations for their emigration. As these progress, Moodie interweaves two highly melodramatic interludes involving first, a fisherman, Jarvis and his faithful dog, Neptune and next a version of the night-visiting genre in which a drowned mariner appears outside the window of his beloved before it is known that he is lost.[11]

When the time comes for departure, Moodie describes two failed attempts to board a passing steamer at sea. The first is undertaken in what she calls a pilot boat, *King William*, though she doesn't make clear whether it is a yawl or gig. The passengers wait for ten hours, eight miles off in appalling wind and rain, all becoming sea-sick before the captain, Palmer decides the expected ship will not show. Assisted by Cragie, and others, it is anyway expedient to return given the conditions and state of the passengers. A crowd has gathered on the beach thinking the boat is lost but Palmer guides her over the 'formidable breakers which thundered on the beach' and the 'foam flew in feathery volumes high above their head, until 'the keel grated on the shingles.'[12] The second attempt is made a week later. This time the cliffman in charge is the surly and unsociable Sam Rogers. They rendezvous with the wrong ship to discover the expected one has been delayed. Again, there is nothing for it but to return. This time the cliffmen's worst fear descends, a blanketing fog. Though they avoid collision, 'the fog was so dense and bewildering that they made little way, and the long day was spent wandering to and fro without being able to ascertain where they were.'[13] Only when a breeze sprang up and the moon appeared were they able to hoist sail and return, after midnight, onto the deserted shore. The embarkation succeeds at the third attempt.

Novelists were not the only ones to take up the pen to depict the longshoremen. An unusual writer was the marvellously named Walter Scott Montgomery, a blind itinerant organ-grinder who, with such a name, could only have been a balladeer. His was an interesting life, told first by Ronald Fletcher in *In a Country Churchyard* (1980) and also noted by Richard Fisk, Southwold's stalwart postman for nearly forty-seven years. Both of them had it from Montgomery's daughter who saved his now lost diary. Montgomery tramped between Southwold, Westleton and the surrounding villages pulling his barrel organ and selling his work.

Montgomery's ballads were traditional in purpose, subject matter and form. They functioned as ballads always had, as a means of passing on news or stories of disasters and catastrophic incidents. He wrote of national and local events – the death of Edward VII, of Lord Kitchener, incidents of the First World War such as the execution of Nurse Edith Cavell; of tragedies at sea, the sinking of the *S.S Lusitania*; of shipwrecks and local lifeboat rescues; of longshoremen who drowned at home or whilst serving in the Navy; he liked to prick the pompous behaviour of Southwold Town Council particularly in relation to the events surrounding the 1912 Trinity Fair, or ingeniously to inventory in a thirty-four-verse epic – *Old Friends of Long Ago Part 1 and Part 2* – the deaths of 150 Southwold people. His style also honoured the tradition in that he suggested tunes to which the ballads and their choruses could be sung and he adopted the customary rhythm and rhyme. Overall it is estimated he wrote over 200 such ballads.

Poem in loving memory of Edward Rogers and his son Esau who were drowned off Dunwich by the swamping of their boat "Clara" on Friday 14th June 1901 is his version of the tragedy with which this book begins:

> By and by as the wind kept rising
> The boats made a rush for the shore
> And all landed safe but the "Clara,"
> She was swamped by the waves dashing o'er.
>
> With the child on his back tightly clinging
> He was plunged in the pitiless sea
> And being a very good swimmer
> He fought with the waves manfully.
> The sight must have been most heartrending

Poor Ted struggling there midst the foam

His poor little son loudly crying,

Crying for mother and home.

A mate who was near, but to leeward,

Did his utmost to rescue and save;

But the wind and the tide were against him,

He alas! Saw them sink 'neath the wave.[14]

A plaque in the Reading Room commemorates Alfred Rogers one of five Southwold Naval reserves from longshoring families who, just after the First World War was declared, were posted to two elderly cruisers, *Aboukir* and *Cressy*. The others were Arthur Green, Robert Ladd, Robin Barber and Bertie Goldsmith.[15] On September 22nd, 1914 they, with a sister ship, *Hogue* were patrolling the Dutch coast. Ordered to maintain a speed of ten to twelve knots and to zig-zag, they did neither as no German submarines were known to have ever been in the area. At 6:25 a.m. *Aboukir* was torpedoed by U9, commanded by Otto Widdigan. *Hogue*, thinking *Aboukir* had hit a mine went to rescue survivors only to be torpedoed herself. Widdigan surfaced and then aimed at *Cressy*. All three ships were sunk. 1,459 lives were lost, including the five Southwold lads, and 837 rescued.

Montgomery's response was: *In Loving Memory of* FIVE BRAVE SOUTHWOLD LADS *Who perished when the three cruisers, the "Aboukir" the "Hogue" and the "Cressy" were torpedoed off the Dutch Coast, September 22nd, 1914.* The ballad is patriotic and sentimental:

Far away from dear old Southwold

Out upon the treacherous blue,

Fighting for old England's honour

'Neath the Union Jack so true.

Five brave lads we've loved have perished

At the call of duty stern

Gone to swell the roll of heroes

Who can never more return…

Each of the lads was commemorated in his own verse, thus:

Alfred Rogers, gone for ever
Sank exhausted 'neath the foam
Never more to see his loved ones,
Nor his native town or home.
With a thousand gallant comrades
Who have for their country died
Cheering to the last for England
As they sank beneath the tide.

As in the previous ballad, the last verse seeks consolation in the next world.

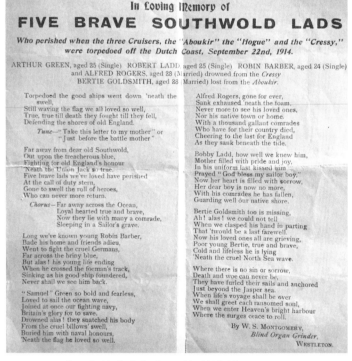

A typical ballad distributed by W. S. Montgomery

When the subject demanded it, Montgomery always championed the ordinary man who often perished through selflessness and heroism. The proceeds from the sale of his ballads were frequently donated to the suffering family. It is extraordinary to think that thanks to Montgomery, the ballad survived in its traditional form and purpose well into the 20th century in coastal East Suffolk. According to Fletcher,

'Little girls used to dance to his music in the streets' when he came into the villages towing his barrel-organ accompanied by his family and sometimes his friend, the peg-legged, Snowden.[16]

Occasionally the beachmen themselves took up the pen. One such was Ben Lowsey, *Masterpiece* to his peers, for he was also an artist. He sailed as bosun in big ships for much of his life and when he was done, returned to the beach where he ran pleasure boats for the visitors and the *camera obscura*. E. R. Cooper called him 'a poet of sorts'. I have only come across three of his pieces, idiosyncratic takes on the form. *Lines on the Gallant Rescue of Five of the* CREW OF THE DAY STAR *by the Southwold and Dunwich Life-boats, December 27th, 1896* tells the story and sings the praises of Southwold's brave Lifeboat men.

After word has reached Southwold from Dunwich that three ships are in distress in Dunwich bight, the Lifeboat (*London Coal Exchange*) is launched and approaches the *Day Star* with cox'n John (Jack) Cragie at the helm:

> And high above the howling sea is heard John Cragie's cheer
> Lower away boys and stand by, as the Day Star we drift near
> See lashed in the ship's rigging against the stinging blast
> Are seen five poor fellows, bold Catchpole was the first.

Four are rescued, leaving only the captain aboard. As the lifeboat approaches:

> They tried to get the boat to him, brave Cragie at the helm
> The great seas they came rolling on the Life-boat did o'er whelm.
> Ah! Well may ye stand on old Thorpe beach and hold your bated breath
> When you watch the boat with her brave crew so near the jaws of death
> Oh Heavens! He's washed from the boat and struggling in the sea,
> But see, he's rescued, once again with his brave crew to be.[17]

The Dunwich Lifeboat, also standing by, manages to save the captain after Cragie is rescued by his men, so in a remarkable episode, all five of the crew are brought safely ashore.

No matter that Lowsey writes in clichés and is occasionally

ambiguous – it's not immediately clear that it is Cragie and not the captain who is washed overboard, literary merit is not the point; the celebration of bravery by local lifeboatmen most certainly is. Lowsey honours his fellow cliffmen in a heartfelt tribute. Emerson, who befriended Cragie, also wrote about this incident having got it from Cragie himself and Cragie's own version was reported verbatim in the local press.[18] Not unlike the English incident, the doom of the sea was compelling.

Heartfelt, sentimental and elegiac also are Lowsey's lines on Cragie's predecessor, *On the Death of Benjamin Herrington one of our Life-boat Heroes who died May 8th, 1890.* Lowsey begins with childhood memories:

> When I was once a happy boy, I have stood beside his place
> Have heard his kindly voice to me, and seen his happy face…

He goes on to praise Herrington's skills as cox'n:

> The lifeboat many a time has launched, when stormy seas
>   overwhelm;
> We've seen our coxswain take his place all fearless at the helm;
> And oft have heard his cherry [*sic*] voice, a voice that we well knew,
> Above the tempest's howling roar, cheer on his daring crew;
> What could excel that noble heart, amid the billows strife,
> As with his brave and daring crew, they risked each precious life…

Before lamenting his passing:

> Our dear old friend is gone, for he has done his part
> Yes! for ever gone: now rest that noble heart;
> The loved ones he have left behind, he's only gone before;
> May they meet him there, above all on that happy shore.[19]

'Cherry voice' is so much more appealing than the intended 'cheery voice' and seems so appropriate for the 'lion-maned' Herrington.

Ben Lowsey's neighbours on the beach under Gun Hill happened to be the Herringtons, 'young Bennicks' succeeding his father. One of the latter's sons, William also served in the Lifeboat before the First World War. When war broke out, he became the gunner on a requisitioned drifter, *Golden Chance* (LT 1215) patrolling the coast in anti-submarine activity. On one occasion an incident occurred about which he composed a ballad, if it can be called that. I have a recording of it which I have transcribed. At 8 a.m. on January 14th, 1916 whilst on patrol between the Mull of Kintyre, Sandy Island and Ailsa Craig awaiting orders that were late:

> Our watches changed around again
> And to my gun I climbed my way
> Scanning the swell rough sea
> A swirling mine was straight in our path.
> O saviour! Was my flashing thought
> Just seconds left for me!
>
> I could not tell a soul
> But to leap and try to keep her free
> As I rushed along the deck
> And breathless climbed the bridge and opened the door
> I pushed past my shipmate at the wheel
> And gripped the telegraph
> 'Full speed astern!' I rang it down
> As our ship trembled like a leaf.
> Thank God my deed was done in time
> I had saved them all by just seven feet.

What follows is disappointment:

> I can always see that picture of that storm-tossed Irish sea
> And that dear old land of Scotland as that dawn was breaking free.
> I have tried to tell my story how I saved these lives at sea
> But I was never reported by one
> Who should have done
> Who knew I saved his life as all others did, you see.[20]

The 'one' was the superior officer in command who for whatever reason, did not want it known that a gunner had given the order to go full speed astern in breach of regulations. So, despite his heroism, Herrington was overlooked for recognition of his life-saving deed, about which he clearly felt resentful. On the page this is barely a ballad, resembling one occasionally only in rhythm and the odd rhyme.

However, to hear Herrington speak the verse is extraordinary because his voice – clear, resonant, accented and rhythmic is marvellous. The oral tradition overrides the written one here in a very interesting way, asserting the older way of transmission.

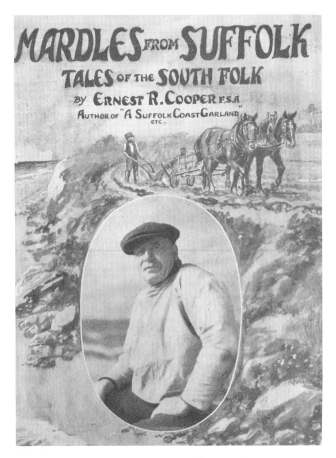

Mardles from Suffolk (1932) dust jacket

The doom of the sea also interested E.R. Cooper, and much more besides. Lawyer, Town Clerk, indefatigable member of innumerable committees, writer and journalist using the pseudonym *Suffolk Coast*, there wasn't much to do with the sea and beach life that escaped his attention. In books, articles and pamphlets he recorded a vanishing way of life. Though he never recorded longshoring as Emerson had, he wrote about almost everything that surrounded it. As lifeboat secretary, he often went out with his box camera in the *Alfred Corry*, his great friend the cox'n, Sam May at the helm, snapping life aboard. He wrote the history of the Lifeboat, recording the rescues (and failures) the beachmen attempted, clearly in awe of their skills. Similarly, in *Storm Warriors of the Suffolk Coast* (1937) he recorded the biographies and rescues made by Lifeboat men along the coast. *A Suffolk Coast Garland* (1928) gathered together much of his journalism showing his wide range of interests. *Mardles from Suffolk* (1932) showed his good ear for dialect. The cover, an echo of Emerson's *Pictures of East Anglian Life*, has Charles *Champagne* Rogers in its centre. In many pamphlets he wrote for example, about Southwold's struggle against erosion, a serious problem in his time; about smuggling along the coast and about wrecks which littered the shore. His more obscure pieces are worth the effort of tracking down, for instance *The Suffolk and Norfolk Beach Yawls*, a detailed piece on the origins, construction and history of the craft, which:

'…will never again be seen launching off the beach in a smother of sea, or thrashing out seaward with a pilot and his black canvas bag in the stern sheets and a crew of hairy, hardy amphibians piling up the bags of shingle ballast in the weather bilge, and working the foresheet to every squall.'[21]

Four volumes of his scrapbooks were donated to Southwold Museum by his daughter in which ephemera feature prominently. Only Cooper could have kept a note about the wife of Jacob Spenser, a cliffman who drowned in 1802 when his yawl, *Sailors' Friend* capsized beaching to board a pilot. Previously married to a member of the Fish family, she had a sole tattooed on her thigh,[22] surely the definitive Southwold inking.

Notes

1   Maggs Vol 1 p.127

2   *Minute Book* Lifeboat Society p.29

3   Cooper, E.R. *Seventy Years* p.10

4   Bell, Neil *My Writing Life* p.213

5   Bell, Neil *Forgive Us Our Trespasses* p.24

6   Ibid p.61

7   Ibid p.139

8   Ibid p.194

9   Ibid p.264

10   Ibid p.268

11   Moodie, Susanna *Flora Lyndsay* p.52-71

12   Ibid p.85

13   Ibid p.91

14   Author's collection.

15   A photograph can be seen in Barrett Jenkins *Reminiscences of Southwold* p.4

16   Fletcher, Ronald *In A Country Churchyard* Ch.2

17   Southwold Museum

18   Press Cutting Dec 29th, 1886 in Maggs Vol 5, Southwold Museum

19   Southwold Museum

20   Author's collection

21   Cooper, E. R. *The Suffolk and Norfolk Beach Yawls* p.213

22   Cooper, E.R. *Old Southwold Vol 1* p.140

20

Masterpiece

If the longshoremen were not extensively written about, they fared better in works of art. Walberswick is well-known as having been an artists' colony but Southwold also attracted its share of painters. Many artists and their works have been collected by Ian Collins in *Making Waves* (2005). Geoffrey Munn has also liberally illustrated *Southwold: An Earthly Paradise* (2006) with paintings of the town including beach scenes. While there is no point repeating what Collins and Munn have done, it is possible to look at works by or in which longshoremen and longshore life feature in interesting ways.

Emerson was typically sniffy about artists who 'wander along the beach with canvas or camera, pondering on the rich harmonies of dark sea-stained sand and sea-washed moss.'[1] and elsewhere of 'amateurs' around the Blyth 'of the pretty, niggling, beautified-Nature school'.[2] Twenty years later W. A. Dutt noted: 'Scarcely any exhibition of paintings can now be considered complete without some picture of Southwold, and during several months of the year artists are so numerous round about the town as almost to constitute a character-istic feature of the scenery…'[3]

Emerson would have had no time at all for the artistic merits of longshoremen who picked up a brush, though Dutt, I suspect, would have been more sympathetic. The commonest subject, unsurprisingly, was shipwreck. Among the best of the so-called 'shore-artists' were Ted Syer and Ben Lowsey. Theirs is folk art. Three examples of *Masterpiece* Lowsey's work can be seen in the Reading Room. The *Loss of the Elizabeth Kilner* 1892, a small but good example (Plate IV).

On February 15th the vessel was observed in difficulties in a south easterly or an easterly gale. Though she had managed to stand off, it was clear that sooner or later she would be driven on to the lee shore. The lifeboat men in anticipation, hauled the surf lifeboat, *Quiver II* with the aid of horses north, right through the town along the top of the cliff at Easton, almost as far as the broad, where the cliff descended again to the beach. Arthur Grubbe and his brother, Edmund were eye witnesses. Arthur recorded that:

'…by the time we got there, there were at least a hundred men, women and children. The doomed vessel was still on the same tack [starboard] close-hauled and making slow progress. Three or four times I saw her attempt to 'go about' and of course every time she lost ground getting nearer to the shoal. She made no signal of distress whatever and the skipper appeared to be doing his damnedest to keep her off. She was carrying too much canvas and was labouring heavily. After about an hour of this sort of thing she had gradually been driven by the wind into the broken water of the outer shoal which was very heavy. She now half-hoisted the red ensign as a signal of distress and Sergeant [the Lifeboat Secretary] and the chief Coastguard waved the Board of Trade Flag for her to come ashore. It was nearly high water but though she looked light I don't believe anyone expected to see her clear the shoal easily. She lowered her main peak but though she had little or no weigh on it was a good many seconds before she paid off. At last she came round and made straight for the shoal. It was a grand sight to see her come through... She gave one bump on the shoal and broached-to a bit but came round again all right and sailed straight ashore. There was some little difficulty getting a line to her, the rocket missed her but eventually the chief boatman of the Coastguard [Bill Davis] threw a line to her. The crew were numbed and stupefied. There was a boy & four men. The boy was in a Training Ship uniform and I believe had run away a few days before. One of the men – a lad – was in a black bob-tail coat and looked like a landsman. We afterwards heard that the Captain & mate were efficient sea-men. The boy had never been to sea before: one of the men was just out of prison and presented himself as AB [able bodied] though he knew nothing about the sea: and the third man was little more than the ex-convict. The schooner was the *Elizabeth Kilner,* eighty tons, built in 1871 bound from London to Scotland with a hundred and twenty tons of bone dust.'[4]

Grubbe doesn't make clear that once the crew had made the line to the ship fast and the men on the beach had pulled it taut, some of them went into the sea to give what help they could. The crew attached themselves to the line by means of a thin rope and holding on, edged forward one by one to the shore. Sometimes they were smothered by the waves, sometime pushed up as the ship rolled, snatched to safety by the shoremen out in the breakers when they neared the beach.

The incident is interesting in so many ways: the sheer effort of transporting the lifeboat through the town and along the cliff at Easton, shadowing the schooner, is remarkable of the dedication of the lifeboatmen; the inadequate crew, including a child, unable to sail the boat – Grubbe said that the Captain couldn't leave the helm to get the boat about – indicative of the poor standards so often encountered aboard ships; the potential wreck as an event in the town attracting so many spectators; the difficulty of operating the rocket apparatus; the shoals off and the lee shore, the perennial danger. Board of Trade maps which marked wrecks with dots show these were more numerous off the East Anglian coast than anywhere else in the country.

Lowsey's painting shows the schooner broadside on the beach. So low is the beach line that he has only enough room to suggest the figures gathered there as stick men. The rocket apparatus can be seen in the centre and to the right are those holding the line ashore and in the waves. The focus is on the schooner, or more accurately on the grey-green white-topped waves which overwhelm her, whipped up by the easterly gale. The seas are enormous, taking up the majority of the canvas. Cooper called it a 'bitter wild day' and that the ship approached the beach 'sometimes perched on the crest of a monster sea and next minute half-mast down in the trough.' She was lucky to pick up a 'thundering boiling crest' to cross the shoal and had she not been lifted at that moment she would surely have struck.[5] You can hear it in your imagination, the roaring and thundering in the gnawing, numbing gale and you can feel the tension of all as she crossed that furious white threshold.

A tiny book in the Museum contains a small series of photographed pictures of wrecks collected by Cooper, each accompanied by a few interesting notes. One shows another painting of the incident by Lowsey, this time from an impossible viewpoint above the sea. The beach, a thin dark line about half-way up the canvas is dotted with tiny figures looking out to the schooner rolling towards the shoal. The beach is almost obliterated by the sky which descends in fast-driving clouds and by the sea, a mass of white-breaking waves pulverising the shore. It has a remarkable energy. Commenting, Cooper wrote that when he first saw the picture, he remarked to Lowsey that he had omitted the houses on top of the cliff. Lowsey replied that he could do ships but not houses.

Loss of the Elizabeth Kilner February 15th, 1892, Ben Lowsey

Cooper was one of those who helped haul *Quiver II* to Easton. When he got home, he made a sketch of the incident which was published in the *Daily Graphic*; he also wrote an account which appears at the end of *Storm Warriors of the Suffolk Coast*. He used another version for the cover of *A Suffolk Coast Garland* (Plate V). The schooner's cargo, Cooper calls it guano and Grubbe bone dust, both fertilisers, was taken off and the boat sold and broken up on the beach where she had grounded safely, though not without much concern.

Many paintings have a topographical element which give an indication of ways in which beach life was organised. A beautiful watercolour, *Below East Cliff* made in 1886 by Walter Crane (Plate VI) shows the Kilcock Cliff Company's look-out perched above Critten's workshop and in the distance looking north, the sheds and punts of the Kilcock men. Hidden behind Critten's shop the masts of the Company's yawl, the first *Bittern* rise up. The reverse view is also well captured in Edward Edwards' *Southwold Suffolk* (Plate VII). *Bittern* is clearly visible among the crabs. The three sheds at the the curve of the cliff bottom are *Royalist, Belle Isle* and *Rosebud*. Punts line up towards Critten's workshop jutting out in the distance. The picture is also of interest showing no development beyond St James's Green where the flagpoles stand by the two-gun battery. These are wonderfully captured in Henry Davy's *Kill Cock Cliff, Southwold* (Plate VIII), on display in the Museum, where the stern of a yawl and a punt are hauled up the score, a gig can be seen on the beach and boats in the offing are being regarded through telescopes.

Another picture of interest is Thomas Smythe's of the Long Island lookout painted around 1880. A cliffman is scanning the traffic through a telescope mounted on a metal stand placed on a timber stud. Three other figures, two in sea-boots, are seated on a wooden bench waiting. The third plays with a dog. As soon as a ship is sighted, this one will run for the pilot and the two in boots will go down to the beach below to gather a crew and launch the yawl. Smythe adds a lot of detail of the fishing life, an anchor, dan, a beam trawl, baskets and drying sails.

The Long Island Company's Lookout c.1880, Thomas Smythe

This picture also gives a good indication of the scene of the fracas that took place here in 1842. On the evening of the 17th November, a group of longshoremen and others had gathered: Edward Palmer, Robert Land, Robert and William Herrington, Foster Bokenham and Abraham Girling. Girling and Palmer were Harbour pilots. Girling suffered from respiratory problems which often prevented him from working. For some reason a dispute between Bokenham and Girling arose about Girling's berth in a pilot boat that would be taking herrings to London and Bokenham jeered at him. Girling said Bokenham could take his place for five shillings. After more words, Girling grew angry and, as Bokenham left the look-out with William Herrington, he allegedly said to another, 'My fingers did kinder itch at him'. Bokenham overheard the remark and challenged Girling to fight at which they duly removed their jackets. At the inquest, Robert Herrington said that they squared up in the north-east corner of the look-out which was dark because of the shutter being closed. He opened it so 'that they might have fair play.' As he was going up the steps to go home, he saw Girling come out 'reeling like a drunken man.' Bokenham followed and then struck Girling on the face, at which Girling 'got upon his legs and staggered towards the the edge of the Cliff. He fell on his right side from weakness and slid over the rail, [clearly visible in Smythe's painting] and then fell upon the beach.' The inquest returned a verdict of death from a fit of apoplexy occasioned by extravasation of blood upon the brain, but it could not decide whether this was due to the violence or the exertion. Bokenham was summonsed to Court in Yarmouth on January 11th and for further examination on February 1st. At the ensuing Assizes at Bury St Edmunds on March 25th, he was sentenced to four months imprisonment for manslaughter. The case caused 'much excitement.'[6]

The South end of the beach was less frequently painted. An oil by Thomas Smythe painted before 1862 when the Lifeboat shed was moved, shows in the distance Gun Hill descending to the beach with the town behind (Plate IX). The Casino can be easily identified on the hill. In the foreground a punt is beached, beside which a seated figure appears to be transferring the catch from the beam-trawl beside him into a basket. Smythe has also shown three fishermen *draw-netting*, exactly as described earlier by Mr English. Two fishermen stand on the beach holding a net rope while the third rowing off in his punt will pay out the net to make a semi-circle. When he beaches the two ends will be drawn together and the catch landed. Much later, A. Heaton Cooper made a watercolour used to illustrate *Norfolk and Suffolk* (1921) showing the sheds at the back of the beach, some punts and crabs seaward and the lifeboat sheds in the distance (Plate X).

Punts were often of interest in themselves to artists. In another beautiful watercolour by Walter Crane, *Southwold A Study of Sails* (Plate XI) made in 1886 probably on the same visit as *Below East Cliff*, punts at Kilcock face the sea, sails up. Three in the foreground have hauled their nets up the mainmast to dry. On the beach the *stools* used to chock the punts upright can be seen and most interestingly in the foreground, Crane has shown a *sett* with its swan-neck lying on the beach waiting to be used.

Joseph Southall has been referenced both by Collins and Munn. His tempera paintings are perhaps the most graphic of beach life, superbly detailed scenes both of longshoremen and their punts. In almost all his images the longshoreman is at work, steadying the punt on landing, hauling it up the beach with others, mending nets, fetching a bucket of water to sluice down the inside of the punt, carrying a basket, winding a crab. Only in *The Old Fisherman* (1903) do we see a contemplative figure leaning against his punt, looking away from the sea, waiting for his partner or simply resting for a minute or so (Plate XIII). Just as Emerson saw in the 'fisherfolk' a glimpse of an older pre-industrial order, Southall's longshoremen seem intent on older rhythms, on work passed from generation to generation, obeying the call of the sea. They often seem oblivious to the visitors, some lithe in their swimsuits, desporting round them.

Southall's attention to detail is impressive. Time and again he paints the paraphernalia of longshore life. In *Fishermen and Boat* (Plate XII), for example we see the *ways* over which the boat is being hauled up the beach, the rig of the sails on the punts behind – the *traveller* ringing the mast, attached to the *yard* along whose length the lugsail is threaded and a net-barrow with basket in the foreground.

Fisherman Carrying a Sail (Plate XIV) shows a finely detailed *crab*. In *The Old Fisherman*, who was William *Rose* Deal,[7] we cannot miss the floats and ballast bags. Southall also included the *snoozle*, the hole in the curve of the stem post where it meets the keel, through which a chain, attached to the cable running from the crab, was threaded to pull it up the beach. The longshoremen's dress-slops both tanned and white, crotch-boots, variety of headgear are vividly true to life. It is colour that fascinates Southall above all, however, vibrant, luminous, washing Southwold beach with a golden light, more Mediterranean than East Anglian.

Southall recorded the names of some of his subjects. *Blondin* Stannard sits on the beach by his punt mending his net with his son, Christmas looking on in *Mending the Net* (1904) and is probably the moustached figure on the far side in *Fishermen and Boat*. Mr Barber remembered that towering thunderheads were named for him as *Blondin's Bishops*. There appear to be no LT numbers on punts in pre-1900 works. Southall's, all post-1900 however, show them clearly. LT 790 is *Boy Frank* belonging to F Stannard; LT 793 is Sam May's *Rose*; LT 829 is William Deal's *Kate*.

Two *Studies of Thomas Rogers* made in 1928 and '30 show him in typical dress: hat, slop and sea-boots carrying a bucket in the one and in profile, hatted and bearded in the other. Southall noted that he died aged 75 in December 1930 and in another study that he lived in Church Street. Maggs recorded that as a boy, he and John Crickmore junior narrowly escaped drowning in July 1866. A newspaper cutting reported that the boat in which the two were beating through the Kessingland Gat 'was suddenly capsized by a squall; Fortunately the oars floated and were seized by Crickmore, who by some exertion, was able to give one to Rogers and thus prevented him from sinking under the weight of his clothes.'[8] In 1903 he is recorded as owning two punts LT 852 *Boy Albert* and LT 853 *Boy Ernest*. He could be the uncle who upbraided Mr Rogers for his barmskin but there is no way of knowing now. It will be remembered that Mr Rogers said that when he was boy, *Bather* Rogers, who lived in Church Street, owned the shed at Ferry Road decorated with the nameboard *Nyl-Ghau*, so perhaps Thomas was Bather. And so we return to Emerson.

A platinum print made in 1886, *East Coast Fishermen* features the name board prominently. Although clearly posed, it is another fine example of Naturalistic photography. Like Southall, Emerson rarely named his subjects but from other evidence it is highly likely that standing at the back in the white slop is *Skinny* Rogers. Seated in front of him are two others. The one on our right bears a remarkable facial resemblance to the Southall study of Thomas Rogers. Thomas would have been thirty-one or thirty-two in 1886 Is he Bather? If so it is a

Two Studies of Thomas Rogers, 1928-30, Joseph Southall

remarkable coincidence that the Rogers family supplied subjects for two of the town's artists. *East Coast Fishermen* also uses props, a *dan*, a conical wooden float threaded with a flagpole known as a *Dutch bowl float*, which would have been used to mark the position of an anchor when swiping or marking the dan anchor when longlining; a net barrow with a net piled on top of it, its flat corks on the net-rope clearly visible. Emerson was particularly taken with *Skinny*: there are two striking portraits of him and he is in four interior shots of a fisherman's cottage, the sitters perhaps all Rogers. William Rogers and his son appear in two of these and also in the image of eel-picking. In contrast to Southall, Emerson's prints record the grubbiness of the longshoremen's clothes, their filthy trousers, smeared smocks, scuffed boots. Their poverty is evident, no golden glow shines on them however much they might stand for old England.

East Coast Fishermen c.1886 P. H. Emerson

Though the longshoremen left the beach after the First World War and then slowly, the harbour with its muddle of sheds and gear, they have endured in the town in other ways. Until the recent refurbishment (2017), no one looking aloft at the church tower could have failed to see that its weather vane was not the usual cock, which would have been appropriate enough standing as it does for the fisherman, Peter, but a punt with only its mizzen sail rigged, keeping it, as at sea, head to wind. This was a different fisher of souls. Mr Winter had a memory of being told that the cock which the boat replaced was shot by one of the Crickmores. In 1923 the children of the church raised the funds to pay for the new punt which Andrew Critten, then a churchwarden, designed. Though it has had to be repaired from time to time, its loss would be an absence. A model of the *Alfred Corry* hangs suspended in the nave. Outside the Reading Room a punt still sails the wind, as does another outside the Alfred Corry Museum at the harbour.

We have already noted the herrings in the town's St Edmund insignia and the contested species on the Town pump. A relief of what could be a herring shaped out of beach pebbles can also be seen over the houses in Park Lane which once belonged to Sam May.

Salvaged from wrecks, figureheads used to be placed around the town. When I was a child the figurehead of *Princess Augusta* stood on the corner of 1, East Green, opposite the Sole Bay. It can be seen in a photograph taken in the 1950s by the brilliant photographer, Edwin Smith. Those of *Lucille* and *Augusta* can now be seen in the Museum and *William 1V* with others in the Reading Room. Dwellings are (or were until recently) named for longshoremen, the shoals or wrecks. *Dutchman's Cottage* for *Dutchman* Upcraft but now renamed, an emblem of the town's change, and *Adelaide Cottage*, reputedly for Adelaide Critten, both on St James's Green. *Caneway Cottage* on Skilman's Hill for the shoal. *Idun House* in Stradbroke Road for the barque driven ashore in 1912. Concerning this, Mr Winter told me that Mr Jarvis always spoke of the Customs Officer, armed with a pistol, who threatened to shoot anyone who went aboard the beached wreck. It didn't stop the fishermen trying to get the copper off the hull, he added. And magnificently of course there is the Sailors' Reading Room, where, on the small shingle strip at its side, as if on the beach below, is a replica of a crab made by John Barber and the rudder of the yawl *Bittern* saved by Andrew Critten before she was broken up. Inside, amongst its many delights, is the nameboard from *Nordhavet*, a Norwegian bark carrying coal which came ashore in 1887.

In the graveyard are the tombs of many whose names are mentioned in this book. An interesting inscription records the death of Edward Palmer 'drowned off this beach by the upsetting of a yawl' on October 22nd, 1844. 'And there was no more Sea', the verse chosen for him from *Revelations*. The yawl was *Jubilee*, Ben

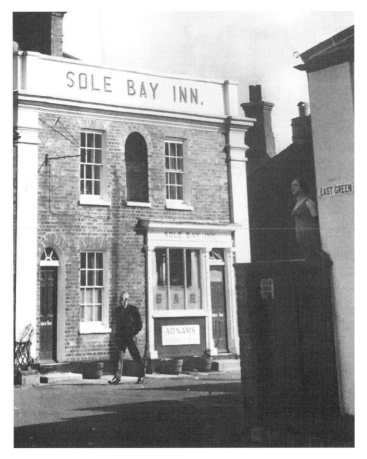

East Green, Edwin Smith, from Angus Wilson's *England*, 1971

Herrington at the helm. Palmer, it will be remembered, was found beneath the boat with an agate in his mouth. Another carving, possibly of a three-masted yawl can be seen on the stone of Mary Everard. A piece of *graffito* of a sailing boat incised into the bench top in the choir of the church by, one presumes, a bored choirboy, is also of interest. A nod to the Californians is given in the black sheds at the bottom of Skilman's Hill, and though none are now original they have not long replaced ones that survived from earlier days. The *Alfred Corry*, found abandoned in an Essex mud berth, resurrected first as *Alba* and now magnificently restored, is housed at the harbour, in which shed can also be seen wonderful displays of the fishermen. She rests only a little further south of her original berth, the long-gone Lifeboat sheds opposite the *Sail Loft* on Ferry Road. Formerly called the *Dutch Barn*, this renaming reflects one of that building's earlier functions.

The longshoreman was directly referenced in Adnams' older brews (Plate XV). A ruddy faced longshoreman in a sou'wester and a smock smoking a Dunwich clay helped to sell their Strong Ale as well as a bottled beer called *Fisherman's*. It was possible to confound non-locals by asking the landlord for a *Fish* or a *Fish and mild*. At the *Harbour Inn* above the bar billiards table, now also long gone, there used to be a comical print depicting a drunken fisherman and his mate attempting to play the game. With the light above the table swinging madly, his blurred vision has transformed the green baize of the table into a rolling wave heading menacingly towards them. It was called *A Rough Night Ashore* (Plate XVI) and beneath the title the fisherman is saying: 'Luff, Jimmy, Luff, 'Ere come a big 'un!'. The longshoremen's last trace is in the Reading Room, the Alfred Corry Museum and the Museum and their last living trace is to be seen at the summer regattas where a few of the small boats they made still sail the Model Yacht Pond.

Notes

1 Emerson, P.H. *Pictures of East Anglian Life* p.46

2 Ibid p.76

3 Dutt, W. A. *The Norfolk and Suffolk Coast* p.93

4 Grubbe, A. *Diary* February 28th, 1892

5 Cooper, E. R. *Storm Warriors* p.171

6 Maggs *Diary Vol 2* p.341

7 I am indebted to Paul Denny for this information. William Deal was his maternal great grandfather.

8 Maggs *Diary Vol 4* p.43

The Return

A woman swam up who made it known, as if water itself was whispering in my ear, that she wanted me to follow. Swimming high then dropping beneath me like a seal, her movements were strong, swift and supple. Resting, she kept turning back to see that I was there. After some time, I knew that we were close to the beach.

She waited and when I was standing on the Kaneway, just a little below the surface, the whispering sounded both like music and words. The tide is at the flood. Go now. You have but a short way to swim.

I waded to the end of the bank, kicked off, and rose to the surface, first hair, then forehead, then face. And I breathed in air, air so pure it filled my lungs and lifted me.

When I came to the beach, the others were looking out, just as I had left them. That same wind was tugging mercifully in keening notes and the shingle rattled down the shore. Blue sky above me, so blue. The others did not appear to be moving. My eyes clouded and when I opened them again, I was in my dry clothes alongside them looking into the waves and pointing at the now unpeopled sea, as if not a minute had passed.

21

The Sea Is History

Apart from Emerson's focused lens and some of Bell's novels, the Southwold longshoremen have mostly been in peripheral vision, whether in documents or cultural representations. Putting their voices into historical contexts has shone some light on the depth of their culture, on how others saw them and on the beach as workplace, a place of transition, and, far too often, a place of some considerable danger. The men often proved as vulnerable as the coast itself in the face of the relentless sea. At the same time, they were remarkable sailors and seamen, not just in their own boats but as cliffmen or lifeboatmen, equal to any on the East Anglian coast or indeed in the British Isles.

I would have loved to have seen them on the beach, to have tried to get to know them, even to have gone off with them. I would have loved to have seen how their lives worked, to have sailed a punt, to have gone into a shed, to have looked through a telescope in one of the lookouts, to have spent an hour or two with John Critten in his workshop, to have smelt the fishy beach, to have listened to them yarning, to have seen the patterns on their ganseys. I wouldn't have wanted to go off on a cold December morning longlining, knowing my hands would soon be frozen or, if I was unlucky, to get my finger snagged on a hook, nor to broach when launching or landing, nor to be ruled by the tides, nor to lose my gear fouled on an underwater obstruction or by another fisherman, nor to lug fish up from the beach in baskets and boxes to the merchant's after hours at sea and be unable to negotiate a good price, nor to worry how to feed my children in the winter, nor to leave my family to go big boating, nor, with my wife, to be in debt to the shopkeepers, understanding though they were.

I imagine all this when I am on the cliff at St James's Green looking down at vanished Kilcock, driving down Ferry Road, past California to buy fish from the harbour and, most often, standing on Long Island Cliff, outside the Reading Room. I like to walk the beach in my head to be in that other time. And sometimes morbidly, I imagine the men calling or beckoning from that grey vault. Subtexts.

Irretrievable now. But not quite, or not quite for me. When I was a boy, I was desperate to learn how to sail. Aged about eleven, I plucked up courage, mounted my bike, cycled past the water tower, down the hill, over the *cansey*, the causeway crossing the marshes, and on to Blackshore and the Blyth to the pound where the members of the Sailing club were rigging up to go to sea for the morning's races. In the prime position nearest the hard, I saw a man and asked if I could learn to sail. "You can come along with me, boy. What's your name? Come back here next week, about 9 o' clock." Though I didn't know it, this was Syd Brown, the commodore and the club's driving force. He took me with him, three-up, with his regular crew, Elvin Forster, every Sunday for about two years. He was the best sailor in the club. He could read the water like no other and he was fearless. I have sat out a force eight with him in the dinghy with rain pummelling our bodies, sky ink-black, waves steaming beneath us, wind screaming through the rigging. The only time we ever capsized, he never got wet. His dinghy was called *Schh... You Know Who* and he made it fizz. He was the son of a Kessingland longshoreman. Later, I got one of my first jobs in the same school at which he taught. We would share lifts. Every October he got his herring nets out and went night fishing. Sometimes when I picked him up, he had had only a couple of hours sleep. Why he was so good to me I do not know, but I was privileged to know him and now, I realise, to have been to sea with one who had been bred to it, who had the extraordinary qualities of seamanship of his ancestors. He was still one of them though in different form. I followed clumsily. He was a remarkable man, taken too soon after retirement by cancer. The church was packed for his funeral, the wake filled the Sailing club and that night, the *Harbour Inn*. His ashes were scattered at sea.

A few years ago, on a November morning, I decided to walk the beach to Easton Bavents, north of the town. On top of the cliff, teetering on the edge was a house. I wanted to see what it was like to be so close. As I descended the steps that zig-zagged through the concrete sea wall, the early morning sun was already igniting the sea in a glitter-path that led to the horizon. On either side it was its usual leaden grey. As if slumbering, for there was no wind to speak of, it seemed hardly to rise and fall, nor could it be said to be breaking on the shore, more to wash it with a shushing sound, a long exhalation running ahead and behind me. There were no punts spratting, off.

On my left, the cliffs, friable and crumbling glacial deposits, led the eye north. In the sun they stood clear. The umber top-soil, a yard or so deep, was pebble-dashed with small white stones. Beneath, ripples of sand undulated in bands now almost white, now tawny, now orange. Absorbing the sunlight they glowed. Where there had been falls, concave scoops had been hollowed out. On the beach the debris had piled up in pyramids so that the topsoil with its grasses and weeds camouflaged the cliff halfway. Near the top in several places sand martins' nests pockmarked the face. They were dark, empty and silent.

Walking, I kept seeing sea-rolled bricks, some fragments, some whole, their square ends rounded as if they had been poured into loaf tins. They shone red, unnaturally, in the shingle. These had been washed out of the spoil that had been used to gang up the cliff against the sea. Or they were from older buildings that had stood on the cliffs, Second World War defences perhaps or from earlier still, deposited by the tide. A stump of tree from Covehithe had been dumped at the base. It was too calm for amber. In places, threading out of the cliff just below the surface, rusting cables or blue water pipes hung perpendicularly or looped like necklaces against the yellow bands. Looking down, the low sun made isolated pebbles on the sand cast long shadows. I felt I was an astronaut.

Above the high-water line, the sand and shingle were churned up with yesterday's footprints, dog prints and, inexplicably, a single tyre mark, as if someone had been pushing a wheelbarrow. Below it, the tide had erased all marks leaving only the smooth ochre of the sand and broadcasts of gleaming shingle. By one of those quirks of land and line, the house on the cliff in the distance had now disappeared. I noticed the window handle of a car in the shingle. Wagtails bopped along the cliff.

A little further and there was the house again. Its grey and steep triangular gable had been decorated in a lozenge-shape, fashioned out of tiles. A rusting Sky satellite-dish pointed south. Now the house was above me. A fresh fall had brought down the topsoil, its greenery still intact. Soon the cliff began to curve down to the beach at an angle like that of an old Citroen.

Where it met the sand, I turned back on myself and began to walk the cliff top, rising with every step as if in a slow-motion aerial shot, the beach receding beneath me. On my right was an unploughed stubble field and the path which formed its margin showed patches of frost here and there, grey thistles whose seeds had long flown from their drooping heads, skeletal umbellifers and desiccated grasses.

At the highest point instead of following the path round, I stepped over the green link-fence already at ground level and entered the garden of the house which I now could see was not a single but a semi-detached dwelling. The garden's inner plots, gone wild, were defended by a row of tall hawthorns. The north-east winds had slicked back their tops so that in the morning light their black branches looked like a brylcreemed quiff. There were two outhouses. The first contained an open and rusting freezer, carpet tiles, rotting plasterboard and several abandoned FOR SALE signs. The second had once been an outside toilet. A toy rocking horse stood looking out to sea.

The semi was entered through a lean-to. Letters and junk mail were on the floor. In every room were plastic boxes filled with children's toys. A clock with two bears standing in relief against a scene of pastoral kitsch had stopped at 6.30 but it was impossible to tell if it was a.m. or p.m. The boxes suggested that they were meant to be removed but had remained there in anticipation. The parents had simply abandoned it. Washing up was stacked in the kitchen sink. A row of mugs hung neatly on hooks one of them bearing the legend KISSES above a rusting BREAD bin stencilled in red. Upstairs the roll top bath stood stoutly amid the chaos of the room's spilled contents. In a bedroom the only book I saw was entitled: *Your Dreams and What They Mean*. Over the whole house was a film of imminent decay as if the sea had breathed its salty breath in every room and on every object and surface.

In the stairway the yellow paint, which was blistering and peeling off the walls and which crunched when I trod on its flakes, showed traces of earlier colours and in places had reverted to the original plaster. A rusting woodburner in the living room had been wrenched out of the cast-iron fireplace. A chrome lighting unit hung incongruously from the ceiling in the kitchen. It was as if the house was shedding its history. Nor would its beginning be its end for it had once stood much further down the track away from the cliff edge and had slowly moved closer without ever having moved at all. Out in the garden almost on the lip, a computer console stood in a trailer whose wheel had half detached from the rim. Silence. No birdsong. No human noise. Just the sea sighing below.

A few months later, the house went over.

Returning, the tide was coming in. Near the end of the sea-wall I picked up my earlier footprints. The waves of that grey vault [1] were just beginning to catch them.

Notes

1   Walcott, D. *The Sea is History* in *The Star Apple Kingdom*

Glossary

(Including the long-marks and breast-marks of some of the wrecks and obstructions offshore. Supplied by Mr Robert *Dinks* Cooper of Walberswick)

Anchor, The: an anchor in seven fathoms off Southwold pier. Long-mark: Walberswick Church on the foot of Gun Hill. No breast-mark.

Arles: unwritten two-way binding contract made before the season began between the Scotch girls and their employers.

Ballast bags: small canvas bags filled with shingle used to keep the longshore punt upright at sea especially going to windward. They were shifted on each tack.

Barmskin: oilskin apron worn when sorting and gutting catches.

Beachman: one who worked on the beach. Usually a longshoreman. He might also be employed in Cliff company work.

Beam Trawl: a trawl net attached to a wooden beam at the top and a ground rope at the bottom.

Beat: to make or repair nets.

Belle Isle, The: a wreck lying in two parts in six and seven fathoms off Dunwich. Breast-mark: road open just clear of the cliff at Minsmere.

Berth/barth: the area of beach where a longshoreman kept his punt(s) with usually enough space for two.

Big boating: taking a berth in one of the Lowestoft drifters or trawlers. Big boating often meant being away for long periods and could earn more money than that made longshoring.

Blondin's Bishops: banks of thick cloud coming especially from an easterly direction. A sign of bad weather. Named for *Blondin* Stannard.

Bottom-fying: a winter job involving the clearing of ditches.

Brass Gun, The: a wreck in eight fathoms off Dunwich. Breast-mark: when you can see through the arch of the monastery.

Breast-mark: a landmark used to triangulate a position at sea. Usually used in conjunction with the long-mark.

Bridles: the two ropes attached to the beam-trawl lutes joining to form a V-shape, to which the trawl warp was attached.

Brig, The: a wreck in seven fathoms. Breast-mark: Walberswick Church over the west chimney of Westwood Lodge. Long-mark: The lighthouse over the dome on Centre cliff.

Brown shrimp: (*Crangon vulgaris*) or common shrimp. A Southwold speciality about which the following doggerel was written in *Punch*:

> Yet with heartfelt delight will the epicure say
> 'He is simply sublime is the shrimp of Sole Bay.'

Buff: a canvas covered buoy used on a deep-sea herring net to keep it afloat.

Bull: the top part of the post in a crab with a slot through its centre.

Bumpkin: the hook extending from the stem of the punt to which the tack of the dipping lug was attached.

Burton: the rope staying the mast in a longshore punt.

Butts: flounders (*Platichthys flesus*).

Calabash: a Dunwich clay pipe with a broken stem smoked upside down.

California: the area of the beach extending from the bottom of Gun Hill to the Lifeboat sheds.

Cansey: the road over the marsh leading to the harbour. A diminutive of 'causeway'.

Cast: to capsize, overturn, especially on a shoal when launching or when beaching.

Chimneys-in-one: a breast-mark. When the three chimneys on the coastguards' cottages at Minsmere were aligned in one.

Chittle-nets: nets which become tangled and twisted by the tide.

Chow: to chew tobacco.

Cliffman/Cliftman: one employed by a Cliff company and/or a member of a Cliff company engaged in shipping Trinity House pilots and salvage work.

Clift-house: the lookout on top of or embedded in the cliffs used by the Southwold Cliff Companies.

Cob: common gull (*Larus canus*).

Cod-end: the narrow bag-like end of a trawl net.

Coug: the basket in which the guts of the herrings were deposited by the Scotch-girls when gutting.

Crab: capstan used to haul boats up the beach. It was turned by a long bar inserted through the bull at the top.

Crotch-boots: leather sea-boots up to thirty-six inches long going up to the crotch.

Crow's foot: two broken strands of a mesh. See: *Sprank-mesh*.

Cutch: resin of the tree *Acacia catechu* used to tan nets, sails and slops.

Dan: a buoy used to mark the position of long lines or nets at sea.

Dipping lug: the large foresail of the longshore punt.

Dodge: to keep a deep-sea boat head to wind in rough weather.

Draw/Draw-net/Draw-ground: a method of fishing usually involving three men who make an ever decreasing semi-circle of a net at sea or in the river and draw it together to land the catch.

Drive: to drift with the tide.

Drogue-sail: a bag-like contrivance of hessian or sacking used to drag the boat with the tide when trawling during times of little wind.

Dunwich Bank: a shoal off Dunwich.

Dunwich clay: an unbroken clay pipe.

Dust: a small sample of less valuable fish brough to the fishmonger in a pail. The money exchanged provided the first pint in the pub.

Dutch bowl float: inverted conical wooden float with a flag attached to the pole running through it.

Eel-babbing: method of catching eels by threading worms through wool or worsted so that the eels' teeth became snagged in the wool allowing them to be lifted from the water.

Eel-picking: method of catching eels in the dykes using a trident-like pronged instrument called an *eel-pick*.

Fare: an early modern term referring to a fishing season or a practice at sea e.g. herringfare; swipingfare.

Farlane: wooden trough into which herrings were shot prior to being gutted.

Freaks: visitors to Southwold.

Gansey: blue hand-knitted sweater decorated with symbolic motifs such as anchors, zig-zags or flags.

Go off: to go fishing at sea.

Harnsey: the road over the marsh leading to the harbour. So-called because of the herons that frequented the dykes. O.E. heronsew. Thus in *Hamlet*: 'I know a hawk from a handsaw.' See also *Cansey*.

Hawk: to sell fish either around the town or in the local countryside.

Hayle, The: a shoal to the north off the Harbour mouth.

Heart: a coloured thread running through the centre of a rope.

Hermit, The: same breast-mark as *The Brig*. Long-mark: the lighthouse over the brewery chimney.

Hoveller: large longshore boat used on the North Norfolk coast.

Hovel-money: the same as *Dust*.

Joe's Wreck: a wreck in quarter-less nine fathoms. Breast-mark: Lighthouse and Church open an oar's length. Long-mark: Walberswick Church over Cook's corner.

Kaneway: the *kanery* was the inner shoal off the beach. Also the water between the inner and outer shoals

Kilcock Cliff: the cliff beneath St James's Green extending north. Kilcock was the area below. The Kilcock or North Cliff Company was one of the Southwold Cliff Companies. Its clift-house was situated near the site of the present public toilets.

Kist: the wooden chest containing the Scotch-girls' belongings.

Kitty: kittiwake (*Rissa tridactyla*).

Kittyhawks: an abusive term used of children who got in their fathers' ways when on the beach.

Klondike: area of the beach a little south and more north of the pier to which the Kilcock men moved after the flood of 1897.

Latch lifter: see *Dust* and *Hovel-money*. Enough money to get you into the pub where others might then buy the drinks.

Lead-line: a small lead weight attached to a line marked out in fathoms and half-fathoms denoted by different coloured ribbons, used for taking depth-soundings.

Lee-board: a board carried in the longshore punt and suspended from the tholepins to act as a centreboard. Five to six foot in length and eighteen inches wide, it was made from elm, was flat on one side and oval on the other. A Southwold invention.

Lint: generically a net. Specifically the part of the net beneath the oddy. The name suggests that in older times nets were made of linen threads derived from flax.

Little Broad: a shoal just off Benacre broad.

Loader: a rarely seen type of herring with a red nose.

Long Hundred/Long Tail/Long Tell: herrings were counted in fours, each four known as a warp. Originally thirty warps made the long hundred (120) but later it increased to thirty-three (132).

Long Island Cliff: the length of cliff running north from beneath the Sailors' Reading Room to Kilcock cliff. The Long Island Cliff Company had its clift-house beneath the Reading Room.

Longlines: baited lines of forty fathoms which were sunk by means of anchors and used to catch cod and roker (thornback ray).

Long-mark: a landmark usually taken at the same time as the breast-mark to triangulate a position.

Loon: red-throated diver (*Gavia stellata*).

Loughs/luvs/loves/louvres: parallel bars in a framework going up the smokehouse walls.

Lum: to thread a length of twine through the gills of fish in order to weigh them.

Lute-heads: three-sided iron heads with a flat top attached to each end of the beam on a beam trawl.

Maids: small roker or skate.

Make up: to store gear after the year's fishing.

Margarine: a box used for carting herrings or sprats with a capacity of three-and-a-half stone for herrings and four stone for sprats.

Middlesborough, The: a wreck in twelve fathoms. Breast-mark: Lighthouse and Chimneys-in-one.

Mizzen: standing lugsail attached to the outrigger aft of the longshore punt.

Moprey, The: a wreck in five fathoms. Breast-mark: Plant's house and Chimneys-in-one. Long-mark: the Round house over the middle hut of the pier.

Mudding: see *Slubbing*.

Net-barrow: a wooden bier with handles at each end on which nets were carried.

Net-rope: top rope of a net with a right-hand left-hand lay to prevent it twisting.

New York Cliff: the cliff at South Green. The New York Cliff Company's clift-house stood on top of the cliff until 1853.

Night-lining: eel-catching method using a worm, hook and line left overnight on the bank of a dyke.

Norsel: a length of twine about six to nine inches used to attach the net to the net-rope.

Oddy/Ossel/Hoddy: a piece of herring net nine inches deep used on a sprat net to which the norsels were attached at the top and the lint below.

Oven lids: a shoal of hard pan close in off Dunwich cliffs.

Oysters, The: a shoal in eleven fathoms off Easton broad.

Pack: a Cromer word. A longline to which 250 hooks were attached.

Patch-arsed Solemen: the Southwold longshoremen who inserted a patch of duffel into the rear of their trousers to give extra durability when rowing.

Peck: a measure of sixteen pints used for shrimps.

Pickmire: the black-headed gull (*Larus ridibundus*).

Popple: mildly rough sea.

Punt: a Southwold longshore boat. Its relatively flat bottom enabled launching and beaching.

Red herring: a heavily salted herring smoked for a long period at the top of the smokehouse.

Reefing pennants: five rows of threads on the dipping lug and three on the mizzen sail used for reefing the sails of a longshore punt in heavy weather.

Reining: about four strands of cotton at the bottom of a sprat net to create an edge.

Rixie: the common tern (*Sterna hirundo*).

Road open: a breast-mark. A road could be seen just clear off the cliff at Minsmere.

Roker: thornback ray (*Raja clavata*). The term might include other species of ray.

Rouse/roust: to turn herrings in coarse salt prior to smoking.

Run herring: to hawk herrings around the town.

Saver: a final tow with the trawl net if previous efforts had been unsuccessful.

Score-pair: the measure used for smelts. There were forty in a score-pair.

Scotch girls/lassies: generic term applied to itinerant female Scottish herring gutters.

Scuppet: a wooden shovel with a rounded, coppered bottom-edge and a leather shield at the join of blade and shaft to stop mud travelling up the arm. Used in bottom-fying and slubbing.

Sea-pie: the oyster catcher (*Haematopus ostralegus*).

Set/Sett: a twenty-foot long pole with a z-shaped iron attached to the end, inserted into the cheeks of the punt and used to push it off in heavy weather. Also used with other types of boat e.g yawls.

Shod: a longshoreman's shed on the beach in which he kept his nets, sails and gear.

Shoot: to cast the nets or lines.

Shoreman: those who walked the riverbank or shore when draw or drag-netting.

Sizewell Bank: a shoal off Sizewell which joins on to Dunwich bank.

Skip: two-handled basket of a bushel capacity used for carrying fish.

Sledge: type of way used to float a longshore punt. Shaped like an inverted sledge with irons on either side and attached to a chain.

Slip: a Dover sole measuring less than nine inches.

Slop: t-shaped upper garment worn by longshoremen either white or tanned.

Slubbing: rebuilding the river banks using mud and turf. A back-breaking winter job.

Smooth: a calm sea, usually the sixth or seventh in a sequence of rough ones.

Snoods/snuds: fifteen to eighteen-inch lengths of twine to which the hooks were attached on a longline.

Snoozle: the hole at the base of the stem of the longshore punt. A chain, to which the cable of the crab was attached, was threaded through it to enable the punt to be dragged up the beach.

Sole/Sowl/Sowle: Southwold.

Speet: a rounded length of hazelwood pointed at one end used for hanging fish about to be smoked. The speets were attached to the loughs.

Sprank/sprunk mesh: a single broken mesh.

Stalls: bandages applied to the fingers by the Scotch-girls for protection.

Steam Boat, The: a wreck in quarter-less eleven fathoms off Covehithe. Breast-mark: Covehithe Church in the second gap in the trees on Covehithe cliff. Long-mark: the lighthouse on the end of Southwold pier.

Steam Boat, The: a wreck in quarter-less twelve fathoms outside Sizewell bank buoy. Breast-mark with the buoy on the battery.

Stones, The: a shoal in nine to ten fathoms off Easton broad.

Stool: a triangular wooden construction used to keep the longshore punt upright on the beach.

Sweepers, The: a wreck in twelve and thirteen fathoms. Breast-mark: The House -in-the-clouds at Thorpeness. Long-mark: the buoy on the Coastguards' houses at Minsmere.

Sweeps/swipes: the oars of a longshore punt. They usually carried four.

Swipe/sweep: the practice of recovering anchors from the sea-bed.

Swivel: a way with a revolving channel which housed the keel and enabled the punt to be turned seaward once hauled up the beach.

Thimble: the eye on the yard into which the traveller was hooked.

Thole-pin: a wooden pin, used in pairs, inserted into the top gunwale of the punt through which the oars passed or from which gear was suspended. They were made of wood such as holly which was hard but which would easily snap.

Thorpe Rocks: a shoal just in off Thorpeness. Used in lobster and crab fishery.

Traveller: the iron ring around the mast attached to the thimble.

Trick over: neatly uncoil a longline to look for missing hooks and recoil in a different place. To reposition nets drying on the beach.

Tudor Rose: a wreck in ten fathoms: Breast-mark: Covehithe Church in the second gap in the trees on Covehithe cliff. Long-mark: the lighthouse halfway along the pier.

Warp: a length of heavier rope.

Warp: four herrings which counted as one (two in each hand). Thirty-three warps made a long-hundred (132).

Ways: flat or curved lengths of wood to which a strip of iron was attached. This was kept greased. Used for pulling the boats up and down the beach.

Wigs: Walberswick fishermen.

Willock/willie/wil-duck: guillemot (*Uria aalge*). Guillemot is a diminutive of *Guillaume* in French. A neat circularity.

Wreck in the Bay: breast-mark: water tower over Southwold House. Long-mark: white gable of Moorside in line with Walberswick Church.

Yard: the spar to which the dipping lug was attached.

Bibliography

Allen Collection, Southwold Museum, 2006.62

Arnott, W.G. *Alde Estuary,* Norman Adlard & Co.Ltd., Ipswich 1952

Bacon, S. *Southwold Suffolk,* Segment Publications 1996

Bailey, M., ed. *The Bailiffs' Minute Book of Dunwich 1404-1430,* Boydell Press
  Woodbridge 1992, for the Suffolk Records Society

Barber, G. *My Life Story,* Private Collection

Bell, N. *Bredon And Sons,* Little Brown and Co., Boston 1934
  Forgive Us Our Trespasses, Eyre And Spottiswode, London 1947
  My Writing Life, Alvin Redman, London 1955

Blyth Voices Folk songs collected in Southwold by Ralph Vaughan Williams in 1910
  East Anglian Traditional Music Trust 2003

Bochel, M *The Story of Nairn Fisher Girls at the Gutting*, National Museum of
  Antiquities of Scotland, Edinburgh, for Nairn Fishertown Museum, 1979

Bottomley, A.F. *Papers,* Suffolk Records Office, Lowestoft

Bottomley, A.F., ed. *The Southwold Diary of James Maggs Vols 1 & 2, 1818-1876,*
  Boydell Press, Woodbridge 1983, for the Suffolk Records Society

Box, P. *The Belles of the East Coast,* Tyndale + Panda Publishing Ltd, 1989

Butcher, D. *Fishing Talk: The Language of a Lost Industry Drawn Mainly From East*
  Anglian Sources, Poppyland Publishing, Cromer 2013
  'From the Catcher's Angle', Suffolk Records Office, Lowestoft, L.639.22
  Medieval Lowestoft: The Origins and Growth of a Suffolk Coastal
  Community, The Boydell Press, Woodbridge 2016
  Rigged for River and Sea, North Atlantic Fisheries History Association 2008
  The Driftermen, Tops'l Books, Reading 1979
  The Last Haul: Recollections of the Days before English Fishing Died
  Poppyland Publishing, Lowestoft 2020

Cooper, E.R. *A Suffolk Coast Garland,* Heath Cranton Ltd, London 1928
  Mardles from Suffolk, Heath Cranton Ltd, London 1932
  Notebook of Sixteen Wrecks, Ms. Southwold Museum
  Notes on Southwold Harbour, Ms. Southwold Museum
  Old Southwold, Vols 1-4 Scrapbooks, Southwold Museum
  Seventy Years' Work of the Southwold Lifeboats, Southwold Press 1912
  Storm Warriors of the Suffolk Coast, Heath Cranton Ltd, London 1937
  The Suffolk and Norfolk Beach Yawls, The Mariner's Mirror,
  Vol 13 Issue 3 1927

Cunliffe, T. *Pilot Cutters Under Sail Pilots and Pilotage in Britain and Northern*
  Europe, Seaforth Publishing 2013

Dutt, W.H. *The Coastal Series: The Suffolk and Norfolk Coast,* T. Fisher Unwin,
  London 1909

Dyson, J. *Business in Great Waters: The Story of British Fishermen,* Angus & Robertson 1977

East Suffolk Mercury and Lowestoft Weekly News

Emerson, P.H. *Pictures of East Anglian Life,* Samson, Low, Marston, Searle and Rivington, London 1888

    The English Emersons, David Nutt, London 1898

Evans, G.E. *The Pattern Under the Plough,* Faber & Faber 1966

Fletcher, R. *In A Country Churchyard,* Paladin Grafton Books, London 1980

Flood's Register of Vessels for the Port of Lowestoft, Feb. 1903, Private Collection

Gale's Almanacs, Southwold Museum

Gooding, D. J. *Notebook,* The A.B. Jenkins Collection, Southwold Museum

Graham W.S. *New Collected Poems,* Faber & Faber 2004

Grubbe, A. *Diary,* Southwold Museum

Herrington, J.C. *The Story of a Cliffman,* Southwold Parish Magazine 1928

Higgins, D. *The Beachmen,* Terence Dalton, Lavenham 1987

Ipswich Journal

Jenkins, A.B. *A Selection of Ghost Stories Smuggling Stories and Poems Connected with Southwold*, Southwold Press 1986

    Reminiscences of Southwold During the Two World Wars, Southwold Press 1984

Lawrence, R. *Southwold River: Georgian Life in the Blyth Valley,* Suffolk Books 1990

Lethbridge, T.C. *Boats and Boatmen,* Thames and Hudson, London 1952

Lewis, Rev. R.W.M. *Walberswick Churchwardens' Accounts AD 1450-1499,* Headley Brothers, London 1947

Logan, J. *Fishing for Ganseys,* The Moray Firth Gansey Project

Maggs, J. *Diary Vols 1-5,* Ms., Southwold Museum

Maitland, P. S. *The status of smelt osmerus eperlanus in England*, English Nature Research Report no 516, 2002/3

March, E.J. *Inshore Craft of Great Britain in the Days of Sail and Oar Vol 1,* David and Charles 1970

Mayhew, H. *Life and Labour of the London Poor Vol 1*, Griffith, Bohn and Co., London 1861

Middleton, E.E. *The Cruise of the Kate,* 1870

Moodie, S. *Flora Lyndsay, Or Passages in an Eventful Life*, ed., M. Peterman, University of Ottowa Press 2014

Moore, E.W. *Scrapbook,* Southwold Museum

Newhall, N. *P.H.Emerson,* Aperture, New York 1975

Nicolson, A. *The Mighty Dead: Why Homer Matters,* William Collins 2015

Bibliography

Patterson, A.H. *Rough Notes on the Fish and Fisheries of East Suffolk*, The Zoologist 1909

Pilotage Committee Minutes, Ms.30158, Trinity House, London Metropolitan Archives

Pope, D. ed., *The Sailors' Reading Room The First 150 Years from 2nd June 1864*, Southwold Press 2013

Rogers, S. *Sea-Lore,* Harrap 1928

Southwold Borough Collection, Suffolk Records Office, Lowestoft

Southwold Lifeboat Society Minute Book, Private Collection

Letter Book, Private Collection

Suffolk Chronicle

Taylor, J. *The Old Order and The New: P.H.Emerson and Photography 1885-1895,* Prestel 2007

The Gooding Collection, Southwold Museum

Thompson, G. *Guernsey and Jersey Patterns,* Batsford, London 1955

Tolhurst, P. *East Anglian Folk Art,* Black Dog Books, forthcoming

This Hollow Land: Aspects of Norfolk Folklore, Black Dog Books 2018

Vertue, F.W. *Notebook 2,* Southwold Museum

Wake, R. *Southwold and its Vicinity,* F. Skill, Yarmouth 1839

Walcott, D. *The Sea is History* in *The Star Apple Kingdom,* New York Farrar, Strauss & Giroux 1979

Williams, R. *The Country and The City,* Chatto and Windus, London 1973

Williamson, T. *An Environmental History of Wildlife in England 1650-1950,* Bloomsbury 2013

Other References

www.soundsurvey.org.uk/index.php/radio recordings/1930s/1543/

southwoldandson.co.uk